THE
SHAKESPEARE
HANDBOOK

R W MASLEN
and MICHAEL SCHMIDT

Quercus

Contents

Introduction

This handbook takes the form of an anthology of fifty great scenes, or parts of scenes, from the works of Shakespeare. It is based on the conviction that reading them side by side can provide an unrivalled sense of Shakespeare's astonishing range as a playwright, and of the radical changes he underwent in the course of roughly twenty-five years as a man of the theatre.

Each extract is a kind of miniature play in itself, distilling the essence of the larger dramatic unit of which it is part. Each comes equipped with a guide in the form of an introduction and notes; and this general introduction aims to alert you to some of the motifs and trends you may notice as you read.

Traditional editions of Shakespeare's complete plays sort them into three distinct genres – tragedy, comedy, history – arranged as in the first edition of his works, published in 1623. This book follows instead the example of the Oxford *Complete Works* of 1986 by presenting the plays in approximate order of their first performance. The advantages of this ordering are several. It helps us identify the periods when he became obsessed by a certain kind of drama (the run of great tragedies in the early 1600s, the fistful of romances he penned as he neared retirement). It lets us track, too, the sudden, amazing shifts in tone he achieved elsewhere (as when he switched in about 1600 from the carefree forest of *As You Like It* to the claustrophobic castle of *Hamlet*).

For another thing, it prevents our understanding of Shakespeare's plays from being limited by preconceptions concerning genre. As comedy follows tragedy, or the delightful surprises of a romance follow on from the political complexities of a Roman play, we discover the extent to which Shakespeare resisted getting stuck for long in a single theatrical mode, even in his periods of greatest obsession with history, tragedy or romance. We discover, too, how a single play can change tone radically from scene to scene (as in our two extracts from *Henry IV* Part I, which invoke quite different moods); or how a single scene can move from one emotional register to another (as in our extracts from *Antony and Cleopatra* and *The Tempest*). This is perhaps the most startling thing about Shakespeare: diversity and mutability were in his bones, so that his characters and the language they utter can be transformed at a moment's notice, while retaining continuities that make us believe Shakespeare knows, or instinctively senses, the social, political and personal pressures that bring about those transformations. No arrangement by genre can do justice to his constant metamorphoses; so a chronological arrangement seems the most satisfactory way of organizing his productions.

Nobody knows the exact chronology of his plays, and scholars disagree over which came first. It is satisfying to begin with *The Two Gentlemen of Verona*, because the play contains so much that Shakespeare returned to again and again: a cross-dressing heroine, unreliable men and courageous women, a court where superficial politeness turns to treachery, a wilderness where tensions between the characters come to a head and find resolution. Shakespeare revisited these motifs in *As You Like It* and *Cymbeline*. Indeed, his first few plays run the gamut of moods, plots and themes that remained central to his artistic practice. *Two Gentlemen*, with its emphasis on travel, disguise and unexpected reunions, can be called a romance, like some of the middle comedies and many of the late plays. *The Taming of the Shrew* is closer to classical Roman comedy, a mode he revisited in *The Merry Wives of Windsor* and *Twelfth Night*. *Titus Andronicus* is a bloody tragedy – though it also displays the interest in civic policy that marks all the plays Shakespeare set in ancient Rome, and the satirical bent he explored in his plays about the world of the ancient Greeks, *Troilus and Cressida* and *Timon of Athens*. The rest of the early plays draw on English history – a subject Shakespeare made peculiarly his own (he was the most prolific Elizabethan writer of history plays) and to which he returned in one of his last compositions, *Henry VIII*. If variety is Shakespeare's hallmark, so is a remarkable consistency in his concerns and fascinations. The same situations, the same social institutions, the same kinds of people continued to ignite his imagination throughout his theatrical career.

The early plays show, too, how these fascinations crop up in plays of very different types. His interest in civil war, for instance (whether in a household or a nation), as opposed to conflicts between strangers or nations, is evident in comedy (*The Taming of the Shrew*), history (*Henry VI* Parts II and III) and tragedy (*Titus Andronicus*). So is his fascination with the sources of attraction and conflict between men and women, and the inventiveness with which they articulate their antagonisms. His interest in race finds its first expression in Aaron, an isolated Moor among the Romans in *Titus Andronicus*, who is the shockingly exuberant villain of the piece. Aaron's descendants are the Jew Shylock, the North African Othello, the Egyptian Cleopatra, the islander Caliban. But Aaron is just one manifestation of Shakespeare's passion for outsiders, from the comically disobedient daughter Katherina in *The Taming of the Shrew* to the tragically intractable soldier Coriolanus. And Aaron's sense of humour – the 'extreme laughter' to which he succumbs as he tortures his victims – is a drastic example of one of Shakespeare's most remarkable traits: his ability to find humour in every situation, no matter how appalling. Time and again in our scenes you will see laughter or some other form of lightness breaking out at the moment of greatest emotional intensity: Romeo's cheerfulness before his suicide; Hamlet joking with the gravedigger as he approaches his final showdown with Claudius; the clown coming in with the poisonous snakes that will kill Cleopatra. It's at points like these that Shakespeare's capacity to marry changefulness with continuity is at its most daring.

Shakespeare's development can be separated into five phases, reminiscent of the five acts into which his plays are traditionally divided. After the first phase, when he sets out his wares as a young playwright, comes a period of explosive linguistic playfulness, which extends from *Love's Labour's Lost* to *Richard II*, full of puns, unexpected comparisons, clever arguments and exquisite lyricism. This is followed by the confident plays of his maturity: his greatest histories (such as *Henry V*) and most ebullient comedies (such as *Much Ado*). Next comes a darker period, when he wrote his most celebrated tragedies (from *Hamlet* to *Macbeth*), and his most emotionally and morally ambiguous comedies or 'problem plays' (from *Troilus* to *Timon*). The final phase is dominated by romance, whose geographical expansiveness and optimism in the face of adversity is delightfully anticipated by *Antony and Cleopatra*, and whose antithesis is the rigorously self-disciplined protagonist of *Coriolanus*.

If you were to progress through these five phases, you would notice certain stylistic alterations. You would see, for instance, how Shakespeare's verse becomes more rhythmically liberated, escaping from the regularity of his early use of iambic pentameter – the ten-syllable line in which he wrote most of his plays – by abandoning the practice of making us pause at the end of each line, and by introducing adventurous variations in sound and rhythm. These changes can be appreciated by comparing the disrupted rhythms of Iachimo's speech in our scene from *Cymbeline* with the far more formal patterns of Julia's speech beginning 'How many women would do such a message?' in *Two Gentlemen of Verona*.

Shakespeare's increasingly inventive use of metaphor, too, becomes obvious when you consider an early extract – say, the meeting of Talbot and his son in *Henry VI* Part 1 – alongside a late one – such as the death of Cleopatra in our second extract from her tragedy. In the speech beginning 'When from the Dauphin's crest', Talbot's stress on blood as a means of distinguishing his closeness to his own son from his distance from the son of his enemy dominates the first few lines; whereas Cleopatra's speech beginning 'Give me my robe' mixes notions of mortality and immortality, distance and intimacy, pain and pleasure, in a complex metaphorical knot that has no equivalent in the early drama. The extracts from *The Tempest* and *Antony and Cleopatra* show too how in his late plays Shakespeare slips easily between verse and prose in a single scene, whereas in his first works these are segregated by their deployment in different contexts. The distance between Shakespeare's apprenticeship as a dramatic poet and his achievement of full poetic mastery is a vast one, and our selection is intended to bring this out.

The selection also aims to bring out the continuities that bind his plays to one another. Some extracts chose themselves: the balcony scene from *Romeo and Juliet*, for instance, or Bottom with his ass's head from *A Midsummer Night's Dream*, or the storm scene from *King Lear*. But where the choice was less obvious, I have often been guided by a desire to show Shakespeare's tendency to play variations on themes he had already handled. So the banter between Petruchio and Katherina in *The Taming of the Shrew* finds echoes in Richard III's seduction of Lady Anne; then in Hero's chastisement of her cousin Beatrice for the kind of aggressive wit that got Katherina into trouble (*Much Ado About Nothing*, extract 1); and finally in Rosalind's witty taunting of her lover Orlando in *As You Like It*. The assassination of York in *Henry VI* Part III introduces us to an aristocrat whose ambitions were parodied by the rebellious commoner Jack Cade in our scene from Part II; while its focus on the death of father and son (before he dies, York laments the murder of his young son Rutland) is intensified in our extract from Part I (the death of Talbot and his son), and casts its shadow over the scenes from *King John* (where an assassin refuses to torture a boy prince) and *Macbeth* (where an ambitious warrior plans to massacre all the children who stand in the way of his accession to the throne of Scotland). I have tried to follow each extract with another of contrasting tone and pace; but every scene has one or more companion-pieces in the volume, and you will see more themes and variations as you read than I can hint at in this introduction.

Some of the echoes and contrasts between the scenes are picked out in introductions to individual plays. Others are mentioned in the notes. Many more will occur to you unaided, as you grow familiar with the Shakespearean terrain you are covering. In the end you may find that some of this terrain has become your own, and that your imaginative landscape has grown larger and richer in consequence. If so, the book will have achieved its purpose.

The Two c.*1590-91*
Gentlemen
of Verona

ACT **4** SCENE **4**

❝ **I did play a lamentable part ...**
Which I so lively acted with my tears
That my poor mistress, movèd therewithal,
Wept bitterly *❞*

This play is packed with motifs that continued to fascinate Shakespeare throughout his life: friendships betrayed, cross-dressing, a forest where damaged relationships are healed. Two male friends go their separate ways, Valentine to seek preferment at court, Proteus to court Julia at home. Later Proteus too goes to court, where he falls in love with Silvia, Valentine's girlfriend.

The duplicitous Proteus succeeds in getting Valentine banished to the woods, leaving him free to woo Silvia – until she runs away to join her lover. Proteus pursues and tries to rape her; Valentine stops him; and there follows one of the strangest episodes in Shakespeare's work. Proteus begs his friend's forgiveness, and Valentine 'gives' him Silvia to cement their reconciliation. At this point Silvia's father arrives, accompanied by her fiancé Thurio. When Valentine gets aggressive, Thurio backs down and 'gives' him Silvia, after which her father 'gives' her to Valentine once more. So Silvia is given away three times by different men in a matter of minutes; it's hardly surprising if the situation leaves her speechless.

Luckily, there's another woman present who is very far from speechless. This is Julia, Proteus's first love, who has disguised herself as a page, Sebastian, and followed him through all his misadventures. Julia is Shakespeare's most charming early heroine, who sees men's faults clearly, yet remains determined to see the right man joined to the right woman despite all the odds against it. Her disguise as an adolescent boy puts her in a liminal space between male and female, possessing elements of either sex and attractive to both. This permits her to judge how far gender roles are a matter of performance, capable of being modified or manipulated by any skilful performer. It was Proteus' changeful behaviour, she tells him in Act 5, that forced her to change into a boy, as the only available means of retaining her identity as a lover. Shakespeare was always fascinated by the question of how constant love survives in an inconstant environment, and Julia's pursuit and conquest of Proteus is one of his most touchingly implausible answers to this question.

The extract we have selected begins with Proteus handing Julia/Sebastian a ring that Julia once gave him, with instructions to give it to his new love, Silvia. This leads to a wonderfully knotty soliloquy in which Julia puzzles over the confusion of 'truth' and 'falsehood' caused by her disguise, since as Sebastian she must remain true to her false master, but as Julia this is to be false to herself. And the scene ends, naturally, with a sophisticated meditation on the theatre. Sebastian tells Silvia about a time when he put on women's clothes and delivered a tragic speech to Julia. Julia, he says, was moved to tears by his performance, which made him cry too; while Silvia is moved to tears in her turn by this tear-filled narrative. The hearts of two women come together through this web of fictions, and the hearts of the theatre audience, too, are stirred by its sheer complexity – rendered yet more complex by the fact that all Shakespeare's women were played by boys. Shakespeare never wrote better about the miraculous way in which truth can emerge from a tissue of lies; and about how acting helps to achieve this miraculous emergence.

OPPOSITE Estelle Kohler as Sylvia and Helen Mirren as Julia (disguised as a page, Sebastian) in the Royal Shakespeare Company's 1970 production.

[*Enter* **PROTEUS** *and* **JULIA** *disguised as Sebastian*]

PROTEUS Sebastian, I have entertainèd thee,
Partly that I have need of such a youth
That can with some discretion do my business,
But chiefly for thy face and thy behaviour,
Which, if my augury deceive me not,
Witness good bringing up, fortune, and truth.
Therefore know thou, for this I entertain thee.
Go presently, and take this ring with thee,
Deliver it to Madam Silvia.
She loved me well delivered it to me.

JULIA It seems you loved not her, to leave her
   token.
She is dead, belike?

PROTEUS   Not so; I think she lives.

JULIA Alas!

PROTEUS Why dost thou cry 'Alas'?

JULIA   I cannot choose
But pity her.

PROTEUS Wherefore shouldst thou pity her?

JULIA Because methinks that she loved you as well
As you do love your lady Silvia.
She dreams on him that has forgot her love;
You dote on her that cares not for your love.
'Tis pity love should be so contrary;
And thinking on it makes me cry 'Alas'.

PROTEUS Well, give her that ring, and therewithal
This letter. That's her chamber. Tell my lady
I claim the promise for her heavenly picture.
Your message done, hie home unto my chamber,
Where thou shalt find me sad and solitary. [*Exit*]

And now am I, unhappy messenger,
To plead for that which I would not obtain,
To carry that which I would have refused,
To praise his faith, which I would have dispraised.
I am my master's true-confirmèd love,
But cannot be true servant to my master
Unless I prove false traitor to myself.
Yet will I woo for him, but yet so coldly
As, heaven it knows, I would not have him speed.
[*Enter* **SILVIA**]
Gentlewoman, good day! I pray you be my mean
To bring me where to speak with Madam Silvia.

SILVIA What would you with her, if that I be she?

JULIA If you be she, I do entreat your patience
To hear me speak the message I am sent on.

SILVIA From whom?

JULIA From my master, Sir Proteus, madam.

SILVIA O, he sends you for a picture?

JULIA Ay, madam.

SILVIA Ursula, bring my picture there.
Go, give your master this. Tell him from me,
One Julia, that his changing thoughts forget,
Would better fit his chamber than this shadow.

JULIA Madam, please you peruse this letter.
[*She gives Silvia a letter from Proteus to Julia*]
Pardon me, madam; I have unadvised
Delivered you a paper that I should not.
[*She takes back the first letter and gives Silvia
   a second*]
This is the letter to your ladyship.

SILVIA I pray thee, let me look on that again.

*And now am I, unhappy messenger,
To plead for that which I would not obtain*

JULIA How many women would do such
   a message?
Alas, poor Proteus! Thou hast entertained
A fox to be the shepherd of thy lambs.
Alas, poor fool! Why do I pity him
That with his very heart despiseth me?
Because he loves her, he despiseth me;
Because I love him, I must pity him.
This ring I gave him when he parted from me,
To bind him to remember my good will;

JULIA It may not be. Good madam, pardon me.

SILVIA There, hold!
I will not look upon your master's lines.
I know they are stuffed with protestations
And full of new-found oaths, which he will break
As easily as I do tear his paper.
[*She tears the letter*]

JULIA Madam, he sends your ladyship this ring.
[*She gives Silvia a ring*]

The Two Gentlemen of Verona

SILVIA The more shame for him that he sends it me;
For I have heard him say a thousand times
His Julia gave it him at his departure.
Though his false finger have profaned the ring,
Mine shall not do his Julia so much wrong.

JULIA She thanks you.

SILVIA What sayst thou?

JULIA I thank you, madam, that you tender her.
Poor gentlewoman! My master wrongs her much.

SILVIA Dost thou know her?

JULIA Almost as well as I do know myself.
To think upon her woes I do protest
That I have wept a hundred several times.

SILVIA Belike she thinks that Proteus hath
forsook her?

JULIA I think she doth; and that's her cause of sorrow.

SILVIA Is she not passing fair?

'Come, shadow, come, and take this shadow up'

In Elizabethan English, 'shadow' could mean a copy or imitation, as well as having its modern sense. Thus, actors could be shadows, and so could pictures. Julia is telling herself (as a girl acting a boy) to pick up the picture of Silvia – and implying that she has as much chance of enjoying Proteus's caresses as the portrait does.

JULIA She hath been fairer, madam, than she is.
When she did think my master loved her well,
She, in my judgment, was as fair as you.
But since she did neglect her looking-glass
And threw her sun-expelling mask away,
The air hath starved the roses in her cheeks
And pinched the lily tincture of her face,
That now she is become as black as I.

SILVIA How tall was she?

JULIA About my stature; for at Pentecost,
When all our pageants of delight were played,
Our youth got me to play the woman's part,
And I was trimmed in Madam Julia's gown,
Which servèd me as fit, by all men's judgments,
As if the garment had been made for me;
Therefore I know she is about my height.
And at that time I made her weep agood,
For I did play a lamentable part.
Madam, 'twas Ariadne passioning
For Theseus' perjury and unjust flight;

Which I so lively acted with my tears
That my poor mistress, movèd therewithal,
Wept bitterly; and would I might be dead
If I in thought felt not her very sorrow.

SILVIA She is beholden to thee, gentle youth.
Alas, poor lady, desolate and left!
I weep myself to think upon thy words.
Here, youth, there is my purse. I give thee this
For thy sweet mistress' sake, because thou lov'st her.
Farewell. [*Exit*]

JULIA And she shall thank you for't, if e'er you
know her.
A virtuous gentlewoman, mild and beautiful.
I hope my master's suit will be but cold,
Since she respects my mistress' love so much.
Alas, how love can trifle with itself!
Here is her picture. Let me see; I think
If I had such a tire, this face of mine
Were full as lovely as is this of hers.
And yet the painter flattered her a little,
Unless I flatter with myself too much.
Her hair is auburn, mine is perfect yellow;
If that be all the difference in his love,
I'll get me such a coloured periwig.
Her eyes are grey as glass, and so are mine;
Ay, but her forehead's low, and mine's as high.
What should it be that he respects in her
But I can make respective in myself,
If this fond Love were not a blinded god?
Come, shadow, come, and take this shadow up,
For 'tis thy rival. O thou senseless form,
Thou shalt be worshipped, kissed, loved and adored!
And, were there sense in his idolatry
My substance should be statue in thy stead.
I'll use thee kindly for thy mistress' sake,
That used me so; or else, by Jove I vow,
I should have scratched out your unseeing eyes,
To make my master out of love with thee. [*Exit*]

'Madam, 'twas Ariadne passioning For Theseus' perjury and unjust flight'

In Greek myth, Ariadne was abandoned by her lover Theseus on a desert island, after helping him to defeat the Minotaur. In some versions of the story she found consolation in the arms of the god of wine, Dionysus or Bacchus. Shakespeare could have read her story in Ovid's *Heroides*, an Elizabethan school text, which tells it from Ariadne's point of view.

The Taming of the Shrew

c. 1592

ACT **2** SCENE **1**

❝ O, you are novices! 'Tis a world to see
How tame, when men and women are alone,
A meacock wretch can make the curstest shrew. ❞

The Taming of the Shrew

In Shakespeare's early plays, men and women occupy separate spheres, so that men fabricate ridiculous fantasies about women, while women devise ingenious stratagems to resist the pressures these fantasies exert upon them. Nowhere in Shakespeare's work are male illusions more extravagant than they are in the *Shrew*; and no play has generated more controversy over Shakespeare's personal attitude to women.

Hortensio and Lucentio both wish to marry the lovely Bianca, whose father Baptista has sworn she shall stay single till he has found a husband for her sister, Katherina. But no man wants Katherina because of her fearsome reputation as a termagant or 'shrew'. Along comes Petruchio, a wit who wants a wealthy wife and doesn't care how he gets her. Hortensio persuades him to woo Katherina, while Hortensio and Lucentio pose as private tutors to get close to Bianca. Our extract begins at the point when Petruchio is about to meet Katherina for the first time.

Before this comes a display of her formidable temper. Hortensio, posing as a music master, has his lute smashed over his head when he questions her technique. When Katherina meets Petruchio, her tongue proves as vigorous as her fists, and the pair of them launch into a blazing war of words. Petruchio seeks to eroticize Katherina (she is 'gamesome' and 'sweet as springtime flowers'), while she repeatedly denigrates his masculinity (he is 'no cock' because he 'crows like a craven' [coward]). The war ends in victory for Petruchio; but it's won by underhand means. At the beginning of our extract, he tells us his strategy for taming this recalcitrant girl: he intends to ignore what she says altogether. And in the ensuing verbal battle he tells her how the 'sland'rous world' will do exactly the same thing, spreading malicious gossip about her no matter how she behaves. Afterwards Petruchio does just this – except that his lies are not obviously malicious. Describing the battle to her father, he makes it sound like a stroll in the park: Katherina loves him, he says, and has accepted his proposal, but they have agreed that she will act 'curstly' until the wedding. These lies effectively rob Katherina of her voice, since they register nothing of what she has actually said. And after their marriage Petruchio continues to ignore her dissent, until in her desperation to be heard she consents to his most ridiculous assertions: that the sun is the moon, for instance, or that Lucentio's aged father is a 'budding virgin'.

In the process, Petruchio demonstrates the absurdity of the premises on which patriarchy is founded. Hortensio and Lucentio fall for Bianca without any knowledge of her character; they merely assume her to be compliant on the basis of her looks. Petruchio's assertions about the sun are no madder than their assumptions about Bianca – as we learn in Act 5, when Bianca pays no attention to the commands of her new husband Lucentio. Meanwhile Katherina obeys Petruchio unquestioningly, even launching into a notorious anti-feminist diatribe as she does so. But after witnessing Katherina's forcefulness in our extract, it's hard to take this diatribe at face value. The audience is left wondering whether Shakespeare meant it, or whether he meant us to believe that Katherina has finally learned to wield Petruchio's most potent weapon: irony.

OPPOSITE Richard Burton as Petruchio and Elizabeth Taylor as Katherina in the 1967 film, directed by Franco Zeffirelli.

[PETRUCHIO *on stage, alone*]

PETRUCHIO I will attend her here,
And woo her with some spirit when she comes.
Say that she rail, why then I'll tell her plain
She sings as sweetly as a nightingale.
Say that she frown, I'll say she looks as clear
As morning roses newly washed with dew.
Say she be mute and will not speak a word,
Then I'll commend her volubility,
And say she uttereth piercing eloquence.
If she do bid me pack, I'll give her thanks
As though she bid me stay by her a week.
If she deny to wed, I'll crave the day
When I shall ask the banns, and when be marrièd.
But here she comes; and now, Petruchio, speak.

[*Enter* **KATHERINA**]

Good morrow, Kate; for that's your name, I hear.

KATHERINA Well have you heard, but something
  hard of hearing:
They call me Katherina that do talk of me.

PETRUCHIO You lie, in faith, for you are called
  plain Kate,
And Bonny Kate, and sometimes Kate the curst,
But Kate, the prettiest Kate in Christendom,
Kate of Kate Hall, my super-dainty Kate –
For dainties are all cates, and therefore 'Kate' –
Take this of me, Kate of my consolation:
Hearing thy mildness praised in every town,
Thy virtues spoke of, and thy beauty sounded –
Yet not so deeply as to thee belongs –
Myself am moved to woo thee for my wife.

KATHERINA Moved! In good time! Let him that
  moved you hither
Remove you hence. I knew you at the first
You were a moveable.

PETRUCHIO   Why, what's a moveable?

KATHERINA A joint-stool.

PETRUCHIO   Thou hast hit it. Come, sit on me.

KATHERINA Asses are made to bear, and so are you.

PETRUCHIO Women are made to bear, and so are you.

KATHERINA No such jade as you, if me you mean.

PETRUCHIO Alas, good Kate, I will not burden thee,
For knowing thee to be but young and light.

KATHERINA Too light for such a swain as you
  to catch,
And yet as heavy as my weight should be.

PETRUCHIO Should be? Should buzz!

KATHERINA   Well ta'en, and like a buzzard.

PETRUCHIO O slow-winged turtle, shall a buzzard
  take thee?

KATHERINA Ay, for a turtle, as he takes a buzzard.

PETRUCHIO Come, come, you wasp, i' faith you
  are too angry.

KATHERINA If I be waspish, best beware my sting.

PETRUCHIO My remedy is then to pluck it out.

KATHERINA Ay, if the fool could find it where it lies.

PETRUCHIO Who knows not where a wasp does
  wear his sting? In his tail.

KATHERINA In his tongue.

PETRUCHIO Whose tongue?

KATHERINA Yours, if you talk of tales, and so
  farewell.

PETRUCHIO What, with my tongue in your tail?
  Nay, come again,
Good Kate, I am a gentleman.

KATHERINA   That I'll try.

[*She strikes him*]

PETRUCHIO I swear I'll cuff you if you strike again.

KATHERINA So may you lose your arms.
If you strike me you are no gentleman,
And if no gentleman, why then no arms.

PETRUCHIO A herald, Kate? O, put me in thy books!

KATHERINA What is your crest – a coxcomb?

PETRUCHIO A combless cock, so Kate will be my hen.

KATHERINA No cock of mine; you crow too like
  a craven.

PETRUCHIO Nay, come, Kate, come. You must not
  look so sour.

KATHERINA It is my fashion when I see a crab.

PETRUCHIO Why, here's no crab, and therefore
  look not sour.

KATHERINA There is, there is.

PETRUCHIO Then show it me.

KATHERINA   Had I a glass I would.

'Should be? Should buzz!'

The banter between Petruchio and Kate is so
dense with double meanings that it's hard to
gloss, though the speed of the exchange is
easy to appreciate. So for instance, 'Should be?
Should buzz' begins a series of allusions to
bees and other buzzing insects or 'buzzards',
which could also be the untrainable hawks
that still roam the English countryside. When
Petruchio shrinks Katherina's name to 'Kate'
he turns her into a tasty morsel, since 'cates'
are delicacies. And when Katherina tells
Petruchio he will lose his arms if he strikes
her, she means his coat of arms as a
gentleman as well as his upper limbs.

The Taming of the Shrew

PETRUCHIO What, you mean my face?

KATHERINA Well aimed, of such a young one.

PETRUCHIO Now, by Saint George, I am too young for you.

KATHERINA Yet you are withered.

PETRUCHIO   'Tis with cares.

KATHERINA   I care not.

PETRUCHIO Nay, hear you, Kate. In sooth you scape not so.

KATHERINA I chafe you if I tarry. Let me go.

PETRUCHIO No, not a whit. I find you passing gentle.
'Twas told me you were rough and coy and sullen,
And now I find report a very liar,
For thou are pleasant, gamesome, passing courteous,
But slow in speech, yet sweet as springtime flowers.
Thou canst not frown, thou canst not look askance,
Nor bite the lip, as angry wenches will,
Nor hast thou pleasure to be cross in talk,
But thou with mildness entertain'st thy wooers,
With gentle conference, soft and affable.
Why does the world report that Kate doth limp?
O sland'rous world! Kate like the hazel twig
Is straight and slender, and as brown in hue
As hazelnuts, and sweeter than the kernels.
O, let me see thee walk. Thou dost not halt.

KATHERINA Go, fool, and whom thou keep'st command.

PETRUCHIO Did ever Dian so become a grove
As Kate this chamber with her princely gait?
O, be thou Dian, and let her be Kate,
And then let Kate be chaste and Dian sportful!

KATHERINA Where did you study all this goodly speech?

PETRUCHIO It is extempore, from my mother-wit.

KATHERINA A witty mother, witless else her son.

PETRUCHIO Am I not wise?

KATHERINA   Yes, keep you warm.

PETRUCHIO Marry, so I mean, sweet Katherina, in thy bed.
And therefore, setting all this chat aside,
Thus in plain terms: your father hath consented
That you shall be my wife; your dowry 'greed on;
And, will you, nill you, I will marry you.
Now, Kate, I am a husband for your turn,
For by this light, whereby I see thy beauty
(Thy beauty that doth make me like thee well),
Thou must be married to no man but me;
For I am he am born to tame you, Kate,
And bring you from a wild Kate to a Kate

Conformable as other household Kates.
[*Enter* **BAPTISTA**, **GREMIO**, *and* **TRANIO**]
Here comes your father. Never make denial;
I must and will have Katherina to my wife.

BAPTISTA Now, Signior Petruchio, how speed you with my daughter?

PETRUCHIO How but well, sir? How but well?
It were impossible I should speed amiss.

BAPTISTA Why, how now, daughter Katherina! In your dumps?

KATHERINA Call you me daughter? Now I promise you
You have showed a tender fatherly regard,
To wish me wed to one half-lunatic,
A madcap ruffian and a swearing Jack,
That thinks with oaths to face the matter out.

PETRUCHIO Father, 'tis thus: yourself and all the world
That talked of her have talked amiss of her.
If she be curst, it is for policy,
For she's not froward, but modest as the dove;
She is not hot, but temperate as the morn;
For patience she will prove a second Grissel,
And Roman Lucrece for her chastity.
And to conclude, we have 'greed so well together
That upon Sunday is the wedding day.

KATHERINA I'll see thee hanged on Sunday first.

GREMIO Hark, Petruchio, she says she'll see thee hanged first.

TRANIO Is this your speeding? Nay then, good-night our part!

PETRUCHIO Be patient, gentlemen. I choose her for myself.
If she and I be pleased, what's that to you?
'Tis bargained 'twixt us twain, being alone,
That she shall still be curst in company.
I tell you, 'tis incredible to believe
How much she loves me. O, the kindest Kate!
She hung about my neck, and kiss on kiss
She vied so fast, protesting oath on oath,
That in a twink she won me to her love.
O, you are novices! 'Tis a world to see
How tame, when men and women are alone,
A meacock wretch can make the curstest shrew.
Give me thy hand, Kate. I will unto Venice,
To buy apparel 'gainst the wedding day.
Provide the feast, father, and bid the guests;
I will be sure my Katherina shall be fine.

[*Exeunt* **PETRUCHIO** *and* **KATHERINA** *severally*]

Henry VI
Part II

c.1591

| ACT **4** | SCENE **2** |

> ❝ Away with him, I say!
> Hang him with his pen
> and inkhorn about his neck. ❞

The three plays now known as *Henry VI* Parts I, II and III were Shakespeare's ambitious first attempts to dramatize English history. Many scholars believe that the second part was written first, but whatever the order of composition, the three plays form a tightly organized narrative, which redistributes the complex material of the chronicles so as to foreground recurring issues and generate suspense.

The choice of subject was bold; this period was a touchy topic for the Tudors, focusing attention on their shaky claim to the English throne and reminding the audience of rival claims. But the risk paid off. Taken together, the trilogy became one of the biggest box-office draws of the early 1590s, and helped to establish Shakespeare's reputation as a serious dramatist.

The second part compresses into five acts the events of a decade, 1445–55. It opens with a succession of scenes in which contending factions range themselves in opposition to one another, clustered round the flags of two noble houses, those of Lancaster and York. Each house contains one or more candidates for kingship, and the impression we get from these early scenes is that the English crown is imaginatively up for grabs, available to whatever member of the ruling classes proves trickiest and most unscrupulous. One by one the weaker candidates fall away, leaving the unworldly Lancastrian Henry VI – supported by his powerful wife Margaret – and the ambitious Duke of York as the sole remaining contenders. As hostility between their factions mounts, Shakespeare signals the approach of war with repeated references to a rising storm: the 'black storm' invoked by York in Act 3 Scene 1. The storm breaks in Act 4, when Jack Cade's rebellion erupts in Kent, stirred up by supporters of the Yorkist cause.

In our extract, the commoner Cade provides a brilliant satirical riposte to the insanely self-centred ambitions of the aristocracy in the play. He invents a spurious genealogy to support his claim to the throne, in daft mimicry of the genealogy supplied by York in Act 2 Scene 2. But unlike his fellow claimants, his aim as monarch is solely to benefit his people. In Cade's projected commonwealth all things 'shall be in common', and the trappings that exclude commoners from power shall be forbidden, from Latin and reading to lordships and fine clothes. Cade's incoherent dreams here serve to stress the fact that the power games of the aristocracy have little to do with the living conditions of ordinary citizens; that they are founded, in fact, on nothing but splendid language, of which the ruling classes seek to have a monopoly. The point is driven home a few scenes later when Lord Clifford disperses Cade's followers with a rousing speech, in which he invokes the memory of Henry V to persuade them that it would be better to fight the French than engage in political action at home. Cade dies alone and starving, a victim of the ruling-class monopoly of fine words, good weapons and sustaining food that he sought to question.

His death leaves the aristocracy free to continue their wars unimpeded, with a savagery that is rendered more dreadful by Cade's exposure of its irrelevance to most of its victims. In this play, Shakespeare depicts English history not as heroic but as horribly farcical.

OPPOSITE The rebellious commoner Jack Cade (Oliver Cotton), in the Royal Shakespeare Company's 1988 production.

[*Enter* CADE, DICK *the Butcher*, SMITH *the Weaver, a Sawyer, and a Drummer, with infinite numbers*]

CADE We, John Cade, so termed of our supposed father –

DICK [*Aside*] Or rather of stealing a cade of herrings.

CADE For our enemies shall fall before us, inspired with the spirit of putting down kings and princes – command silence!

DICK Silence!

CADE My father was a Mortimer –

DICK [*Aside*] He was an honest man and a good bricklayer.

CADE My mother a Plantagenet –

DICK [*Aside*] I knew her well, she was a midwife.

CADE My wife descended of the Lacies –

DICK [*Aside*] She was indeed a pedlar's daughter, and sold many laces.

SMITH [*Aside*] But now of late, not able to travel with her furred pack, she washes bucks here at home.

CADE Therefore am I of an honourable house.

'He can write and read and cast account.'

The crimes of the Clerk of Chatham, as the rebels see them, are as follows: he can do arithmetic ('cast account'); set writing exercises ('copies') for boys; owns a book, perhaps a Latin Primer to teach from, that looks like a book of spells; can prepare binding contracts ('obligations') and can write in legal script ('court hand'). His name (Emmanuel, meaning 'God with us') was used on official documents. For these reasons, they see him as a tool of the ruling classes and a corrupting influence on the young. Ironically, the ruling classes in *Henry VI* Part II are indeed as corrupt as the rebels believe the unfortunate clerk to be.

DICK [*Aside*] Ay, by my faith, the field is honourable, and there was he born, under a hedge, for his father had never a house but the cage.

CADE Valiant I am –

SMITH [*Aside*] A must needs, for beggary is valiant.

CADE I am able to endure much –

DICK [*Aside*] No question of that, for I have seen him whipped three market days together.

CADE I fear neither sword nor fire.

SMITH [*Aside*] He need not fear the sword, for his coat is of proof.

DICK [*Aside*] But methinks he should stand in fear of fire, being burnt i' th' hand for stealing of sheep.

CADE Be brave, then, for your captain is brave and vows reformation. There shall be in England seven halfpenny loaves sold for a penny, the three-hooped pot shall have ten hoops, and I will make it felony to drink small beer. All the realm shall be in common, and in Cheapside shall my palfrey go to grass. And when I am king, as king I will be –

ALL God save your majesty!

CADE I thank you, good people! – there shall be no money. All shall eat and drink on my score, and I will apparel them all in one livery, that they may agree like brothers and worship me their lord.

DICK The first thing we do let's kill all the lawyers.

CADE Nay, that I mean to do. Is not this a lamentable thing, that of the skin of an innocent lamb should be made parchment? That parchment, being scribbled o'er, should undo a man? Some say the bee stings, but I say 'tis the bee's wax; for I did but seal once to a thing, and I was never mine own man since. How now! Who's there?
[*Enter some, bringing forward the* CLERK *of Chatham*]

SMITH The Clerk of Chatham. He can write and read and cast account.

CADE O monstrous!

SMITH We took him setting of boys' copies.

CADE Here's a villain!

SMITH Has a book in his pocket with red letters in't.

CADE Nay, then he is a conjuror!

DICK Nay, he can make obligations and write court hand.

CADE I am sorry for't. The man is a proper man, of mine honour. Unless I find him guilty, he shall not die. Come hither, sirrah, I must examine thee. What is thy name?

CLERK Emmanuel.

DICK They use to write it on the top of letters – 'twill go hard with you.

CADE Let me alone. Dost thou use to write thy name? Or hast thou a mark to thyself, like an honest plain-dealing man?

CLERK Sir, I thank God I have been so well brought up that I can write my name.

ALL He hath confessed. Away with him! He's a villain and a traitor.

CADE Away with him, I say! Hang him with his pen and inkhorn about his neck.

[*Exit one with the* **CLERK**. *Enter* **MICHAEL**]

MICHAEL Where's our general?

CADE Here I am, thou particular fellow.

MICHAEL Fly, fly, fly! Sir Humphrey Stafford and his brother are hard by with the King's forces.

CADE Stand, villain, stand, or I'll fell thee down. He shall be encountered with a man as good as himself. He is but a knight, is a?

MICHAEL No.

CADE To equal him, I will make myself a knight presently. [*He kneels and knights himself*] Rise up, Sir John Mortimer. [*Rises*] Now have at him!

[*Enter* **SIR HUMPHREY** *and* **WILLIAM STAFFORD**, *with drum and Soldiers*]

SIR HUMPHREY Rebellious hinds, the filth and scum of Kent,
Marked for the gallows, lay your weapons down;
Home to your cottages, forsake this groom.
The King is merciful, if you revolt.

WILLIAM STAFFORD But angry, wrathful, and inclined to blood,
If you go forward. Therefore, yield or die.

CADE As for these silken-coated slaves, I pass not.
It is to you, good people, that I speak,
Over whom, in time to come, I hope to reign –
For I am rightful heir unto the crown.

SIR HUMPHREY Villain, thy father was a plasterer;
And thou thyself a shearman, art thou not?

CADE And Adam was a gardener.

WILLIAM STAFFORD And what of that?

CADE Marry, this: Edmund Mortimer, Earl of March, Married the Duke of Clarence' daughter, did he not?

SIR HUMPHREY Ay, sir.

CADE By her he had two children at one birth.

WILLIAM STAFFORD That's false.

CADE Ay, there's the question; but I say 'tis true.
The elder of them, being put to nurse,
Was by a beggar-woman stol'n away,
And, ignorant of his birth and parentage,
Became a bricklayer when he came to age.
His son am I – deny it if you can.

DICK Nay, 'tis too true; therefore he shall be king.

SMITH Sir, he made a chimney in my father's house, and the bricks are alive at this day to testify. Therefore deny it not.

SIR HUMPHREY And will you credit this base drudge's words
That speaks he knows not what?

ALL Ay, marry, will we; therefore get ye gone.

WILLIAM STAFFORD Jack Cade, the Duke of York hath taught you this.

CADE [*Aside*] He lies, for I invented it myself. [*Aloud*] Go to, sirrah, tell the King from me that for his father's sake, Henry the Fifth, in whose time boys went to span-counter for French crowns, I am content he shall reign; but I'll be Protector over him.

DICK And furthermore, we'll have the Lord Say's head for selling the dukedom of Maine.

CADE And good reason, for thereby is England maimed, and fain to go with a staff, but that my puissance holds it up. Fellow kings, I tell you that that Lord Say hath gelded the commonwealth, and made it an eunuch; and more than that, he can speak French, and therefore he is a traitor!

SIR HUMPHREY O gross and miserable ignorance!

CADE Nay, answer if you can: the Frenchmen are our enemies; go to, then, I ask but this: can he that speaks with the tongue of an enemy be a good counsellor or no?

ALL No, no – and therefore we'll have his head!

WILLIAM STAFFORD Well, seeing gentle words will not prevail,
Assail them with the army of the King.

SIR HUMPHREY Herald, away, and throughout every town
Proclaim them traitors that are up with Cade;
That those which fly before the battle ends
May, even in their wives' and children's sight,
Be hanged up for example at their doors.
And you that be the King's friends, follow me!
[*Exeunt* **WILLIAM STAFFORD** *and* **SIR HUMPHREY**, *and Soldiers*]

CADE And you that love the commons, follow me!
Now show yourselves men; 'tis for liberty.
We will not leave one lord, one gentleman;
Spare none but such as go in clouted shoon,
For they are thrifty honest men, and such
As would, but that they dare not, take our parts.

DICK They are all in order and march toward us.

CADE But then are we in order when we are most out of order. Come, march forward!

[*Exeunt*]

Henry VI
Part III

c.1592

ACT **1** | SCENE **4**

'O tiger's heart wrapped in a woman's hide!'

Our chosen scene from this play was well known in Shakespeare's time. In 1592 the playwright Robert Greene incorporated a line from it (York's description of Queen Margaret as having a 'tiger's heart wrapped in a woman's hide') into a notorious attack on Shakespeare in one of his popular pamphlets. Greene branded the young commoner from Stratford as an arrogant upstart with a 'tiger's heart wrapped in a player's hide', thus paying him the accidental compliment of quoting from the most emotionally powerful episode he had so far penned.

In it, Queen Margaret taunts her captured enemy, the Duke of York, for aspiring to the throne; she crowns him with a paper crown, wipes his eyes with a napkin stained with the blood of his murdered son, the Earl of Rutland, and finally stabs him to death, thereby unleashing on her family the vengeful fury of his surviving offspring. Greene's comment may have been intended to kick off a civil war among playwrights – university-educated wits like himself against young pretenders fresh from grammar school. But although Greene's university friend Thomas Lodge had written a half decent civil war play in 1590 (*The Wounds of Civil War*), by the time Greene launched his attack on Shakespeare the upstart playwright was the acknowledged master of the topic in Elizabethan London.

Henry VI Part III is the most mournfully contemplative of Shakespeare's early histories. Here, war is a family affair. The play begins and ends with the deaths of two sets of fathers and sons, caught in a vicious cycle of murder and revenge from which the warring families of Lancaster and York see little chance of emerging. In the first act the Lancastrian Clifford kills young Rutland, thus exacting a dreadful revenge for the death of his own father in the previous play. Soon afterwards Margaret, Henry VI's aggressive wife, helps Clifford kill Rutland's father, the Duke of York. In the last act tragedy afflicts the Lancastrians in their turn, as first Henry's son Prince Edward and then Henry himself are murdered by Richard of Gloucester, the future Richard III. Between these two sets of double murders, alliances and betrayals, victories and defeats follow one another with bewildering rapidity, as combatants struggle – and inevitably fail – to reconcile familial ties with political expediency.

At one point in Act 2, the ineffectual but saintly monarch Henry VI sees a man who has inadvertently killed his son in battle, and observes that 'The red rose and the white are on his face, / The fatal colours of our striving houses'. Each inhabitant of England, then, is symbolically embroiled in civil war by the colours of his or her complexion, their bodies marking them out as doomed to perpetual internecine conflict. The cycle is only broken with the emergence of a character who acknowledges no family ties whatever, and whose body defines him as different: the hunchback Richard of Gloucester. After his murder of Henry VI, Richard announces 'I am myself alone', and by saying so he offers an escape route from violence, even if that route lies through the horrors of his reign as king. In depicting the instability of fifteenth-century England, Shakespeare was careful to imply that all the issues raised in that epoch would be resolved in his own – while leaving his more sceptical spectators room to doubt it.

OPPOSITE York (Clive Wood) in his paper crown, in the Royal Shakespeare Company's 2000 production.

[YORK *is on stage. Enter* QUEEN MARGARET, CLIFFORD, NORTHUMBERLAND, PRINCE EDWARD, *and Soldiers*]

YORK Come, bloody Clifford, rough Northumberland,
I dare your quenchless fury to more rage!
I am your butt, and I abide your shot.

NORTHUMBERLAND Yield to our mercy, proud Plantagenet.

CLIFFORD Ay, to such mercy as his ruthless arm,
With downright payment, showed unto my father.
Now Phaethon hath tumbled from his car,
And made an evening at the noontide prick.

YORK My ashes, as the phoenix, may bring forth
A bird that will revenge upon you all,
And in that hope I throw mine eyes to heaven,
Scorning whate'er you can afflict me with.
Why come you not? What! Multitudes, and fear?

CLIFFORD So cowards fight when they can fly no further;
So doves do peck the falcon's piercing talons;
So desperate thieves, all hopeless of their lives,
Breathe out invectives 'gainst the officers.

YORK O Clifford, but bethink thee once again,
And in thy thought o'errun my former time,
And, if thou canst for blushing, view this face
And bite thy tongue that slanders him with cowardice
Whose frown hath made thee faint and fly ere this.

CLIFFORD I will not bandy with thee word for word,
But buckle with thee blows, twice two for one.

QUEEN MARGARET Hold, valiant Clifford: for a thousand causes
I would prolong awhile the traitor's life.
Wrath makes him deaf; speak thou, Northumberland.

NORTHUMBERLAND Hold, Clifford! Do not honour him so much
To prick thy finger, though to wound his heart.
What valour were it when a cur doth grin
For one to thrust his hand between his teeth
When he might spurn him with his foot away?
It is war's prize to take all vantages,
And ten to one is no impeach of valour.
[*They lay hands on* YORK, *who struggles*]

CLIFFORD Ay, ay, so strives the woodcock with the gin.

NORTHUMBERLAND So doth the cony struggle in the net.

YORK So triumph thieves upon their conquered booty;
So true men yield, with robbers so o'ermatched.

NORTHUMBERLAND What would your grace have done unto him now?

> *'Now Phaethon hath tumbled … made an evening at the noontide prick.'*
>
> In classical myth, Phaethon was the son of Phoebus, god of the sun, who borrowed his father's chariot and nearly burned up the world before being burned up himself by one of Zeus's thunderbolts. The emblem of the house of York was the sun; so throughout this scene the Lancastrians associate York with destructive flames like those that killed Phaethon.

QUEEN MARGARET Brave warriors, Clifford and Northumberland,
Come, make him stand upon this molehill here,
That wrought at mountains with outstretchèd arms
Yet parted but the shadow with his hand.
What, was it you that would be England's king?
Was't you that revelled in our Parliament,
And made a preachment of your high descent?
Where are your mess of sons to back you now?
The wanton Edward and the lusty George?
And where's that valiant crookback prodigy,
Dicky your boy, that with his grumbling voice
Was wont to cheer his dad in mutinies?
Or with the rest where is your darling Rutland?
Look, York, I stained this napkin with the blood
That valiant Clifford with his rapier's point
Made issue from the bosom of thy boy;
And if thine eyes can water for his death,
I give thee this to dry thy cheeks withal.
Alas, poor York! But that I hate thee deadly
I should lament thy miserable state.
I prithee grieve to make me merry, York.
What, hath thy fiery heart so parched thine entrails
That not a tear can fall for Rutland's death?
Why art thou patient, man? Thou shouldst be mad,
And I, to make thee mad, do mock thee thus.
Stamp, rave, and fret, that I may sing and dance.
Thou wouldst be fee'd, I see, to make me sport.
York cannot speak unless he wear a crown.
A crown for York, and, lords, bow low to him.
Hold you his hands whilst I do set it on.
[*Putting a paper crown on his head*]

Ay, marry, sir, now looks he like a king!
Ay, this is he that took King Henry's chair,
And this is he was his adopted heir.
But how is it that great Plantagenet
Is crowned so soon and broke his solemn oath?
As I bethink me, you should not be king
Till our King Henry had shook hands with death.
And will you pale your head in Henry's glory,
And rob his temples of the diadem
Now, in his life, against your holy oath?
O 'tis a fault too too unpardonable!
Off with the crown, and with the crown his head,
And whilst we breathe, take time to do him dead.

CLIFFORD That is my office for my father's sake.

QUEEN MARGARET Nay, stay; let's hear the
  orisons he makes.

YORK She-wolf of France, but worse than wolves
  of France,
Whose tongue more poisons than the adder's tooth!
How ill-beseeming is it in thy sex
To triumph like an Amazonian trull
Upon their woes whom fortune captivates!
But that thy face is visor-like, unchanging,
Made impudent with use of evil deeds,
I would essay, proud Queen, to make thee blush.
To tell thee whence thou cam'st, of whom derived,
Were shame enough to shame thee, wert thou not
  shameless.
Thy father bears the type of King of Naples,
Of both the Sicils and Jerusalem –
Yet not so wealthy as an English yeoman.
Hath that poor monarch taught thee to insult?
It needs not, nor it boots thee not, proud Queen,
Unless the adage must be verified
That beggars mounted run their horse to death.
'Tis beauty that doth oft make women proud;
But, God he knows, thy share thereof is small.
'Tis virtue that doth make them most admired;
The contrary doth make thee wondered at.
'Tis government that makes them seem divine;
The want thereof makes thee abominable.
Thou art as opposite to every good
As the Antipodes are unto us,
Or as the south to the septentrion.
O tiger's heart wrapped in a woman's hide!
How couldst thou drain the life-blood of the child
To bid the father wipe his eyes withal,
And yet be seen to bear a woman's face?
Women are soft, mild, pitiful, and flexible;
Thou stern, obdurate, flinty, rough, remorseless.
Bids't thou me rage? Why, now thou hast thy wish.
Wouldst have me weep? Why, now thou hast thy will.

For raging wind blows up incessant showers,
And when the rage allays the rain begins.
These tears are my sweet Rutland's obsequies,
And every drop cries vengeance for his death
'Gainst thee, fell Clifford, and thee, false
  Frenchwoman.

NORTHUMBERLAND Beshrew me, but his
  passions move me so
That hardly can I check my eyes from tears.

YORK That face of his the hungry cannibals
Would not have touched, would not have stained
  with blood;
But you are more inhuman, more inexorable,
O ten times more than tigers of Hyrcania.
See, ruthless Queen, a hapless father's tears.
This cloth thou dipp'dst in blood of my sweet boy,
And I with tears do wash the blood away.
Keep thou the napkin and go boast of this,
And if thou tell'st the heavy story right,
Upon my soul the hearers will shed tears,
Yea, even my foes will shed fast-falling tears
And say, 'Alas, it was a piteous deed!'
There, take the crown, and with the crown my curse;
And in thy need such comfort come to thee
As now I reap at thy too cruel hand!
Hard-hearted Clifford, take me from the world.
My soul to heaven, my blood upon your heads!

NORTHUMBERLAND Had he been slaughter-man
  to all my kin,
I should not for my life but weep with him,
To see how inly sorrow gripes his soul.

QUEEN MARGARET What, weeping-ripe, my
  Lord Northumberland?
Think but upon the wrong he did us all,
And that will quickly dry thy melting tears.

CLIFFORD Here's for my oath, here's for my
  father's death.
[*He stabs* YORK]

QUEEN MARGARET And here's to right our
  gentle-hearted King.
[*She stabs* YORK]

YORK Open thy gate of mercy, gracious God!
My soul flies through these wounds to seek
  out thee.
[*He dies*]

QUEEN MARGARET Off with his head and set
  it on York gates;
So York may overlook the town of York.
[*Flourish. Exeunt*]

Titus Andronicus

c.1592

> Even now I curse the day – and yet I think
> Few come within the compass of my curse –
> Wherein I did not some notorious ill

Ancient Rome lay at the heart of the Elizabethan school system. At Stratford grammar school, Shakespeare would have learned to see Roman culture as the source of all good writing, the touchstone by which any modern society must measure its claim to be 'civilized'. So when he set his first non-English tragedy in Rome, one might have expected him to approach the subject with timidity, overawed by the prospect of dramatizing the lives of the supreme exponents of drama, abashed at the thought of testing his rhetorical skills on the historical home of rhetoric …

Not a bit of it. Shakespeare chose instead to cock a snook at Rome. Instead of drawing on Roman history, he invented a story of his own, rewriting the decline and fall of the empire as a series of violent set pieces riddled with derisory laughter. He responded to the belief that Italy was the cradle of civilization by depicting it as fundamentally barbaric. And he mocked his old schoolmasters by filling his play with allusions to the schoolroom, where an appreciation of Latin was thumped into him with a stick. In *Titus*, Shakespeare had the temerity to mock the culture that shaped him; and having done so, he must have seemed to his audiences to be capable of anything.

On the face of it, *Titus* deals with the infiltration of a metropolis by the forces of savagery, as the queen of the Goths Tamora and her Moorish lover Aaron take a terrible revenge on the Roman general Titus for humiliating them in combat. But it soon becomes clear that savagery was endemic in Rome long before these foreigners got there. In the first act, Titus presides over a bloody ritual that horrifies Tamora – the sacrificial killing of an unarmed prisoner-of-war, Tamora's eldest son. In the last, he feeds Tamora's other offspring to her in a cannibalistic orgy. Between these framing atrocities, Rome's affinity with barbarism signals itself repeatedly: for instance, in the speed with which the Roman Emperor Saturninus woos and weds Tamora, or the ease with which the Romans catch on to the lessons she has to teach concerning the intimate relationship between revenge and laughter.

In the chosen scene, Tamora's lover Aaron has been captured by an army of Goths led by Lucius, who was banished for his loyalty to his father Titus and who then made common cause with the Goths against their former queen, now Empress of Rome. Here Aaron describes himself as a perverse schoolmaster, instructing Tamora's younger sons in the art of comic vengeance by showing them how to read Ovid's *Metamorphoses* – a standard Elizabethan school text – as an instruction manual in the art of rape. From it, the boys learned how to deflower Titus's daughter Lavinia, then cut off her hands and tongue to prevent her revealing their crime. And from this dreadful example Titus learns how to cook up a yet more dreadful revenge on Aaron's pupils. Aaron finds this and his other crimes against humanity hilarious. And the funniest of the pranks he pulls is to force the Romans to adopt his son by Tamora, in token of the arbitrariness of their attempts to separate their own 'civilization' from the 'barbarism' of non-Romans – like himself and his creator, Shakespeare.

OPPOSITE Detail of a 19th-century engraving depicting American-born actor Ira Aldridge as Aaron the Moor.

[*Enter* LUCIUS *with an army of Goths. Enter a*
GOTH, *leading* AARON, *his child in his arms*]

GOTH Renownèd Lucius, from our troops I strayed
To gaze upon a ruinous monastery,
And as I earnestly did fix mine eye
Upon the wasted building, suddenly
I heard a child cry underneath a wall.

Tut, I have done a thousand dreadful things
As willingly as one would kill a fly

I made unto the noise, when soon I heard
The crying babe controlled with this discourse:
'Peace, tawny slave, half me and half thy dam!
Did not thy hue bewray whose brat thou art,
Had nature lent thee but thy mother's look,
Villain, thou mightst have been an emperor;
But where the bull and cow are both milk-white
They never do beget a coal-black calf.
Peace, villain, peace!' – even thus he rates the babe –
'For I must bear thee to a trusty Goth
Who, when he knows thou art the Empress' babe,
Will hold thee dearly for thy mother's sake.'
With this, my weapon drawn, I rushed upon him,
Surprised him suddenly, and brought him hither
To use as you think needful of the man.

LUCIUS O worthy Goth, this is the incarnate devil
That robbed Andronicus of his good hand.
This is the pearl that pleased your Empress' eye,
And here's the base fruit of her burning lust.
[*To* AARON] Say, wall-eyed slave, whither wouldst
thou convey
This growing image of thy fiend-like face?
Why dost not speak? What, deaf? What, not a word?
A halter, soldiers! Hang him on this tree,
And by his side his fruit of bastardy.

AARON Touch not the boy, he is of royal blood.

LUCIUS Too like the sire for ever being good.
First hang the child, that he may see it sprawl –
A sight to vex the father's soul withal.
Get me a ladder.
[*A ladder is brought, which* AARON *climbs*]

AARON   Lucius, save the child,
And bear it from me to the Empress.

If thou do this, I'll show thee wondrous things
That highly may advantage thee to hear.
If thou wilt not, befall what may befall,
I'll speak no more but 'Vengeance rot you all!'

LUCIUS Say on, and if it please me which thou
speak'st
Thy child shall live, and I will see it nourished.

AARON And if it please thee! Why, assure thee,
Lucius,
'Twill vex thy soul to hear what I shall speak;
For I must talk of murders, rapes and massacres,
Acts of black night, abominable deeds,
Complots of mischief, treason, villainies
Ruthful to hear yet piteously performed,
And this shall all be buried in my death
Unless thou swear to me my child shall live.

LUCIUS Tell on thy mind. I say thy child shall live.

AARON Swear that he shall, and then I will begin.

LUCIUS Who should I swear by? Thou believest
no god.
That granted, how canst thou believe an oath?

AARON What if I do not? – as indeed I do not –
Yet for I know thou art religious
And hast a thing within thee callèd conscience,
With twenty popish tricks and ceremonies
Which I have seen thee careful to observe,
Therefore I urge thy oath; for that I know
An idiot holds his bauble for a god
And keeps the oath which by that god he swears,
To that I'll urge him, therefore thou shalt vow
By that same god, what god soe'er it be,
That thou adorest and hast in reverence,
To save my boy, to nurse and bring him up,
Or else I will discover naught to thee.

LUCIUS Even by my god I swear to thee I will.

AARON First know thou, I begot him on the
Empress.

LUCIUS O most insatiate and luxurious woman!

Titus Andronicus

'Ay, that I had not done a thousand more.'

Aaron's extravagant crimes recall those of a character in Marlowe's *The Jew of Malta* (c. 1592), the Turk Ithamore, who claims (among other things) that 'Once at Jerusalem, where the pilgrims kneeled, / I strewèd powder on the marble stones, / And therewithal their knees would rankle so / That I have laughed a-good to see the cripples / Go limping home to Christendom on stilts.' Shakespeare's early tragedies and histories are much indebted to his famous contemporary Marlowe, who was killed in 1593.

AARON Tut, Lucius, this was but a deed of charity
To that which thou shalt hear of me anon.
'Twas her two sons that murdered Bassianus.
They cut thy sister's tongue and ravished her,
And cut her hands, and trimmed her as thou sawest.

LUCIUS O detestable villain! Call'st thou that
trimming?

AARON Why, she was washed and cut and
trimmed, and 'twas
Trim sport for them that had the doing of it.

LUCIUS O barbarous beastly villains, like thyself!

AARON Indeed, I was their tutor to instruct them.
That codding spirit had they from their mother,
As sure a card as ever won the set.
That bloody mind I think they learned of me,
As true a dog as ever fought at head.
Well, let my deeds be witness of my worth.
I trained thy brethren to that guileful hole
Where the dead corpse of Bassianus lay.
I wrote the letter that thy father found,
And hid the gold within that letter mentioned,
Confederate with the Queen and her two sons;
And what not done that thou hast cause to rue
Wherein I had no stroke of mischief in it?
I played the cheater for thy father's hand,
And, when I had it, drew myself apart
And almost broke my heart with extreme laughter.
I pried me through the crevice of a wall
When for his hand he had his two sons' heads,
Beheld his tears, and laughed so heartily
That both mine eyes were rainy like to his;
And when I told the Empress of this sport
She swoonèd almost at my pleasing tale,
And for my tidings gave me twenty kisses.

A GOTH What, canst thou say all this and
never blush?

AARON Ay, like a black dog, as the saying is.

LUCIUS Art thou not sorry for these heinous deeds?

AARON Ay, that I had not done a thousand more.
Even now I curse the day – and yet I think
Few come within the compass of my curse –
Wherein I did not some notorious ill,
As kill a man, or else devise his death;
Ravish a maid, or plot the way to do it;
Accuse some innocent and forswear myself;
Set deadly enmity between two friends;
Make poor men's cattle break their necks;
Set fire on barns and haystacks in the night,
And bid the owners quench them with their tears.
Oft have I digged up dead men from their graves
And set them upright at their dear friends' door,
Even when their sorrows almost was forgot,
And on their skins, as on the bark of trees,
Have with my knife carvèd in Roman letters,
'Let not your sorrow die, though I am dead.'
Tut, I have done a thousand dreadful things
As willingly as one would kill a fly,
And nothing grieves me heartily indeed
But that I cannot do ten thousand more.

LUCIUS Bring down the devil, for he must not die
So sweet a death as hanging presently.

AARON If there be devils, would I were a devil,
To live and burn in everlasting fire,
So I might have your company in hell
But to torment you with my bitter tongue!

LUCIUS Sirs, stop his mouth, and let him speak
no more.
[*Goths gag* **AARON**]

'I played the cheater for thy father's hand'

Earlier, Aaron framed two of Titus's sons for murder, then persuaded Titus they would be spared from execution if he lopped off his hand and sent it to the Senate. 'Cheater' means escheator, an officer appointed to look after property forfeited to the crown. Aaron also means he cheated, as if in a game of cards, to win Titus's 'hand' by trickery.

Henry VI Part I

c. 1592

ACT 4 | **SCENES 5–7**

❝ Poor boy! He smiles, methinks, as who should say,
'Had death been French, then death had died today.' ❞

In this, perhaps the third of Shakespeare's histories, England's military triumphs in France are undermined by political in-fighting at home. The play opens with the funeral of the legendary warrior-king Henry V; and before he is buried the kingdom starts to fall apart. A squabble breaks out between a duke and a bishop, whose acrimonious rivalry anticipates the approaching civil wars between Lancaster and York. For a time the shreds of English unity are held together by Lord Talbot, indomitable commander of the English troops on the continent; but when he dies the nation plunges into internecine strife.

In 1592, Thomas Nashe wrote of Shakespeare's play that Talbot's death was greeted 'with the tears of ten thousand spectators at least' in its first performances. Clearly audiences found the passing of this English hero deeply poignant at a time when the country's stability was again under threat, both from continental invasion and internal divisions, in the final years of Elizabeth I.

For much of the play, Shakespeare stresses the integrity and masculinity of the English forces under Talbot at the expense of the French, whom he represents as effeminate turncoats. The French put their trust in Joan La Pucelle, one of several strong women in the early history plays who throw themselves wholeheartedly into the power struggles between men. Joan finds herself reviled for her involvement, and her body subject to attack, first by bawdy innuendo, then by fire. She defends herself by forging sexual alliances – first with the king of France, then with the spirits that give her superhuman strength in combat – but all her lovers betray her. The French dependence on Joan sets them in stark opposition to the English, whose monarch is the saintly and virginal Henry VI.

In our extract, however, it is Talbot's son John who is depicted as virginal. As the French close in, Talbot tries to persuade the boy to withdraw from action. John refuses, since 'The world will say he is not Talbot's blood / That basely fled when noble Talbot stood'. What follows is a strange male bonding ritual, in which the two men reinforce their familial relationship through a series of re-enactments, on the battlefield, of the legitimate sexual act by which young John was conceived. John loses his military 'maidenhood' by having his blood shed by the Bastard Orleans, and is then rescued from death by his father, who becomes thereby (as John puts it) 'twice my father'. Soon afterwards the boy rescues Talbot, which makes him a kind of parent in his turn. And when the boy is finally killed, the dying Talbot imagines them flying together to heaven like sexless angels – 'Two Talbots wingèd through the lither sky' – or like the mythical father and son Daedalus and Icarus, who fled from tyranny on artificial wings. The comparison transforms them into fugitives from a more heroic age, and marks too that age's passing. Their deaths here are brought about (unhistorically) by a dispute between the Duke of York and his Lancastrian rival Somerset over who should send them reinforcements. Once they have gone, and Joan has been burned, all that is left for England is the prospect of civil bloodshed, and a landscape littered with the corpses of fathers and sons who have died killing each other.

OPPOSITE Lord Talbot (Keith Bartlett) and Joan La Pucelle (Katy Stephens) in the Royal Shakespeare Company's 2006 production.

❦ | ACT 4 | SCENE 5
A battlefield near Bordeaux – the English Camp

[*Enter* **TALBOT** *and* **JOHN** *his son*]

TALBOT O young John Talbot! I did send for thee
To tutor thee in stratagems of war,
That Talbot's name might be in thee revived
When sapless age and weak unable limbs
Should bring thy father to his drooping chair.
But – O malignant and ill-boding stars! –
Now thou art come unto a feast of death,
A terrible and unavoided danger.
Therefore, dear boy, mount on my swiftest horse,
And I'll direct thee how thou shalt escape
By sudden flight. Come, dally not, be gone.

JOHN Is my name Talbot, and am I your son,
And shall I fly? O, if you love my mother,
Dishonour not her honourable name
To make a bastard and a slave of me!
The world will say he is not Talbot's blood
That basely fled when noble Talbot stood.

TALBOT Fly to revenge my death if I be slain.

JOHN He that flies so will ne'er return again.

TALBOT If we both stay, we both are sure to die.

JOHN Then let me stay and, father, do you fly.
Your loss is great, so your regard should be;
My worth unknown, no loss is known in me.
Upon my death the French can little boast;
In yours they will, in you all hopes are lost.
Flight cannot stain the honour you have won,
But mine it will, that no exploit have done.
You fled for vantage, everyone will swear,
But if I bow, they'll say it was for fear.
There is no hope that ever I will stay
If the first hour I shrink and run away.
Here on my knee I beg mortality
Rather than life preserved with infamy.

TALBOT Shall all thy mother's hopes lie in one tomb?

JOHN Ay, rather than I'll shame my mother's womb.

TALBOT Upon my blessing, I command thee go.

JOHN To fight I will, but not to fly the foe.

TALBOT Part of thy father may be saved in thee.

JOHN No part of him but will be shamed in me.

TALBOT Thou never hadst renown, nor canst not lose it.

JOHN Yes, your renownèd name; shall flight
abuse it?

TALBOT Thy father's charge shall clear thee
from that stain.

JOHN You cannot witness for me, being slain.
If death be so apparent, then both fly.

TALBOT And leave my followers here to fight and die?
My age was never tainted with such shame.

JOHN And shall my youth be guilty of such blame?
No more can I be severed from your side
Than can yourself your self in twain divide.
Stay, go, do what you will, the like do I;
For live I will not if my father die.

TALBOT Then here I take my leave of thee, fair son,
Born to eclipse thy life this afternoon.
Come, side by side together live and die,
And soul with soul from France to heaven fly.
[*Exeunt*]

ACT 4 | SCENE 6
The battlefield

[*Alarum. Excursions, wherein* **JOHN** *is hemmed about,
and* **TALBOT** *rescues him*]

TALBOT Saint George and victory! Fight, soldiers, fight!
The Regent hath with Talbot broke his word
And left us to the rage of France his sword.
Where is John Talbot? Pause and take thy breath.
I gave thee life, and rescued thee from death.

JOHN O twice my father, twice am I thy son!
The life thou gav'st me first was lost and done
Till with thy warlike sword, despite of fate,
To my determined time thou gav'st new date.

TALBOT When from the Dauphin's crest thy sword
struck fire
It warmed thy father's heart with proud desire
Of bold-faced victory. Then leaden age,
Quickened with youthful spleen and warlike rage,
Beat down Alençon, Orleans, Burgundy,
And from the pride of Gallia rescued thee.
The ireful Bastard Orleans, that drew blood
From thee, my boy, and had the maidenhood
Of thy first fight, I soon encounterèd,

*Surely, by all the glory you have won,
An if I fly I am not Talbot's son.*

And interchanging blows, I quickly shed
Some of his bastard blood, and in disgrace
Bespoke him thus: 'Contaminated, base,
And misbegotten blood I spill of thine,
Mean and right poor, for that pure blood of mine
Which thou didst force from Talbot, my brave boy.'
Here, purposing the Bastard to destroy,
Came in strong rescue. Speak, thy father's care;
Art thou not weary, John? How dost thou fare?
Wilt thou yet leave the battle, boy, and fly,
Now thou art sealed the son of chivalry?
Fly, to revenge my death when I am dead;
The help of one stands me in little stead.
O, too much folly is it, well I wot,
To hazard all our lives in one small boat.
If I today die not with Frenchmen's rage,
Tomorrow I shall die with mickle age.
By me they nothing gain, and if I stay
'Tis but the short'ning of my life one day.
In thee thy mother dies, our household's name,
My death's revenge, thy youth, and England's fame.
All these and more we hazard by thy stay;
All these are saved if thou wilt fly away.

JOHN The sword of Orleans hath not made
  me smart;
These words of yours draw life-blood from
  my heart.
On that advantage, bought with such a shame,
To save a paltry life and slay bright fame,
Before young Talbot from old Talbot fly,
The coward horse that bears me fail and die!
And like me to the peasant boys of France,
To be shame's scorn and subject of mischance!
Surely, by all the glory you have won,
An if I fly I am not Talbot's son.
Then talk no more of flight; it is no boot.
If son to Talbot, die at Talbot's foot.

TALBOT Then follow thou thy desp'rate sire
  of Crete,

> ### 'The ireful Bastard Orleans, that drew blood … Of thy first fight'
>
> As often in Shakespeare, warfare here bears a perverse resemblance to sex. Talbot refers to the notion that women bleed when they first make love; and he goes on to suggest that his son John's willingness to bleed in battle shows him to be Talbot's legitimate heir, whereas the Frenchman Orleans, who robs him of his 'maidenhood' (virginity) as a soldier, is a bastard.

Thou Icarus; thy life to me is sweet.
If thou wilt fight, fight by thy father's side;
And, commendable proved, let's die in pride.
[*Exeunt*]

ACT **4** | SCENE **7**
Another part of the field

[*Alarum. Excursions. Enter* **TALBOT** *led by
  a* **SERVANT**]

TALBOT Where is my other life? Mine own is gone.
O where's young Talbot? Where is valiant John?
Triumphant death, smeared with captivity,
Young Talbot's valour makes me smile at thee.
When he perceived me shrink and on my knee,
His bloody sword he brandished over me,
And like a hungry lion did commence
Rough deeds of rage and stern impatience.
But when my angry guardant stood alone,
Tend'ring my ruin and assailed of none,
Dizzy-eyed fury and great rage of heart
Suddenly made him from my side to start
Into the clust'ring battle of the French,
And in that sea of blood my boy did drench
His over-mounting spirit; and there died
My Icarus, my blossom, in his pride.
[*Enter English Soldiers, bearing the body of* **JOHN**]

SERVANT O my dear lord, lo where your son is
  borne.

TALBOT Thou antic death, which laugh'st us here
  to scorn,
Anon from thy insulting tyranny,
Coupled in bonds of perpetuity,
Two Talbots wingèd through the lither sky
In thy despite shall scape mortality.
[*To* **JOHN**] O thou whose wounds become hard-
  favoured death,
Speak to thy father ere thou yield thy breath.
Brave death by speaking, whether he will or no;
Imagine him a Frenchman and thy foe.
Poor boy! He smiles, methinks, as who should say,
'Had death been French, then death had died today.'
Come, come, and lay him in his father's arms.
My spirit can no longer bear these harms.
Soldiers, adieu! I have what I would have,
Now my old arms are young John Talbot's grave.
[*Dies*]

Richard III

c. 1592-93

ACT **1** | SCENE **2**

‘ Was ever woman in this humour wooed?
Was ever woman in this humour won? ’

***Richard III* is Shakespeare's most exuberantly self-promoting villain. The charm and skill with which he perpetrates his atrocities have made the story of his rise and fall one of Shakespeare's biggest successes on stage and screen. There is no record of the play's reception on its first performance (*c.* 1592–3), but it was frequently reprinted and often alluded to. Acting as vengeful commentators on Richard's career, the women of the play dub him a 'lump of foul deformity' and an 'elvish-marked, abortive, rooting hog', but his reign in the theatre has proved anything but abortive.**

Much of Richard's appeal derives from his talent for rewriting history. In the three parts of *Henry VI* the warring factions of the aristocracy arranged themselves along familial lines, brother joining with brother to avenge wrongs done to fathers and sons. Richard is the monstrous product of this bloodletting among relatives, a child born and raised in a time of violence, whose physical difference sets him apart from the loyalties of his contemporaries. Nature, he claims at the beginning of *Richard III*, sent him into the world 'scarce half made up', and he spends the rest of the play imaginatively 'making up' the rest of himself in a range of different roles. One by one he takes on every male role that figured prominently in the conflicts of Henry's reign: the innocent child, the lover making a daring political match, the churchman, the warrior, the schemer; and as he does so he revises the history of the Wars of the Roses. With breathtaking dexterity he rearranges the contours of the feuding families to suit his purpose, first by wooing the widow of the prince he has murdered, then by killing his own brother and branding his nephews bastards. On the eve of his defeat at Bosworth he is engineering his most outrageous revision yet: he plans to transform King Edward's daughter, whose two young brothers he has recently murdered, from his enemy into his second wife. His suit consists of narrating to the girl's mother a potted survey of the future – a future in which the audience knows he will have no share: 'Again shall you be mother to a king, / And all the ruins of distressful times / Repaired with double riches of content.' Even as death approaches, Richard has the gall to manipulate future history to put himself at centre stage.

The scene given here begins halfway through his courtship of his first wife, Lady Anne, whose husband and father-in-law he murdered in *Henry VI* Part III. It shows him at his most brilliantly plausible, timing his advances to her with the meticulous precision of a professional musician, and ending with one of the great soliloquies in which he enlists the theatre audience in his dastardly schemes. This murderous chancer builds his claim to the throne on nothing; so that when he ends the play, lost and wounded on the battlefield at Bosworth, offering to exchange his kingdom for something as simple as a horse, we can be forgiven for half-believing that he might make the bargain and evade his doom – riding out from among the massed forces of his enemies to forge some other, equally outrageous history for himself in a more hospitable kingdom.

OPPOSITE Celebrated Shakespearian actor David Garrick playing Richard III in a painting by William Hogarth (1745).

[*Enter gentlemen, bearing the coffin of Henry VI,*
LADY ANNE *being the mourner. Enter* RICHARD
Duke of GLOUCESTER]

GLOUCESTER It is a quarrel most unnatural,
To be revenged on him that loveth thee.

LADY ANNE It is a quarrel just and reasonable,
To be revenged on him that killed my husband.

GLOUCESTER He that bereft thee, lady, of thy
husband,
Did it to help thee to a better husband.

LADY ANNE His better doth not breathe upon
the earth.

GLOUCESTER He lives that loves thee better than
he could.

LADY ANNE Name him.

GLOUCESTER   Plantagenet.

LADY ANNE   Why, that was he.

GLOUCESTER The selfsame name, but one of
better nature.

LADY ANNE Where is he?

GLOUCESTER   Here. [*She spits at him*]
                    Why dost thou spit at me?

LADY ANNE Would it were mortal poison for
thy sake!

GLOUCESTER Never came poison from so sweet
a place.

LADY ANNE Never hung poison on a fouler toad.

Out of my sight! Thou dost infect mine eyes.

GLOUCESTER Thine eyes, sweet lady, have
infected mine.

LADY ANNE Would they were basilisks to strike
thee dead!

GLOUCESTER I would they were, that I might
die at once,
For now they kill me with a living death.
Those eyes of thine from mine have drawn salt
tears,
Shamed their aspects with store of childish drops;
These eyes, which never shed remorseful tear,
No, when my father York and Edward wept
To hear the piteous moan that Rutland made
When black-faced Clifford shook his sword
at him;
Nor when thy warlike father, like a child,
Told the sad story of my father's death,
And twenty times made pause to sob and weep,
That all the standers-by had wet their cheeks
Like trees bedashed with rain. In that sad time
My manly eyes did scorn an humble tear;

> ### 'It is a quarrel … revenged on him that killed my husband.'
> This whole scene takes place in the presence of a coffin holding the body of King Henry VI. Richard – who is here called Gloucester, since he is not yet king – murdered Henry and his son, Prince Edward, at the end of *Henry VI* Part III. Lady Anne was married to Prince Edward – which makes Richard's temerity in courting her quite staggering.

And what these sorrows could not thence exhale
Thy beauty hath, and made them blind with
weeping.
I never sued to friend nor enemy;
My tongue could never learn sweet smoothing word;
But now thy beauty is proposed my fee,
My proud heart sues, and prompts my tongue
to speak.
[*She looks scornfully at him*]
Teach not thy lip such scorn, for it was made
For kissing, lady, not for such contempt.
If thy revengeful heart cannot forgive,
Lo, here I lend thee this sharp-pointed sword,
Which if thou please to hide in this true breast
And let the soul forth that adoreth thee,
I lay it naked to the deadly stroke
And humbly beg the death upon my knee.
[*He lays his breast open: she offers at it with his sword*]
Nay, do not pause; for I did kill King Henry –
But 'twas thy beauty that provokèd me.
Nay, now dispatch; 'twas I that stabbed young
Edward –
But 'twas thy heavenly face that set me on.
[*Here she lets fall the sword*]
Take up the sword again, or take up me.

> ### 'No, when my father York and Edward wept … Clifford shook his sword at him'
> Rutland was the youngest child of Richard's father, the Duke of York, butchered without mercy by Clifford in the opening scene of *Henry VI* Part III. Richard is saying that he never wept for the deaths of his father or his little brother, but that he has now been moved to tears by Lady Anne's beauty.

LADY ANNE Arise, dissembler. Though I wish
thy death,
I will not be thy executioner.

GLOUCESTER Then bid me kill myself, and I
will do it.

LADY ANNE I have already.

GLOUCESTER   That was in thy rage.
Speak it again, and even with the word
This hand, which for thy love did kill thy love,
Shall for thy love kill a far truer love;
To both their deaths shalt thou be accessary.

LADY ANNE I would I knew thy heart.

GLOUCESTER 'Tis figured in my tongue.

LADY ANNE I fear me both are false.

GLOUCESTER Then never man was true.

LADY ANNE Well, well, put up your sword.

But since you teach me how to flatter you,
Imagine I have said farewell already. [Exit]

GLOUCESTER Sirs, take up the corpse.

GENTLEMEN Towards Chertsey, noble lord?

GLOUCESTER No, to Blackfriars; there attend
    my coming.
[*Exeunt all but* GLOUCESTER]
Was ever woman in this humour wooed?
Was ever woman in this humour won?
I'll have her, but I will not keep her long.
What! I, that killed her husband and his father,
To take her in her heart's extremest hate,

He that bereft thee, lady, of thy husband,
Did it to help thee to a better husband.

GLOUCESTER Say then my peace is made.

LADY ANNE That shalt thou know hereafter.

GLOUCESTER But shall I live in hope?

LADY ANNE All men, I hope, live so.

GLOUCESTER Vouchsafe to wear this ring.

LADY ANNE To take is not to give.

GLOUCESTER Look how my ring encompasseth
    thy finger,
Even so thy breast encloseth my poor heart.
Wear both of them, for both of them are thine.
And if thy poor devoted servant may
But beg one favour at thy gracious hand,
Thou dost confirm his happiness for ever.

LADY ANNE What is it?

GLOUCESTER That it may please thee leave these
    sad designs
To him that hath more cause to be a mourner,
And presently repair to Crosby House;
Where – after I have solemnly interred
At Chertsey monast'ry this noble king
And wet his grave with my repentant tears –
I will with all expedient duty see you.
For divers unknown reasons. I beseech you
Grant me this boon.

LADY ANNE With all my heart; and much it joys
    me, too,
To see you are become so penitent.
Tressel and Berkeley, go along with me.

GLOUCESTER Bid me farewell.

LADY ANNE   'Tis more than you deserve.

With curses in her mouth, tears in her eyes,
The bleeding witness of my hatred by;
Having God, her conscience, and these bars
    against me,
And I no friends to back my suit at all
But the plain devil and dissembling looks,
And yet to win her, all the world to nothing?
Ha!
Hath she forgot already that brave prince,
Edward her lord, whom I some three months since
Stabbed in my angry mood at Tewkesbury?
A sweeter and a lovelier gentleman –
Framed in the prodigality of nature,
Young, valiant, wise, and no doubt right royal –
The spacious world cannot again afford;
And will she yet abase her eyes on me,
That cropped the golden prime of this sweet prince
And made her widow to a woeful bed?
On me, whose all not equals Edward's moiety?
On me, that halts and am misshapen thus?
My dukedom to a beggarly denier,
I do mistake my person all this while.
Upon my life, she finds, although I cannot,
Myself to be a marv'llous proper man.
I'll be at charges for a looking-glass,
And entertain some score or two of tailors
To study fashions to adorn my body.
Since I am crept in favour with myself,
I will maintain it with some little cost.
But first I'll turn yon fellow in his grave,
And then return lamenting to my love.
Shine out, fair sun, till I have bought a glass,
That I may see my shadow as I pass. [*Exit*]

The Comedy of Errors *c.1594*

> Am I in earth, in heaven, or in hell?
> Sleeping or waking? Mad or well-advised?

The Comedy of Errors

The only one of Shakespeare's comedies to have 'comedy' in the title, *The Comedy of Errors* reads like a dazzling demonstration of the serious social themes that could be investigated through this, the humblest and most manically inventive of theatrical genres.

The word 'errors' refers to the mistakes that arise when two pairs of identical twins who were separated at birth unwittingly find themselves in the same city, getting confused with one another to hilarious effect. But it refers too to physical and mental wandering (from the Latin *errare*), and invokes the perils of finding oneself cut off from familiar co-ordinates, stranded among strangers without access to the essential support networks provided by family and friends. These perils become obvious in the first scene, when the father of one pair of twins, Egeon, is condemned to death by the Duke of Ephesus simply for being a citizen of Syracuse, a state with which Ephesus is at war. The duke defers Egeon's execution out of pity, recognizing the injustice of the law that has doomed him, but unwilling to waive it. The rest of the comedy, then, takes place in the chronological space between a stranger's sentencing and the time set for his beheading; and this confirms Shakespeare's conviction that comedy exists on a knife-edge between disaster and delight, the distinction between these two outcomes being often little more than a matter of timing.

In our extract, Antipholus of Syracuse is mistaken for his brother Antipholus of Ephesus by his brother's wife Adriana and her sister Luciana. At the same time, his servant Dromio is being mistaken for his twin brother, Dromio of Ephesus, with results that are painful as well as funny, since he gets bullied and beaten for failing to carry out instructions that each of his masters thinks he has given him. Antipholus of Syracuse will find his visit to Ephesus more painful still, should he fall victim to the tyrannical law under which his father stands condemned. But Antipholus is less worried by this very real danger than by his superstitious certainty that Ephesus is infested with malignant fairies (as Dromio puts it here, 'This is the fairy land. O spite of spites! / We talk with goblins, oafs, and sprites'), a conviction that arises from his encounter with Adriana, who 'wafts' him into her home, claiming him as her husband, like the man-eating Fairy Queen of popular tradition. Meanwhile, his brother finds that the 'errors' of the play's title affect his standing as a businessman in Ephesus. Trust that he has built up with clients and tradesmen over the years is abruptly broken, and he finds his sanity questioned, so that his efforts to exonerate himself prove ineffectual. Both brothers learn, in fact, just how precarious identity can be, and how fragile are the alliances on which its confirmation depends.

It's a lesson they could have learned less painfully by listening to Adriana, who here points out the insouciance with which a husband can renege on his nuptial promises, thus effectively calling into question the identity of his wife. Women know about the dangers of arbitrary power from their experience of it in the patriarchal household; and Adriana conveys these dangers in this scene with unnerving eloquence and precision.

OPPOSITE Antipholus of Syracuse (Desmond Barrit) is baffled by the attentions of Adriana (Estelle Kohler) in the Royal Shakespeare Company's 1990 production.

[*Enter* ANTIPHOLUS OF SYRACUSE *and* DROMIO OF SYRACUSE. *To them, enter* ADRIANA *and* LUCIANA]

ANTIPHOLUS OF SYRACUSE
But soft! Who wafts us yonder?

ADRIANA
Ay, ay, Antipholus, look strange and frown.
Some other mistress hath thy sweet aspects.
I am not Adriana, nor thy wife.
The time was once when thou unurged
   wouldst vow
That never words were music to thine ear,
That never object pleasing in thine eye,
That never touch well welcome to thy hand,
That never meat sweet-savoured in thy taste,
Unless I spake, or looked, or touched, or carved
  to thee.
How comes it now, my husband,
   O how comes it
That thou art then estrangèd from thyself?
Thy 'self' I call it, being strange to me,
That, undividable, incorporate,
Am better than thy dear self's better part.
Ah, do not tear away thyself from me;
For know, my love, as easy mayst thou fall
A drop of water in the breaking gulf,
And take unmingled thence that drop again
Without addition or diminishing,
As take from me thyself, and not me too.
How dearly would it touch thee to the quick
Shouldst thou but hear I were licentious,
And that this body, consecrate to thee,
By ruffian lust should be contaminate?
Wouldst thou not spit at me and spurn at me
And hurl the name of husband in my face,
And tear the stained skin off my harlot-brow,
And from my false hand cut the wedding-ring,
And break it with a deep-divorcing vow?
I know thou canst, and therefore see thou do it!
I am possessed with an adulterate blot;
My blood is mingled with the crime of lust.
For if we two be one, and thou play false,
I do digest the poison of thy flesh,
Being strumpeted by thy contagion.

Keep then fair league and truce with thy true bed,
I live unstained, thou undishonourèd.

ANTIPHOLUS OF SYRACUSE
Plead you to me, fair dame? I know you not.
In Ephesus I am but two hours old,
As strange unto your town as to your talk,
Who, every word by all my wit being scanned,
Wants wit in all one word to understand.

> **'How comes it now … estrangèd from thyself?'**
>
> Adriana's speech here draws on the Christian doctrine that marriage makes husband and wife 'one flesh', as expressed in Genesis 2:23-4: 'Then the man said, This now is … flesh of my flesh. She shall be called woman, because she was taken out of man. Therefore shall man leave his father and his mother, and shall cleave to his wife, and they shall be one flesh.'

LUCIANA
Fie, brother, how the world is changed with you!
When were you wont to use my sister thus?
She sent for you by Dromio home to dinner.

ANTIPHOLUS OF SYRACUSE
By Dromio?

DROMIO OF SYRACUSE
By me?

ADRIANA
By thee; and this thou didst return from him –
That he did buffet thee, and in his blows
Denied my house for his, me for his wife.

ANTIPHOLUS OF SYRACUSE
Did you converse, sir, with this gentlewoman?
What is the course and drift of your compact?

DROMIO OF SYRACUSE
I, sir? I never saw her till this time.

ANTIPHOLUS OF SYRACUSE
Villain, thou liest; for even her very words
Didst thou deliver to me on the mart.

What error drives our eyes and ears amiss?

The Comedy of Errors

DROMIO OF SYRACUSE

I never spake with her in all my life.

ANTIPHOLUS OF SYRACUSE

How can she thus then call us by our names?
Unless it be by inspiration.

ADRIANA

How ill agrees it with your gravity
To counterfeit thus grossly with your slave,
Abetting him to thwart me in my mood!
Be it my wrong you are from me exempt,
But wrong not that wrong with a more contempt.
Come, I will fasten on this sleeve of thine.
Thou art an elm, my husband, I a vine,
Whose weakness, married to thy stronger state,
Makes me with thy strength to communicate.
If aught possess thee from me, it is dross,
Usurping ivy, brier, or idle moss,
Who, all for want of pruning, with intrusion
Infect thy sap, and live on thy confusion.

ANTIPHOLUS OF SYRACUSE

To me she speaks; she moves me for her theme.
What, was I married to her in my dream?
Or sleep I now, and think I hear all this?
What error drives our eyes and ears amiss?
Until I know this sure uncertainty,
I'll entertain the offered fallacy.

LUCIANA

Dromio, go bid the servants spread for dinner.

DROMIO OF SYRACUSE [*Aside*]

O, for my beads! I cross me for a sinner.
This is the fairy land. O spite of spites!
We talk with goblins, oafs, and sprites.
If we obey them not, this will ensue:
They'll suck our breath, or pinch us black and blue.

LUCIANA

Why prat'st thou to thyself and answer'st not?
Dromio, thou drone, thou snail, thou slug, thou sot!

DROMIO OF SYRACUSE [*To* ANTIPHOLUS]

I am transformèd, master, am not I?

ANTIPHOLUS OF SYRACUSE

I think thou art in mind, and so am I.

DROMIO OF SYRACUSE

Nay, master, both in mind and in my shape.

ANTIPHOLUS OF SYRACUSE

Thou hast thine own form.

DROMIO OF SYRACUSE

No, I am an ape.

LUCIANA

If thou art changed to aught, 'tis to an ass.

DROMIO OF SYRACUSE

'Tis true she rides me, and I long for grass.
'Tis so, I am an ass; else it could never be
But I should know her as well as she knows me.

ADRIANA

Come, come, no longer will I be a fool,
To put the finger in the eye and weep
Whilst man and master laughs my woes to scorn.
Come, sir, to dinner. Dromio, keep the gate.
Husband, I'll dine above with you today,
And shrive you of a thousand idle pranks.
Sirrah, if any ask you for your master,
Say he dines forth, and let no creature enter.
Come, sister. Dromio, play the porter well.

ANTIPHOLUS OF SYRACUSE

Am I in earth, in heaven, or in hell?
Sleeping or waking? Mad or well-advised?
Known unto these, and to myself disguised!
I'll say as they say, and persever so,
And in this mist at all adventures go.

> ### 'We talk with goblins … or pinch us black and blue.'
>
> Oafs are changelings, fairy children left in place of kidnapped human babies. Sucking the breath from sleepers, or pinching people, were favourite fairy pastimes. The best protection against them was to resort to Christian symbolism: the rosary ('beads') and making the sign of the cross. The rosary, crossing oneself and a belief in fairies were taken as symptoms of Catholic superstition in Protestant England.

DROMIO OF SYRACUSE

Master, shall I be porter at the gate?

ADRIANA

Ay, and let none enter, lest I break your pate.

LUCIANA

Come, come, Antipholus, we dine too late.

[*Exeunt*]

Love's Labour's Lost

c.1594-95

| ACT **4** | SCENE **3** |

❝ Never durst poet touch a pen to write
Until his ink were tempered with Love's sighs. ❞

The title of *Love's Labour's Lost* boldly proclaims its status as a time-wasting trifle, irresponsibly substituting itself for the fruitful labour of real workers and offering little in return. It foreshadows the play's ending, when four courtiers who have been courting four ladies find their efforts frustrated, their suits denied an answer. And it recalls the critique of all sexual passion made by the Elizabethan poetry-haters, for whom love's labour was *always* lost. Either way, the phrase pays wry tribute to the loving labour that has gone into the composition of this comedy, the most dazzling display of verbal pyrotechnics in the Shakespeare canon.

But the title has further resonances. Punctuated as *Love's Labours Lost*, it invokes the most arduous working period of all: the twelve-year labours of Hercules, whose name crops up throughout. Hercules was the most contradictory classical hero of the Renaissance, identified at once with brute strength, intellectual prowess and the comic humiliation of the dominant male. As a mental giant he makes an apt emblem for the aspirations of the King of Navarre and his companions at the start of the play. They plan to turn their court into a 'little academe' and live for three years in studious isolation, waging war against 'the huge army of the world's desires'. Hercules, too, was said to have striven against sensuality in his quest for enlightenment, his labours seen as allegories of the struggle of mind and soul against temptations of the flesh.

But Hercules also embodied the irresistible force of sensuality, since his love for Omphale led him to dress up as a woman and perform traditionally female domestic chores. When the Princess of France and her ladies come to visit, the men fall for them at once, and redirect their intellectual energies towards finding excuses to discard their oaths of chastity and woo their lovely guests. They place all their trust in the power of rhetoric – another sphere in which Hercules reigned supreme. But the courtiers gain nothing from their eloquence but a lashing from the tongues of the women, the verbal equivalent of the whipping Hercules received from his queenly mistress. The women see the men's willingness to break their promises as childish; so that when the courtiers decide to put on a show for their royal visitors it seems appropriate that the role of Hercules should be taken by a child, signalling the drastic diminution of the men's credibility as heroes since the play began.

Our extract starts at the point when the king and his friends have finally revealed that they are all in love. Berowne's climactic argument in favour of oath-breaking is one of the cleverest pieces of false logic in Shakespeare's work. It also shows why the women are right not to trust these puerile aristocrats; and why the play turns solemn in the final act, when news arrives of the King of France's death, and the princess returns home to her royal duties. The men press for an answer to their suits before she goes, but the women refuse to give one. Instead they send away their lovers with instructions to prove their passion by labouring like Hercules, for twelve months rather than twelve years. Only by the end of this protracted parturition can their love-language accumulate sufficient substance to be better than stillborn.

OPPOSITE Kenneth Branagh as Berowne with King Ferdinand (Alessandro Nivola), Longaville (Matthew Lillard) and Dumain (Adrian Lester) in Branagh's unconventional 2000 film adaptation.

[*Enter the* **KING** *of Navarre,* **BEROWNE**,
  LONGAVILLE, *and* **DUMAIN**]

BEROWNE Sweet lords, sweet lovers, O let us
  embrace!
As true we are as flesh and blood can be.
The sea will ebb and flow, heaven show his face;
Young blood doth not obey an old decree.
We cannot cross the cause why we were born,
Therefore of all hands must we be forsworn.

KING What, did these rent lines show some love
  of thine?

BEROWNE 'Did they?' quoth you. Who sees the
  heavenly Rosaline
That, like a rude and savage man of Inde
At the first op'ning of the gorgeous east,
Bows not his vassal head and, strucken blind,
Kisses the base ground with obedient breast?
What peremptory eagle-sighted eye
Dares look upon the heaven of her brow
That is not blinded by her majesty?

KING What zeal, what fury hath inspired thee now?
My love, her mistress, is a gracious moon;
She an attending star, scarce seen a light.

BEROWNE My eyes are then no eyes, nor I
  Berowne.
O, but for my love, day would turn to night!
Of all complexions the culled sovereignty
Do meet as at a fair in her fair cheek,
Where several worthies make one dignity,
Where nothing wants that want itself doth seek.
Lend me the flourish of all gentle tongues –
Fie, painted rhetoric! O, she needs it not.
To things of sale a seller's praise belongs.
She passes praise – then praise too short doth blot.
A withered hermit, five-score winters worn,
Might shake off fifty, looking in her eye.
Beauty doth varnish age as if new-born,
And gives the crutch the cradle's infancy.
O, 'tis the sun that maketh all things shine.

KING By heaven, thy love is black as ebony.

BEROWNE Is ebony like her? O word divine!
A wife of such wood were felicity.
O, who can give an oath? Where is a book,
That I may swear beauty doth beauty lack,
If that she learn not of her eye to look?
No face is fair that is not full so black.

KING O paradox! Black is the badge of hell,
The hue of dungeons and the school of night,
And beauty's crest becomes the heavens well.

BEROWNE Devils soonest tempt, resembling
  spirits of light.

O, if in black my lady's brows be decked,
It mourns that painting and usurping hair
Should ravish doters with a false aspect;
And therefore is she born to make black fair.
Her favour turns the fashion of the days,
For native blood is counted painting now,
And therefore red that would avoid dispraise
Paints itself black to imitate her brow.

> **'What, did these rent lines show some
> love of thine?'**
>
> Before this extract, the peasants Jaquenetta
> and Costard brought a letter to the king in
> the belief that it contained 'treason'. In fact
> it contained a love note from Berowne to
> Rosaline, 'treason' against the oath of
> chastity he swore at the beginning of
> the play. Berowne's praise of the dark
> complexion of his mistress should be
> compared to Shakespeare's 'Dark Lady'
> sonnets (sonnets 127–152).

DUMAIN To look like her are chimney-sweepers black.

LONGAVILLE And since her time are colliers
  counted bright.

KING And Ethiops of their sweet complexion crack.

DUMAIN Dark needs no candles now, for dark is light.

*As true we are as flesh
and blood can be …
Young blood doth not obey
an old decree.*

BEROWNE Your mistresses dare never come in rain,
For fear their colours should be washed away.

KING 'Twere good yours did; for, sir, to tell you plain,
I'll find a fairer face not washed to-day.

BEROWNE I'll prove her fair, or talk till
  doomsday here.

KING No devil will fright thee then so much as she.

DUMAIN I never knew man hold vile stuff so dear.

LONGAVILLE Look, here's thy love: my foot and
  her face see.

BEROWNE O, if the streets were pavèd with
  thine eyes,
Her feet were much too dainty for such tread.

> ### 'For valour, is not Love ... in the Hesperides?'
>
> This refers to the garden of golden apples that Hercules had to pick as the last of his twelve labours. The internal rhyme of this couplet renders the exploit childish, true to Berowne's conviction that love makes even wise old men infantile ('Beauty doth varnish age as if new-born / And gives the crutch the cradle's infancy').

DUMAIN O vile! Then, as she goes, what upward lies
The street should see as she walked overhead.

KING But what of this? Are we not all in love?

BEROWNE Nothing so sure, and thereby all
  forsworn.

KING Then leave this chat, and, good Berowne,
  now prove
Our loving lawful and our faith not torn.

DUMAIN Ay, marry, there: some flattery for this evil.

LONGAVILLE O, some authority how to proceed,
Some tricks, some quillets, how to cheat the devil.

DUMAIN Some salve for perjury.

BEROWNE   'Tis more than need.
Have at you then, affection's men-at-arms.
Consider what you first did swear unto:
To fast, to study, and to see no woman –
Flat treason 'gainst the kingly state of youth.
Say, can you fast? Your stomachs are too young,
And abstinence engenders maladies.
O, we have made a vow to study, lords,
And in that vow we have forsworn our books.
For when would you, my liege, or you, or you,
In leaden contemplation have found out
Such fiery numbers as the prompting eyes
Of beauty's tutors have enrich'd you with?
Other slow arts entirely keep the brain,
And therefore, finding barren practisers,
Scarce show a harvest of their heavy toil.
But love, first learnèd in a lady's eyes,
Lives not alone immuréd in the brain,
But, with the motion of all elements
Courses as swift as thought in every power,
And gives to every power a double power
Above their functions and their offices.
It adds a precious seeing to the eye –
A lover's eyes will gaze an eagle blind.
A lover's ear will hear the lowest sound
When the suspicious head of theft is stopped.
Love's feeling is more soft and sensible
Than are the tender horns of cockled snails.
Love's tongue proves dainty Bacchus gross in taste.

For valour, is not Love a Hercules,
Still climbing trees in the Hesperides?
Subtle as Sphinx; as sweet and musical
As bright Apollo's lute, strung with his hair;
And when Love speaks, the voice of all the gods
Makes heaven drowsy with the harmony.
Never durst poet touch a pen to write
Until his ink were tempered with Love's sighs.
O, then his lines would ravish savage ears,
And plant in tyrants mild humility.
From women's eyes this doctrine I derive.
They sparkle still the right Promethean fire.
They are the books, the arts, the academes,
That show, contain, and nourish all the world,
Else none at all in aught proves excellent.
Then fools you were these women to forswear,
Or keeping what is sworn, you will prove fools.
For wisdom's sake, a word that all men love,
Or for love's sake, a word that loves all men,
Or for men's sake, the authors of these women,
Or women's sake, by whom we men are men,
Let us once lose our oaths to find ourselves,
Or else we lose ourselves to keep our oaths.
It is religion to be thus forsworn,
For charity itself fulfills the law,
And who can sever love from charity?

KING Saint Cupid, then! And, soldiers, to the field!

BEROWNE Advance your standards, and upon
  them, lords;
Pell-mell, down with them! But be first advised
In conflict that you get the sun of them.

LONGAVILLE Now to plain dealing. Lay these
  glozes by.
Shall we resolve to woo these girls of France?

KING And win them, too. Therefore let us devise
Some entertainment for them in their tents.

BEROWNE First, from the park let us conduct
  them thither;
Then homeward every man attach the hand
Of his fair mistress. In the afternoon
We will with some strange pastime solace them,
Such as the shortness of the time can shape;
For revels, dances, masques, and merry hours
Forerun fair Love, strewing her way with flowers.

KING Away, away! No time shall be omitted
That will be time, and may by us be fitted.

BEROWNE *Allons! Allons!* Sowed cockle reaped
  no corn,
And justice always whirls in equal measure.
Light wenches may prove plagues to men forsworn;
If so, our copper buys no better treasure.

[*Exeunt*]

A Midsummer Night's Dream

c.1594-96

| ACT **2** | SCENE **1** |

❝ I know a bank where the wild thyme blows,
Where oxlips and the nodding violet grows ❞

A Midsummer Night's Dream is a comic companion-piece to Romeo and Juliet. Both works play startling games with light and dark, love and hate, gentleness and violence, the rigidity of male authority and the flexibility of the comic. The difference is that Romeo and Juliet ends with the young lovers trapped in sepulchral darkness, while Dream ends with the liberation of laughter, love and youth from all entrapment. How does it achieve this liberation?

The play opens in Athens with the setting of two deadlines. The first is the date of Duke Theseus's wedding to the Amazonian queen, Hippolyta; the second the date by which young Hermia must decide whether she will marry Demetrius, the man favoured by her father, or choose instead either to enter a religious order or be put to death – two punishments prescribed by Athenian law for disobedient daughters. This second deadline threatens to launch us into tragedy; but the threat seems diminished by the fact that the second deadline is set so soon after the first, with the result that Hermia's predicament gets mixed up with the forthcoming marriage festivities. Just as Theseus is looking for entertainment to fill up the time till his wedding, Hermia's father bursts in with a complaint against his daughter as if in answer to the Duke's prayer, bringing with him the promise either of an absorbing legal battle or an engaging romance. The timescale of potential tragedy (Hermia's immurement or execution) and the timescale of what Theseus calls the 'spirit of mirth' (the pre-nuptial pastime he hopes for) have been fused, and remain combined throughout the action.

In fact, the comic world of *Dream* is hardly less unsettling than the tragic universe of *Romeo and Juliet*. In this play, people get their kicks from other people's pain. Theseus's marriage to Hippolyta was brought about by violence – he 'wooed [her] with [his] sword'; the goblin Puck gets his pleasure from watching four runaway lovers (Hermia and Lysander, Demetrius and Helena) fight in a forest; while one of the lovers, Helena, finds it easy to believe that the others have teamed up against her 'for [their] merriment'. In Act 5 the Athenian court finds itself weeping tears of laughter at an incompetent performance of a tragedy, that of the suicidal lovers Pyramus and Thisbe; as one courtier puts it, 'more merry tears / The passion of loud laughter never shed'. Laughter, pain and death are bound together in this play as intimately as anywhere in Shakespeare.

Luckily, however, the potentially tragic world of Athens collides with the world of Shakespeare's fairies, whose benevolence towards mortals runs counter to the widespread Elizabethan view of them as malicious, and whose association with tiny things indicates their unwillingness to take anything very seriously. Hermia flees with her boyfriend Lysander to the forest, pursued by Demetrius and his ex-girlfriend Helena; and here their passions become playthings for the King of Fairies, Oberon, and Puck his mischievous servant, with the help of a mere flower, whose juice can change people's affections in an instant. The scene quoted here shows the first meeting in the play between humans and fairies, and the contrast between Demetrius's cruelty to Helena and the ravishing verse of Oberon hints at the happy transmutation of love's torments that this meeting will accomplish.

OPPOSITE A 19th-century illustration by Sir John Gilbert depicting a somewhat malevolent-looking Puck.

[*Enter* **OBERON** *and* **PUCK**]

OBERON

My gentle Puck, come hither. Thou rememb'rest
Since once I sat upon a promontory,
And heard a mermaid on a dolphin's back
Uttering such dulcet and harmonious breath
That the rude sea grew civil at her song,
And certain stars shot madly from their spheres
To hear the sea-maid's music?

PUCK   I remember.

OBERON

That very time I saw, but thou couldst not,
Flying between the cold moon and the earth
Cupid, all armed. A certain aim he took
At a fair vestal thronèd by the west,
And loosed his love-shaft smartly from his bow,
As it should pierce a hundred thousand hearts;
But I might see young Cupid's fiery shaft
Quenched in the chaste beams of the wat'ry moon,
And the imperial vot'ress passèd on
In maiden meditation, fancy-free.
Yet marked I where the bolt of Cupid fell.
It fell upon a little western flower,
Before, milk-white; now, purple with love's wound,
And maidens call it love-in-idleness.
Fetch me that flower; the herb I showed thee once.
The juice of it on sleeping eyelids laid
Will make or man or woman madly dote
Upon the next live creature that it sees.
Fetch me this herb, and be thou here again
Ere the leviathan can swim a league.

> **'You draw me ... for my heart
> Is true as steel.'**
>
> Adamant is a hard stone believed in
> Shakespeare's time to have magnetic
> properties, and therefore to be capable of
> 'drawing' or attracting steel. Raw iron was
> considered an inferior metal to steel, which
> could be used to make high-quality tools
> and weapons. Helena argues here that
> Demetrius is naturally attractive to her –
> and that his hardness of heart, too, is
> unfortunately natural.

PUCK

I'll put a girdle round about the earth
In forty minutes. [*Exit*]

OBERON

                        Having once this juice
I'll watch Titania when she is asleep,
And drop the liquor of it in her eyes.
The next thing then she waking looks upon,
Be it on lion, bear, or wolf, or bull,
On meddling monkey, or on busy ape,
She shall pursue it with the soul of love.

> **'At a fair vestal thronèd by the west'**
>
> This is a compliment to Elizabeth I, the
> so-called 'Virgin Queen' often identified
> with Diana ('vestal' means virgin). Diana, the
> classical goddess of hunting, chastity and the
> moon, had many names, including Cynthia,
> Hecate and Titania. The fact that Elizabeth is
> shown here as impervious to Cupid's arrow,
> whereas Shakespeare's Titania is not, would
> no doubt have pleased the English monarch.

And ere I take this charm from off her sight –
As I can take it with another herb –
I'll make her render up her page to me.
But who comes here? I am invisible,
And I will overhear their conference.

[*Enter* **DEMETRIUS**, **HELENA** *following him*]

DEMETRIUS

I love thee not, therefore pursue me not.
Where is Lysander and fair Hermia?
The one I'll slay, the other slayeth me.
Thou told'st me they were stol'n unto this wood,
And here am I, and wood within this wood
Because I cannot meet my Hermia.
Hence, get thee gone, and follow me no more.

HELENA

You draw me, you hard-hearted adamant;
But yet you draw not iron, for my heart
Is true as steel. Leave you your power to draw,
And I shall have no power to follow you.

DEMETRIUS

Do I entice you? Do I speak you fair?
Or rather do I not in plainest truth
Tell you I do not nor I cannot love you?

*Tempt not too much the hatred of my spirit,
For I am sick when I do look on thee.*

HELENA

And even for that do I love you the more.
I am your spaniel, and, Demetrius,
The more you beat me, I will fawn on you.
Use me but as your spaniel, spurn me, strike me,
Neglect me, lose me; only give me leave,

> **'We cannot fight for love, …
> not made to woo.'**
>
> Helena here draws attention to the fact
> that she is violating Elizabethan gender
> conventions by chasing the man she loves.
> Many of our scenes involve similar violations:
> Julia pursuing Proteus in *Two Gentlemen*;
> Juliet abandoning conventional female
> modesty in her balcony scene with Romeo;
> Portia teaching Bassanio how to win her in the
> *Merchant*, and Desdemona instructing Othello
> in the art of courtship. In all these cases, as
> here, a woman's willingness to forgo custom
> carries considerable risk to her safety.

Unworthy as I am, to follow you.
What worser place can I beg in your love –
And yet a place of high respect with me –
Than to be usèd as you use your dog?

DEMETRIUS

Tempt not too much the hatred of my spirit,
For I am sick when I do look on thee.

HELENA

And I am sick when I look not on you.

DEMETRIUS

You do impeach your modesty too much,
To leave the city and commit yourself
Into the hands of one that loves you not;
To trust the opportunity of night,
And the ill counsel of a desert place,
With the rich worth of your virginity.

HELENA

Your virtue is my privilege, for that
It is not night when I do see your face;
Therefore I think I am not in the night,
Nor doth this wood lack worlds of company,
For you in my respect are all the world.
Then how can it be said I am alone,
When all the world is here to look on me?

DEMETRIUS

I'll run from thee and hide me in the brakes,
And leave thee to the mercy of wild beasts.

HELENA

The wildest hath not such a heart as you.
Run when you will. The story shall be changed:

Apollo flies, and Daphne holds the chase;
The dove pursues the griffin, the mild hind
Makes speed to catch the tiger – bootless speed,
When cowardice pursues and valour flies.

DEMETRIUS

I will not stay thy questions. Let me go.
Or, if thou follow me, do not believe
But I shall do thee mischief in the wood.

HELENA

Ay, in the temple, in the town, the field,
You do me mischief. Fie, Demetrius!
Your wrongs do set a scandal on my sex.
We cannot fight for love, as men may do;
We should be wooed and were not made to woo.
I'll follow thee and make a heaven of hell,
To die upon the hand I love so well.

[*Exit* DEMETRIUS, HELENA *following him*]

OBERON

Fare thee well, nymph. Ere he do leave this grove
Thou shalt fly him, and he shall seek thy love.
[*Re-enter* PUCK]
Hast thou the flower there? Welcome, wanderer.

PUCK

Ay, there it is.

OBERON

                    I pray thee give it me.
I know a bank where the wild thyme blows,
Where oxlips and the nodding violet grows,
Quite over-canopied with luscious woodbine,
With sweet musk-roses, and with eglantine.
There sleeps Titania sometime of the night,
Lulled in these flowers with dances and delight;
And there the snake throws her enamelled skin,
Weed wide enough to wrap a fairy in;
And with the juice of this I'll streak her eyes,
And make her full of hateful fantasies.
Take thou some of it, and seek through this grove.
A sweet Athenian lady is in love
With a disdainful youth. Anoint his eyes;
But do it when the next thing he espies
May be the lady. Thou shalt know the man
By the Athenian garments he hath on.
Effect it with some care, that he may prove
More fond on her than she upon her love;
And look thou meet me ere the first cock crow.

PUCK

Fear not, my lord, your servant shall do so.

[*Exeunt*]

A Midsummer Night's Dream

c.1594-96

ACT **3** | SCENE **1**

' I see their knavery. This is to make an ass of me, to fright me, if they could. '

In this comedy, craftsmen and actors teach the ruling classes everything they need to know about living in harmony. Athenian courtiers fall out over desire, which leads to threats of execution and duels to the death. Fairies fall out over a plaything, a little Indian boy adopted by Titania, whom Oberon wants as an exotic servant – a supernatural squabble that leads to floods and other natural disasters.

In the midst of these upheavals, a group of artisans plan to put on a play to celebrate the wedding of Theseus and Hippolyta. Their affection for each other is obvious; and the communal love and respect they represent ends by working its magic on both the courtiers and the fairies, reuniting everyone who has been at odds and helping to engineer a happy ending in despite of potential tragedy.

The craftsmen are at home neither in the forest nor the court, neither in Theseus's world nor the fairies'; yet they move with consummate ease between both spheres, protected by their cheerful confidence in their own identity. And they have a better sense of the magic of the stage than anyone else in Shakespeare's work; it both exhilarates and disturbs them. Preparing their show, they are certain that it will possess the imaginations of their audience, so they introduce safety measures (an expository prologue, a speech to explain that the actor playing a lion is a man) to protect their audience from suffering for this state of possession. The brashest of them, Bottom, is certain he can act any role, whether lion, woman, Hercules, lover or tyrant, with equal competence. And his conviction is borne out in 'real life' in our extract, when Puck replaces his head with that of an ass, then makes Titania fall in love with him, as part of a plot to persuade the Fairy Queen to give the little Indian boy to Oberon.

Bottom here plays the role of a queen's lover with a dignity and grace surpassing anything the ruling classes in the play can muster. He is modest, denying both his own wisdom and his beauty; generous, in his wish that all 'honest neighbours' might be friends; courteous, warmly greeting a group of fairy servants whose names ally them with small, useful things: condiments (Mustardseed), sticking plasters (Cobweb), and pulses (Peaseblossom). And when later he is deposed from his brief eminence, he shows no regret; only a profound wonder at the strangeness of his midsummer vision. He is a fitting role model for all classes, from menials to immortals.

No wonder, then, if the silly performance in which he plays a leading role in the final act should inspire Theseus to utter the loveliest of lines about the theatre: 'The best in this kind are but shadows, and the worst are no worse if imagination amend them.' The key to enjoying drama, the duke suggests, is love: the kind of mutually supportive affection that binds together Bottom and his craftsmen colleagues. *A Midsummer Night's Dream* celebrates the love that binds communities, not individuals; and this is what rescues it from becoming the sort of tragedy that occurs when love becomes too specific, too exclusive. It's not for nothing that the play ends in a *multiple* marriage.

OPPOSITE Titania awakens and clings to Bottom, surrounded by attendant fairies, in this late 18th-century painting by Henry Fuseli.

[**TITANIA** *lies asleep. Enter the Clowns,* **QUINCE**, **SNUG**, **BOTTOM**, **FLUTE**, **SNOUT** *and* **STARVELING**. *Enter* **PUCK** *behind*]

PUCK [*Aside*] What hempen homespuns have we
   swagg'ring here,
So near the cradle of the Fairy Queen?
What, a play toward! I'll be an auditor;
An actor too perhaps, if I see cause.

QUINCE Speak, Pyramus. Thisby, stand forth.

BOTTOM *Thisby, the flowers of odious savours sweet –*

QUINCE Odours, odours.

BOTTOM *– odours savours sweet;*
So hath thy breath, my dearest Thisby dear.
But hark, a voice! Stay thou but here awhile,
And by and by I will to thee appear. [*Exit*]

PUCK A stranger Pyramus than e'er played here!
[*Exit*]

FLUTE Must I speak now?

QUINCE Ay, marry, must you; for you must
understand he goes but to see a noise that he heard,
and is to come again.

FLUTE *Most radiant Pyramus, most lily-white of hue,*
Of colour like the red rose on triumphant brier,
Most bristly juvenile, and eke most lovely Jew,
As true as truest horse that yet would never tire,
I'll meet thee, Pyramus, at Ninny's tomb.

QUINCE 'Ninus' tomb', man! Why, you must not
speak that yet. That you answer to Pyramus. You
speak all your part at once, cues and all. Pyramus,
enter: your cue is past; it is 'never tire'.

FLUTE O – *As true as truest horse that yet would*
   never tire.

[*Re-enter* **PUCK**, *and* **BOTTOM** *with an ass's head*]

BOTTOM *If I were fair, Thisby, I were only thine.*

QUINCE O monstrous! O strange! We are haunted.
   Pray, masters! Fly, masters! Help!

[*Exeunt* **QUINCE**, **SNUG**, **FLUTE**, **SNOUT**, *and*
   STARVELING]

PUCK I'll follow you, I'll lead you about a round,
Through bog, through bush, through brake,
   through brier.
Sometime a horse I'll be, sometime a hound,
A hog, a headless bear, sometime a fire,
And neigh, and bark, and grunt, and roar,
   and burn,
Like horse, hound, hog, bear, fire, at every turn.
[*Exit*]

> ### 'Nay, I can gleek upon occasion.'
>
> 'Gleek' is usually glossed as 'crack a joke,
> make a witticism'; but nobody knows exactly
> what it means. If Bottom does mean he has
> made a joke, presumably it's at the expense
> of the 'honest neighbours' who can't love
> one another (as the commandment puts it),
> despite the fact that they have not been
> blessed with 'reason' or good sense, and that
> 'reason and love keep little company together
> nowadays'… The witticism isn't brilliant, but
> the sentiment behind it is pleasing.

BOTTOM Why do they run away? This is a knavery
of them to make me afeard.

[*Re-enter* **SNOUT**]

SNOUT O Bottom, thou art changed! What do I
see on thee?

BOTTOM What do you see? You see an ass-head of
your own, do you?

[*Exit* **SNOUT**. *Re-enter* **QUINCE**]

QUINCE Bless thee, Bottom, bless thee! Thou art
translated. [*Exit*]

BOTTOM I see their knavery. This is to make an ass
of me, to fright me, if they could. But I will not stir
from this place, do what they can. I will walk
up and down here, and I will sing, that they shall
hear I am not afraid. [*Sings*]
   The ousel cock so black of hue,
      With orange-tawny bill,
   The throstle with his note so true,
      The wren with little quill.

TITANIA [*Awaking*] What angel wakes me from my
flow'ry bed?

BOTTOM [*Sings*]
   The finch, the sparrow and the lark,
      The plainsong cuckoo grey,
   Whose note full many a man doth mark,
      And dares not answer nay –
for, indeed, who would set his wit to so foolish a
bird? Who would give a bird the lie, though he cry
'cuckoo' never so?

TITANIA I pray thee, gentle mortal, sing again.
Mine ear is much enamoured of thy note;
So is mine eye enthrallèd to thy shape;
And thy fair virtue's force perforce doth move me
On the first view to say, to swear, I love thee.

BOTTOM Methinks, mistress, you should have little

reason for that. And yet, to say the truth, reason and love keep little company together nowadays. The more the pity that some honest neighbours will not make them friends. Nay, I can gleek upon occasion.

TITANIA Thou art as wise as thou art beautiful.

BOTTOM Not so, neither; but if I had wit enough to get out of this wood, I have enough to serve mine own turn.

TITANIA Out of this wood do not desire to go;
Thou shalt remain here, whether thou wilt or no.
I am a spirit of no common rate;
The summer still doth tend upon my state;
And I do love thee. Therefore go with me.
I'll give thee fairies to attend on thee,

> **'good Master Cobweb. If I cut my finger, I shall make bold with you.'**
>
> Bottom identifies each fairy with the useful things their names stand for. Cobwebs were used to stop bleeding. Peaseblossom is the flower of the pea plant; its 'mother' is Mistress Squash, an unripe pea pod, and its 'father' Master Peascod, a ripe pea pod, which is assumed to be male because its name recalls 'codpiece'. Mustardseed's relatives have often fallen victim to oxen because mustard is often eaten with beef. Bottom does not invite Moth to speak because he would probably have been played by the smallest boy in the theatre company, not yet ready for a speaking role; 'moth' was pronounced like 'mote', a speck of dust.

And they shall fetch thee jewels from the deep,
And sing while thou on pressèd flowers dost sleep;
And I will purge thy mortal grossness so
That thou shalt like an airy spirit go.
Peaseblossom! Cobweb! Moth, and Mustardseed!

[*Enter* **PEASEBLOSSOM**, **COBWEB**, **MOTH**, *and* **MUSTARDSEED**]

PEASEBLOSSOM Ready.

COBWEB And I.

MOTH And I.

MUSTARDSEED And I.

ALL FOUR Where shall we go?

TITANIA Be kind and courteous to this gentleman;
Hop in his walks and gambol in his eyes;
Feed him with apricots and dewberries,
With purple grapes, green figs, and mulberries;
The honey-bags steal from the humble-bees,
And for night-tapers crop their waxen thighs
And light them at the fiery glow-worms' eyes,
To have my love to bed and to arise;
And pluck the wings from painted butterflies
To fan the moonbeams from his sleeping eyes.
Nod to him, elves, and do him courtesies.

PEASEBLOSSOM Hail, mortal!

COBWEB Hail!

MOTH Hail!

MUSTARDSEED Hail!

BOTTOM I cry your worships mercy, heartily.
I beseech your worship's name.

COBWEB Cobweb.

BOTTOM I shall desire you of more acquaintance, good Master Cobweb. If I cut my finger, I shall make bold with you. Your name, honest gentleman?

PEASEBLOSSOM Peaseblossom.

BOTTOM I pray you, commend me to Mistress Squash, your mother, and to Master Peascod, your father. Good Master Peaseblossom, I shall desire you of more acquaintance too. Your name, I beseech you, sir?

MUSTARDSEED Mustardseed.

BOTTOM Good Master Mustardseed, I know your patience well. That same cowardly, giant-like ox-beef hath devoured many a gentleman of your house. I promise you your kindred hath made my eyes water ere now. I desire you of more acquaintance, good Master Mustardseed.

TITANIA Come, wait upon him; lead him to my bower.
The moon, methinks, looks with a wat'ry eye,
And when she weeps, weeps every little flower,
Lamenting some enforcèd chastity.
Tie up my love's tongue, bring him silently.
[*Exeunt*]

*What hempen homespuns have we swagg'ring here,
So near the cradle of the Fairy Queen?*

Romeo
and Juliet *c. 1595*

ACT **2** SCENE **2**

O Romeo, Romeo! Wherefore art thou Romeo?

The story of Romeo and Juliet, two young people from feuding families who fall in love, secretly marry and are driven by circumstances to suicide, is so well known as to need no introduction. The original tale by the Italian writer Matteo Bandello was immensely popular in Elizabethan England, with translations being published in the 1560s by Arthur Brooke and William Painter, and variations on its themes acted out on stage from Shakespeare's own *Two Gentlemen of Verona* (*c.* 1590) to John Ford's *'Tis Pity She's a Whore* (*c.* 1630).

What is less well known is how original Shakespeare's treatment of the story may have seemed in its refusal to condemn the lovers. Painter's version tells us that it shows 'what danger either sort incur which marry without the advice of parents'; and the story's setting in Italy, where passions (so the English thought) ran high, religion and society were corrupt, and youthful disobedience was endemic, might have led Shakespeare's contemporaries to expect him to condemn the rebellious children whose clandestine union leads to tragedy.

Instead, he gave the stage its most exuberant and witty lovers, whose lightness of touch and fleetness of tongue is all the more dazzling for the speed with which they are overwhelmed by the social trap they find themselves in. Condemned to love in secret, the pair meet mostly at night, but they brighten the nocturnal gloom with their youthful love of laughter. Their situation is deadly; yet they are always playing games with it, then getting pulled up short by the seriousness of things, then leaping into playfulness again.

In our extract, for instance – part of the famous balcony scene – Romeo's surname of 'Montague' defines him as the enemy of Juliet's family, the Capulets, and Juliet first toys with the notion that he might change it as easily as he makes a pun; then is filled with horror at the frivolity with which he runs the risk of death; and finally finds herself (after our extract ends) unable to stop repeating his name, no matter how dangerous it might be, no matter how true it is that 'bondage is hoarse and may not speak aloud'.

Romeo, meanwhile, trifles with lightness in celebration of his release from the leaden weight of his attraction to another girl, Rosaline. When Juliet asks him how he got into her garden he answers that he fluttered in on 'love's light wings'; to which Juliet replies bluntly, 'If they do see thee, they will murder thee.' Juliet's own natural buoyancy is inhibited by her fear that he may think her 'light' (that is, sexually promiscuous) – as the moralists among Shakespeare's audience would have done – if she assents to his suit too readily. But urgency, and the fact that Romeo has overheard her talking about him and therefore knows her mind, make it impossible for her to be other than honest: 'Therefore pardon me,' she says, 'And not impute this yielding to light love, / Which the dark night hath so discoverèd'. Hereafter their exchanges are as light as the objects – flowers, birds, stars, hearts and souls – to which they are always alluding, and as full of affection as the city of Verona where they live is full of violence and the smothering self-centredness of the older generation.

OPPOSITE Claire Danes as Juliet in the 1996 film adaptation, directed by Baz Luhrmann.

Verona – outside Capulet's house

[*Enter* **ROMEO**]

ROMEO He jests at scars that never felt a wound.
[**JULIET** *appears above at a window*]
But, soft! What light through yonder window breaks?
It is the east, and Juliet is the sun.
Arise, fair sun, and kill the envious moon,
Who is already sick and pale with grief
That thou, her maid, art far more fair than she.
Be not her maid, since she is envious;
Her vestal livery is but sick and green,
And none but fools do wear it; cast it off.
[*Enter* **JULIET** *aloft*]
It is my lady, O, it is my love.
O that she knew she were!
She speaks, yet she says nothing. What of that?
Her eye discourses; I will answer it.
I am too bold, 'tis not to me she speaks.
Two of the fairest stars in all the heaven,
Having some business, do entreat her eyes
To twinkle in their spheres till they return.
What if her eyes were there, they in her head?
The brightness of her cheek would shame those stars
As daylight doth a lamp; her eyes in heaven
Would through the airy region stream so bright
That birds would sing and think it were not night.
See how she leans her cheek upon her hand!
O that I were a glove upon that hand,
That I might touch that cheek!

JULIET   Ay me!

ROMEO [*Aside*]   She speaks.
O, speak again, bright angel; for thou art
As glorious to this night, being o'er my head,
As is a wingèd messenger of heaven
Unto the white upturnèd wond'ring eyes
Of mortals that fall back to gaze on him
When he bestrides the lazy-pacing clouds
And sails upon the bosom of the air.

JULIET O Romeo, Romeo! Wherefore art thou
  Romeo?
Deny thy father and refuse thy name;
Or if thou wilt not, be but sworn my love,
And I'll no longer be a Capulet.

ROMEO [*Aside*] Shall I hear more, or shall I speak
  at this?

JULIET 'Tis but thy name that is my enemy;
Thou art thyself, though not a Montague.
What's Montague? It is nor hand, nor foot,
Nor arm, nor face, nor any other part
Belonging to a man. O, be some other name!
What's in a name? That which we call a rose
By any other word would smell as sweet;

So Romeo would, were he not Romeo called,
Retain that dear perfection which he owes
Without that title. Romeo, doff thy name,
And for that name, which is no part of thee,
Take all myself.

> ### 'Be not her maid … cast it off.'
>
> The moon is associated with Diana, goddess of chastity. Romeo describes her as envious that Juliet is lovelier than she is, which makes her 'green' with jealousy. But greensickness is also a disease thought to afflict young girls ('vestals', or virgins) suffering from sexual frustration. Put simply, Romeo is urging Juliet to sleep with him. (She can't hear him at this stage!)

ROMEO [*To* **JULIET**]
                    I take thee at thy word.
Call me but love, and I'll be new baptized;
Henceforth I never will be Romeo.

JULIET What man art thou that, thus bescreened
  in night,
So stumblest on my counsel?

ROMEO   By a name
I know not how to tell thee who I am.
My name, dear saint, is hateful to myself
Because it is an enemy to thee.
Had I it written, I would tear the word.

JULIET My ears have not yet drunk a hundred words
Of that tongue's uttering, yet I know the sound.
Art thou not Romeo, and a Montague?

ROMEO Neither, fair maid, if either thee dislike.

JULIET How cam'st thou hither, tell me, and
  wherefore?
The orchard walls are high and hard to climb,
And the place death, considering who thou art,
If any of my kinsmen find thee here.

ROMEO With love's light wings did I o'er-perch
  these walls,
For stony limits cannot hold love out,
And what love can do, that dares love attempt.
Therefore thy kinsmen are no stop to me.

JULIET If they do see thee, they will murder thee.

ROMEO Alack, there lies more peril in thine eye
Than twenty of their swords. Look thou but sweet,
And I am proof against their enmity.

JULIET I would not for the world they saw thee here.

ROMEO I have night's cloak to hide me from their eyes;

Romeo and Juliet

And but thou love me, let them find me here.
My life were better ended by their hate
Than death proroguèd, wanting of thy love.

JULIET By whose direction found'st thou out
this place?

ROMEO By love, who first did prompt me
to enquire;
He lent me counsel, and I lent him eyes.
I am no pilot, yet wert thou as far
As that vast shore washed with the farthest sea,
I should adventure for such merchandise.

JULIET Thou know'st the mask of night is on
my face,
Else would a maiden blush bepaint my cheek
For that which thou hast heard me speak tonight.
Fain would I dwell on form, fain, fain deny

Or if thou wilt, swear by thy gracious self,
Which is the god of my idolatry,
And I'll believe thee.

ROMEO   If my heart's dear love –

JULIET Well, do not swear. Although I joy in thee,
I have no joy of this contract tonight.
It is too rash, too unadvised, too sudden;
Too like the lightning, which doth cease to be
Ere one can say 'It lightens'. Sweet, good night.
This bud of love, by summer's ripening breath,
May prove a beauteous flower when next we meet.
Good night, good night! As sweet repose and rest
Come to thy heart as that within my breast!

ROMEO O, wilt thou leave me so unsatisfied?

JULIET What satisfaction canst thou have tonight?

But, soft! What light through yonder window breaks? It is the east, and Juliet is the sun.

What I have spoke: but farewell compliment.
Dost thou love me? I know thou wilt say 'Ay',
And I will take thy word. Yet if thou swear'st
Thou mayst prove false. At lovers' perjuries,
They say, Jove laughs. O gentle Romeo,
If thou dost love, pronounce it faithfully;
Or if thou think'st I am too quickly won,
I'll frown, and be perverse, and say thee nay,
So thou wilt woo; but else, not for the world.
In truth, fair Montague, I am too fond,
And therefore thou mayst think my 'haviour
light.
But trust me, gentleman, I'll prove more true
Than those that have more cunning to be strange.
I should have been more strange, I must confess,
But that thou overheard'st, ere I was ware,
My true-love passion. Therefore pardon me,
And not impute this yielding to light love,
Which the dark night hath so discoverèd.

ROMEO Lady, by yonder blessèd moon I vow,
That tips with silver all these fruit-tree tops –

JULIET O swear not by the moon, th' inconstant
moon,
That monthly changes in her circled orb,
Lest that thy love prove likewise variable.

ROMEO What shall I swear by?

JULIET   Do not swear at all;

ROMEO The exchange of thy love's faithful vow
for mine.

JULIET I gave thee mine before thou didst request it,
And yet I would it were to give again.

ROMEO Wouldst thou withdraw it? For what
purpose, love?

JULIET But to be frank, and give it thee again.
And yet I wish but for the thing I have.
My bounty is as boundless as the sea,
My love as deep. The more I give to thee
The more I have, for both are infinite.
[**NURSE** *calls within*]
I hear some noise within. Dear love, adieu! –
Anon, good Nurse! – Sweet Montague, be true.
Stay but a little, I will come again. [*Exit, above*]

ROMEO O blessèd, blessèd night! I am afeard,
Being in night, all this is but a dream,
Too flattering-sweet to be substantial.

> The scene ends with the most protracted
> and charming series of goodbyes ever
> written. These include a pair of famous
> lines ('Parting is such sweet sorrow /
> That I shall say good night till it be morrow'),
> which perfectly articulate the fusion of joy
> and grief that draws audiences back to this
> play in every generation.

Romeo and Juliet *c. 1595*

> **O happy dagger! This is thy sheath. There rust, and let me die.**

Romeo's tragedy springs from the link between masculinity and violence. In Shakespeare's Verona, sparring brings men closer together, whether in affection or enmity. They jostle for power by joshing one another on their sexual inadequacies. They use women as a means of defining their relationships with other men, verbally invading women's bodies as freely as they invade each other's bodies with their ever-ready swords. And by probing the hidden desires of their friends they affirm their mutual intimacy, as when Benvolio investigates the reasons for his cousin Romeo's depression at the beginning of the play, or when Mercutio imagines Romeo having sex with Rosaline, who is the inaccessible object of his fantasies before he meets Juliet.

There seems remarkably little difference between this friendly joshing and the insults that provoke mortal combat. When Tybalt calls Romeo 'boy' in Act 3 – an affront to his masculinity that triggers a duel to the death – he seems to insult him rather less than Mercutio did earlier in the play, when he pretended to conjure up phallic spirits in the circle of Rosaline's vagina. Young men kill each other with their blades, yet these fatal sword fights, like the word fights that precede them, serve as a perverse expression of solidarity, a substitute for homoerotic lovemaking. It's for this reason, perhaps, that Juliet sees Romeo's killing of Tybalt – the act that leads to his banishment – as an act of infidelity: 'O serpent heart hid with a flow'ring face! / Did ever dragon keep so fair a cave?' For this reason, too, Romeo's second homicide of the play – his killing of Paris beside Juliet's tomb – is prefaced by a declaration of love for his rival ('I love thee better than myself'), and followed by the honourable interment of Paris alongside Juliet, where Romeo himself intends to lie. In this environment where love and bloodshed are so tightly knit, it seems inevitable that Romeo's relationship with Juliet will be suddenly cut short, like his same-sex friendships; and this is just what happens in the climactic death scene, which provides us with our second extract.

Part of the greatness of this scene is that it begins so unexpectedly with the death of Paris. The young count stumbles on Romeo as he is forcing his way into Juliet's tomb intending to kill himself by her side, unaware that she is not really dead (she has drugged herself to avoid a forced marriage to Paris). Romeo provokes the count into combat in exactly the way that Tybalt provoked the fight that led to his and Mercutio's deaths and Romeo's exile. By inviting Paris to run and calling him 'boy', Romeo leaves the young man with no choice but to draw his sword; and by killing him Romeo shows his continued commitment to the culture of male aggression from which his love of Juliet should have freed him. Once Paris is dead, Romeo recognizes him as a relative of his friend Mercutio. The discovery marks the burial ground where he dies as the graveyard of Verona's future, where Tybalt, Mercutio, Paris, Juliet and Romeo – all tied together by bonds of youth, blood and friendship, all effectively self-slaughtered – lie together in a grotesque parody of the peaceful intimacy they could never achieve in life, thanks to the murderous urban environment in which they were raised.

OPPOSITE Romeo lies dead and Juliet raises a hand in horror as she hears someone approaching in Joseph Wright of Derby's 1790 painting *The Tomb Scene*.

[*Enter* PARIS *and* PAGE. *After them enter* ROMEO
and BALTHASAR, *with a torch, mattock, etc.*]

ROMEO [*To* BALTHASAR] Upon thy life I charge thee,
Whate'er thou hear'st or seest, stand all aloof,
And do not interrupt me in my course.
Why I descend into this bed of death
Is partly to behold my lady's face,
But chiefly to take thence from her dead finger
A precious ring, a ring that I must use
In dear employment. Therefore hence, be gone.
But if thou, jealous, dost return to pry
In what I farther shall intend to do,
By heaven, I will tear thee joint by joint
And strew this hungry churchyard with thy limbs.
The time and my intents are savage-wild,
More fierce and more inexorable far
Than empty tigers or the roaring sea.

O, give me thy hand,
One writ with me in sour misfortune's book!

BALTHASAR I will be gone, sir, and not trouble ye.

ROMEO So shalt thou show me friendship. Take
thou that.
Live, and be prosperous; and farewell, good fellow.

BALTHASAR [*Aside*]
For all this same, I'll hide me hereabout.
His looks I fear, and his intents I doubt. [*Retires*]

ROMEO Thou detestable maw, thou womb of death,
Gorged with the dearest morsel of the earth,
Thus I enforce thy rotten jaws to open,
And, in despite, I'll cram thee with more food.
[*Opens the tomb*]

PARIS This is that banished haughty Montague
That murdered my love's cousin, with which grief
It is supposèd the fair creature died;
And here is come to do some villainous shame
To the dead bodies. I will apprehend him.
[*Comes forward*]
Stop thy unhallowed toil, vile Montague!
Can vengeance be pursued further than death?
Condemnèd villain, I do apprehend thee.
Obey and go with me, for thou must die.

ROMEO I must indeed, and therefore came I hither.
Good gentle youth, tempt not a desp'rate man;
Fly hence, and leave me. Think upon these gone;
Let them affright thee. I beseech thee, youth,
Put not another sin upon my head

By urging me to fury. O, be gone!
By heaven, I love thee better than myself,
For I come hither armed against myself.
Stay not, be gone. Live, and hereafter say
A madman's mercy bid thee run away.

PARIS I do defy thy conjuration,
And apprehend thee for a felon here.

ROMEO Wilt thou provoke me? Then have at thee,
boy! [*They fight*]

PAGE O Lord, they fight! I will go call the watch. [*Exit*]

PARIS O, I am slain! If thou be merciful,
Open the tomb, lay me with Juliet. [*Dies*]

ROMEO In faith, I will. Let me peruse this face.
Mercutio's kinsman, noble County Paris!
What said my man, when my betossèd soul
Did not attend him as we rode? I think
He told me Paris should have married Juliet.
Said he not so? Or did I dream it so?
Or am I mad, hearing him talk of Juliet,
To think it was so? O, give me thy hand,
One writ with me in sour misfortune's book!
I'll bury thee in a triumphant grave.
[*He opens the grave, revealing* JULIET]
A grave? O no, a lantern, slaughtered youth,
For here lies Juliet, and her beauty makes
This vault a feasting presence full of light.
Death, lie thou there, by a dead man interred.
[*He lays* PARIS *in the tomb*]
How oft when men are at the point of death
Have they been merry! Which their keepers call
A lightning before death. O, how may I
Call this a lightning? O my love! My wife!
Death, that hath sucked the honey of thy breath,
Hath had no power yet upon thy beauty.
Thou art not conquered, beauty's ensign yet
Is crimson in thy lips and in thy cheeks,
And death's pale flag is not advancèd there.
Tybalt, liest thou there in thy bloody sheet?
O, what more favour can I do to thee
Than with that hand that cut thy youth in twain
To sunder his that was thine enemy?
Forgive me, cousin. Ah, dear Juliet,
Why art thou yet so fair? Shall I believe
That unsubstantial death is amorous,
And that the lean abhorrèd monster keeps
Thee here in dark to be his paramour?
For fear of that I still will stay with thee,

And never from this palace of dim night
Depart again. Here, here will I remain
With worms that are thy chambermaids. O, here
Will I set up my everlasting rest,
And shake the yoke of inauspicious stars
From this world-wearied flesh. Eyes, look your last.
Arms, take your last embrace, and lips, O you
The doors of breath, seal with a righteous kiss
A dateless bargain to engrossing death.
[*He kisses* JULIET, *then pours poison into the cup*]
Come, bitter conduct, come, unsavoury guide.
Thou desperate pilot, now at once run on
The dashing rocks thy sea-sick weary barque.
Here's to my love.
[*Drinks*]
                              O true apothecary!
Thy drugs are quick. Thus with a kiss I die. [*Dies*]

[*Enter* FRIAR LAURENCE, *with lantern, crow, and spade*]

FRIAR Saint Francis be my speed! How oft tonight
Have my old feet stumbled at graves! Who's there?

BALTHASAR Here's one, a friend, and one that knows you well.

'How oft when men …
A lightning before death.'

This is one of many moments in the play when light and dark, lightness (cheerfulness, weightlessness) and heaviness (weightiness, sorrow) come together, to heartbreaking effect. Lightning and thunder are portentous; lightening up at a solemn moment may also be a sign of imminent death. The rest of Romeo's speech is as full of jokes as of despair, as he turns death into a monster who is trying to steal Juliet from her husband, making it necessary for him to stay beside her for ever. Juliet's death-speech, too, is painfully humorous, as she chides Romeo gently for being so rude as to drink all the poison without leaving any for her.

FRIAR Bliss be upon you! Tell me, good my friend,
What torch is yon that vainly lends his light
To grubs and eyeless skulls? As I discern,
It burneth in the Capels' monument.

BALTHASAR It doth so, holy sir; and there's my master,
One that you love.

FRIAR   Who is it?

BALTHASAR   Romeo.

FRIAR How long hath he been there?

BALTHASAR   Full half an hour.

FRIAR Go with me to the vault.

BALTHASAR   I dare not, sir.
My master knows not but I am gone hence,
And fearfully did menace me with death
If I did stay to look on his intents.

FRIAR Stay then, I'll go alone. Fear comes upon me.
O, much I fear some ill unthrifty thing.

BALTHASAR As I did sleep under this yew tree here
I dreamt my master and another fought,
And that my master slew him.

FRIAR   Romeo!
[*He stoops and looks on the blood and weapons*]
Alack, alack, what blood is this which stains
The stony entrance of this sepulchre?
What mean these masterless and gory swords
To lie discoloured by this place of peace?
Romeo! O, pale! Who else? What, Paris too,
And steeped in blood? Ah, what an unkind hour
Is guilty of this lamentable chance!
[JULIET *wakes*]
The lady stirs.

JULIET O comfortable friar! Where is my lord?
I do remember well where I should be,
And there I am. Where is my Romeo?

FRIAR I hear some noise. Lady,
      come from that nest
Of death, contagion, and unnatural sleep.
A greater power than we can contradict
Hath thwarted our intents. Come, come away.
Thy husband in thy bosom there lies dead,
And Paris too. Come, I'll dispose of thee
Among a sisterhood of holy nuns.
Stay not to question, for the watch is coming.
Come, go, good Juliet. I dare no longer stay. [*Exit*]

JULIET Go, get thee hence, for I will not away.
What's here? A cup, closed in my true love's hand?
Poison, I see, hath been his timeless end.
O churl! Drunk all, and left no friendly drop
To help me after? I will kiss thy lips.
Haply some poison yet doth hang on them,
To make me die with a restorative.
[*Kisses him*]
Thy lips are warm.

WATCHMAN [*Within*] Lead, boy. Which way?

JULIET Yea, noise? Then I'll be brief.
[*She takes* ROMEO's *dagger*]
                              O happy dagger!
This is thy sheath. There rust, and let me die.
[*She stabs herself, falls and dies*]

Richard II

c.1594–96

| ACT **3** | SCENE **2** |

" **For God's sake, let us sit upon the ground**
And tell sad stories of the death of kings **"**

Shakespeare's second tetralogy (a series of four plays) – *Richard II*, *Henry IV* Parts I and II, *Henry V* – represents his most sustained meditation on the constantly shifting relationship between a monarch and his people. In *Richard II*, a king's self-indulgent playfulness, his arrogant assumption that his power is absolute and that he may therefore ignore his obligations to his subjects, unleashes a set of consequences that are described in metaphors of physical debility. And the lexicon of bodies and disease continues to dominate the tetralogy, and to undergo astonishing transmutations as the narrative evolves.

Richard's arbitrariness as ruler first manifests itself when he banishes two nobles in Act 1, with devastating effects on their physiques. The pair abruptly find their limbs out of control, bereft of their former athleticism. One exile tells the king that by sending him abroad 'Within my mouth you have engaoled my tongue, / Doubly portcullised with my teeth and lips'. The other, Bolingbroke, compares his forced removal from England to the parting of flesh from spirit. Meanwhile John of Gaunt – Bolingbroke's father and Richard's uncle – accuses the king of damaging his own constitution as well as that of his kingdom. The monarch 'chokes' himself with a 'rash fierce blaze of riot', and involves that 'teeming womb of royal kings' England in crushing financial bondage to pay for his extravagance. Gaunt's own dying body, as emaciated as his name suggests, is for him the emblem of England's desiccation, bled dry by Richard's rapacity. But it also illustrates the accelerated decrepitude that Richard is bringing on himself as he commits his 'anointed body' to the care of 'those physicians that first wounded thee', his favourites.

Once Gaunt is dead, Richard's diseases accumulate apace. His queen detects 'Some unborn sorrow, ripe in fortune's womb' about to enter his life instead of the son he failed to father; and when Bolingbroke returns illegally to England, ostensibly to reclaim the property Richard stole from him during his exile, the queen recognizes him as her 'sorrow's dismal heir' – anticipating both his seizure of the throne and the bloody civil wars that will blight his reign. The Duke of York compares Bolingbroke to an illness: 'Now comes the sick hour that [Richard's] surfeit made'. And in our extract, Richard notes the symptoms of this illness for the first time in his own body.

Relentlessly the scene inflicts successive hammer blows on Richard's identity as king. His subjects twist their limbs into unnatural contortions to fight against him (young boys 'clap their female joints / In stiff unwieldy arms', elderly men 'learn to bend their bows … against thy state'). Richard rails against his favourites in the belief that they have betrayed him, only to learn that they have lost their heads for his sake. As the regalia and allies of his kingship fall away from him, Richard discovers to his horror that he possesses a body like those of his dead friends, a corporeal 'court' that is already occupied by the grotesque monarch Death, 'grinning at his pomp' with fleshless jaws. Death, he now knows, will be his heir apparent, a barren substitute for the dynasty he never founded. And once he knows this, Richard is elevated as a poet to a greatness he never achieved as king.

OPPOSITE Jeremy Irons as Richard II in the Royal Shakespeare Company's 1987 production.

[*Enter* KING RICHARD, AUMERLE, BISHOP OF CARLISLE, *and Soldiers*]

AUMERLE Comfort, my liege; remember who you are.

KING RICHARD I had forgot myself; am I not King?
Awake, thou coward majesty! Thou sleep'st.
Is not the King's name twenty thousand names?
Arm, arm, my name! A puny subject strikes
At thy great glory. Look not to the ground,
Ye favourites of a king; are we not high?
High be our thoughts. I know my uncle York
Hath power enough to serve our turn. But who comes here?

[*Enter* SCROOP]

SCROOP More health and happiness betide my liege
Than can my care-tuned tongue deliver him.

KING RICHARD Mine ear is open and my heart prepared.
The worst is worldly loss thou canst unfold.
Say, is my kingdom lost? Why, 'twas my care
And what loss is it to be rid of care?
Strives Bolingbroke to be as great as we?
Greater he shall not be; if he serve God,
We'll serve Him too, and be his fellow so.
Revolt our subjects? That we cannot mend;
They break their faith to God as well as us.
Cry woe, destruction, ruin and decay –
The worst is death, and death will have his day.

SCROOP Glad am I that your highness is so armed
To bear the tidings of calamity.
Like an unseasonable stormy day,
Which makes the silver rivers drown their shores
As if the world were all dissolved to tears,
So high above his limits swells the rage
Of Bolingbroke, covering your fearful land
With hard bright steel and hearts harder than steel.
Whitebeards have armed their thin and hairless scalps
Against thy majesty; boys with women's voices
Strive to speak big, and clap their female joints
In stiff unwieldy arms against thy crown.
Thy very beadsmen learn to bend their bows
Of double-fatal yew against thy state;
Yea, distaff-women manage rusty bills
Against thy seat. Both young and old rebel,
And all goes worse than I have power to tell.

KING RICHARD Too well, too well thou tell'st a tale so ill.

Where is the Earl of Wiltshire? Where is Bagot?
What is become of Bushy? Where is Green?
That they have let the dangerous enemy
Measure our confines with such peaceful steps?
If we prevail, their heads shall pay for it.
I warrant they have made peace with Bolingbroke.

> *'that small model of the
> barren earth … to our bones.'*
>
> **The 'model' of the earth is either the
> earth that encloses a corpse when it is
> buried – which can be seen to stand for
> the earth as a whole – or the body or flesh
> of a human being, which is a microcosm
> or tiny working replica of the world. 'Paste'
> is pastry, and the pastry casing for a pie
> was known as a 'coffin'.**

SCROOP Peace have they made with him indeed, my lord.

KING RICHARD O villains, vipers, damned without redemption!
Dogs, easily won to fawn on any man!
Snakes in my heart-blood warmed, that sting my heart!
Three Judases, each one thrice worse than Judas!
Would they make peace? Terrible hell make war
Upon their spotted souls for this offence!

SCROOP Sweet love, I see, changing his property,
Turns to the sourest and most deadly hate.
Again uncurse their souls; their peace is made
With heads, and not with hands. Those whom you curse
Have felt the worst of death's destroying wound
And lie full low, graved in the hollow ground.

AUMERLE Is Bushy, Green, and the Earl of Wiltshire dead?

SCROOP Ay, all of them at Bristol lost their heads.

AUMERLE Where is the Duke my father with his power?

KING RICHARD No matter where – of comfort no man speak.
Let's talk of graves, of worms and epitaphs;
Make dust our paper, and with rainy eyes
Write sorrow on the bosom of the earth.
Let's choose executors and talk of wills;
And yet not so – for what can we bequeath
Save our deposèd bodies to the ground?
Our lands, our lives, and all are Bolingbroke's,
And nothing can we call our own but death,

Richard II

within the hollow crown
That rounds the mortal temples of a king
Keeps Death his court

And that small model of the barren earth
Which serves as paste and cover to our bones.
For God's sake, let us sit upon the ground
And tell sad stories of the death of kings:
How some have been deposed, some slain in war,
Some haunted by the ghosts they have deposed,
Some poisoned by their wives, some sleeping killed,
All murdered. For within the hollow crown
That rounds the mortal temples of a king
Keeps Death his court; and there the antic sits,
Scoffing his state and grinning at his pomp,
Allowing him a breath, a little scene,
To monarchize, be feared, and kill with looks;
Infusing him with self and vain conceit,
As if this flesh which walls about our life
Were brass impregnable; and humoured thus,
Comes at the last, and with a little pin
Bores through his castle wall, and farewell king!
Cover your heads, and mock not flesh and blood
With solemn reverence. Throw away respect,
Tradition, form, and ceremonious duty,
For you have but mistook me all this while.
I live with bread like you, feel want,
Taste grief, need friends. Subjected thus,
How can you say to me I am a king?

BISHOP OF CARLISLE My lord, wise men ne'er
   sit and wail their woes,
But presently prevent the ways to wail.
To fear the foe, since fear oppresseth strength,
Gives in your weakness strength unto your foe,
And so your follies fight against yourself.
Fear and be slain – no worse can come to fight;
And fight and die is death destroying death,
Where fearing dying pays death servile breath.

AUMERLE My father hath a power. Inquire of him,
And learn to make a body of a limb.

KING RICHARD Thou chid'st me well. Proud
   Bolingbroke, I come
To change blows with thee for our day of doom.
This ague-fit of fear is overblown;
An easy task it is to win our own.
Say, Scroop, where lies our uncle with his power?
Speak sweetly, man, although thy looks be sour.

SCROOP Men judge by the complexion of the sky
The state and inclination of the day;
So may you by my dull and heavy eye,
My tongue hath but a heavier tale to say.
I play the torturer, by small and small
To lengthen out the worst that must be spoken.
Your uncle York is joined with Bolingbroke,
And all your northern castles yielded up,
And all your southern gentlemen in arms
Upon his party.

KING RICHARD
                    Thou hast said enough.
[*To* **AUMERLE**] Beshrew thee, cousin, which didst
   lead me forth
Of that sweet way I was in to despair!
What say you now? What comfort have we now?
By heaven, I'll hate him everlastingly
That bids me be of comfort any more.
Go to Flint castle; there I'll pine away;
A king, woe's slave, shall kingly woe obey.
That power I have, discharge, and let them go
To ear the land that hath some hope to grow,
For I have none. Let no man speak again
To alter this, for counsel is but vain.

> ### 'Fear and be slain – no worse ... destroying death'
>
> **Some of Shakespeare's counsellor figures speak in very convoluted terms (compare Nestor in *Troilus and Cressida*). The bishop means that no worse can happen in fighting than to be afraid and to be killed; and that to die fighting is to destroy death's power by dying. The latter contention in particular doesn't seem to make a lot of sense.**

AUMERLE My liege, one word.

KING RICHARD   He does me double wrong
That wounds me with the flatteries of his tongue.
Discharge my followers. Let them hence away,
From Richard's night to Bolingbroke's fair day.
[*Exeunt*]

King John
c.1596

ACT 4 | SCENE 1

❛ **Must you with hot irons burn out both mine eyes?** ❜

This peculiar history play has almost nothing to do with history as it was told in the Tudor chronicles. Shakespeare based it on an anonymous play published in 1591, and many of its episodes look like versions of events in Elizabeth's reign.

John's split with Rome, for instance, recalls Elizabeth's excommunication by the pope in 1570; his fears concerning the better claim to the throne of his nephew Arthur evoke Elizabeth's similar fears concerning her cousin, Mary Queen of Scots; the French Armada destroyed by storms echoes the fate of the Spanish Armada in 1588; and so on. But these echoes are hardly calculated to compliment the Elizabethans. John's reign is an 'iron age', as Prince Arthur says in our chosen scene, when the honour England won under John's dead brother, Richard the Lionheart, has been lost completely. The ruling classes are always making promises and breaking them; one-time allies are always changing sides; and aristocratic friendships are always on the verge of becoming murderous enmities. Characters constantly emerge from nowhere or vanish into obscurity, as if to accentuate the radical instability of the times they live in. If this world is intended to resemble Elizabethan England, the comparison is an unsettling one.

The most fascinating people in the play are those who are forgotten or marginalized by the historians: Constance, the mother and champion of Prince Arthur; Hubert, the hired assassin with a heart; and above all, the Bastard Falconbridge, who stands out as the only figure of consistent strength and substance in the narrative. His status as Richard the Lionheart's illegitimate son promotes him to the rank of general in King John's army, but dispossesses him of lands and title. He uses his displaced condition to speak with hilarious bluntness at times when the landed aristocracy is engaged in prevarication, lies and double-dealing. But when he urges England to stay 'true' to itself in the play's last lines – to break free from the cycle of betrayals we have witnessed – his marginal position suggests that he is swimming against the tide of English history.

Prince Arthur, innocent pawn of the play's political operators, furnishes the most memorable scene in the play, which provides our extract. Here he pleads to be spared from torture by the king's grim servant Hubert, appealing to the love and pity that most other characters have forgotten. The torture in question – John has ordered Hubert to burn out Arthur's eyes with red-hot irons – seems calculated to shock the audience into an almost physical reaction. As the boy begs Hubert to imagine himself in the position of his victim, he appeals too to the senses of the playgoers: 'O God, that there were but a mote in [your eyes]… Then, feeling what small things are boisterous there / Your vile intent must needs seem horrible'. The fact that the pleader is a young child, and that his name links him with a mythical British golden age, drives home the horrors of this 'iron age' more powerfully than any massacre. No wonder Hubert is prepared to spare him at the risk of his own life. The boy dies anyway a few scenes later; but in this scene Shakespeare paints a convincing picture of the weak, just once in the play successfully resisting the intolerable pressure of the strong.

OPPOSITE The young Prince Arthur pleads with Hubert, the hired assassin, not to blind him in this 19th-century painting by George Henry Harlow.

A castle in England

[*Enter* **HUBERT** *and* **EXECUTIONERS**]

HUBERT Heat me these irons hot, and look thou stand
Within the arras. When I strike my foot
Upon the bosom of the ground, rush forth
And bind the boy which you shall find with me
Fast to the chair. Be heedful. Hence, and watch.

EXECUTIONER I hope your warrant will bear out the deed.

HUBERT Uncleanly scruples. Fear not you. Look to't.
[*Exeunt* **EXECUTIONERS**]
Young lad, come forth; I have to say with you.

[*Enter* **ARTHUR**]

> **'Must you with hot irons burn out both mine eyes?'**
>
> The order to blind Arthur contradicts King John's order to murder him in Act 3. Shakespeare may have included this scene so as to emphasize the appalling physical consequences of the political machinations with which the play is filled. As Arthur points out, the eye is a highly sensitive organ, and the threat to destroy a child's eyes demonstrates how far England has become desensitized.

ARTHUR Good morrow, Hubert.

HUBERT   Good morrow, little Prince.

ARTHUR As little prince, having so great a title
To be more prince, as may be. You are sad.

HUBERT Indeed, I have been merrier.

ARTHUR   Mercy on me!
Methinks nobody should be sad but I.
Yet I remember, when I was in France,
Young gentlemen would be as sad as night
Only for wantonness. By my christendom,
So I were out of prison and kept sheep,
I should be as merry as the day is long;
And so I would be here, but that I doubt
My uncle practises more harm to me.
He is afraid of me and I of him.
Is it my fault that I was Geoffrey's son?
No, indeed, is't not, and I would to God
I were your son, so you would love me, Hubert.

HUBERT [*Aside*] If I talk to him, with his innocent prate
He will awake my mercy, which lies dead;
Therefore I will be sudden and dispatch.

ARTHUR Are you sick, Hubert? You look pale today.
In sooth, I would you were a little sick,
That I might sit all night and watch with you.
I warrant I love you more than you do me.

HUBERT [*Aside*] His words do take possession of my bosom.
[*He shows* **ARTHUR** *a paper*]
Read here, young Arthur. [*Aside*] How now: foolish rheum,
Turning dispiteous torture out of door?
I must be brief, lest resolution drop
Out at mine eyes in tender womanish tears.
[*Aloud*] Can you not read it? Is it not fair writ?

ARTHUR Too fairly, Hubert, for so foul effect.
Must you with hot irons burn out both mine eyes?

HUBERT Young boy, I must.

ARTHUR   And will you?

HUBERT   And I will.

ARTHUR Have you the heart? When your head did but ache
I knit my handkerchief about your brows,
The best I had – a princess wrought it me,
And I did never ask it you again –
And with my hand at midnight held your head,
And like the watchful minutes to the hour,
Still and anon cheered up the heavy time,
Saying, 'What lack you?' and 'Where lies your grief?'
Or 'What good love may I perform for you?'
Many a poor man's son would have lain still
And ne'er have spoke a loving word to you;
But you at your sick service had a prince.
Nay, you may think my love was crafty love,
And call it cunning. Do, an if you will.
If heaven be pleased that you must use me ill,
Why then you must. Will you put out mine eyes,
These eyes that never did, nor never shall,
So much as frown on you?

HUBERT   I have sworn to do it,
And with hot irons must I burn them out.

ARTHUR Ah, none but in this iron age would do it.
The iron of itself, though heat red-hot,

O, save me, Hubert, save me! My eyes are out
Even with the fierce looks of these bloody men.

Approaching near these eyes would drink my tears,
And quench his fiery indignation
Even in the matter of mine innocence;
Nay, after that, consume away in rust,
But for containing fire to harm mine eye.
Are you more stubborn-hard than hammered iron?
An if an angel should have come to me
And told me Hubert should put out mine eyes,
I would not have believed him – no tongue but
   Hubert's.

HUBERT Come forth!
[**HUBERT** *stamps his foot. Re-enter*
   EXECUTIONERS]
Do as I bid you do.

ARTHUR O, save me, Hubert, save me! My eyes
   are out
Even with the fierce looks of these bloody men.

HUBERT Give me the iron, I say, and bind him here.

ARTHUR Alas, what need you be so boisterous-
   rough?
I will not struggle; I will stand stone-still.
For God's sake, Hubert, let me not be bound!
Nay, hear me, Hubert! Drive these men away,
And I will sit as quiet as a lamb;
I will not stir, nor wince, nor speak a word,
Nor look upon the iron angerly.
Thrust but these men away, and I'll forgive you,
Whatever torment you do put me to.

HUBERT Go, stand within. Let me alone with him.

EXECUTIONER I am best pleased to be from such
   a deed.
[*Exeunt* **EXECUTIONERS**]

ARTHUR Alas, I then have chid away my friend!
He hath a stern look, but a gentle heart.
Let him come back, that his compassion may
Give life to yours.

HUBERT   Come, boy, prepare yourself.

ARTHUR Is there no remedy?

> **'Ah, none but in this
> iron age would do it.'**
>
> **The iron age is the age of cruelty, as
> opposed to the golden and silver ages of
> classical myth. Arthur is reminded of it by
> Hubert's threat to use a red-hot iron on his
> eyes. Arthur's own name allies him with a
> mythical golden age of England – he is
> even titled 'Arthur of Britain' (Brittany), as
> if to recall the legendary Arthur's unification
> of the British isles.**

HUBERT   None but to lose your eyes.

ARTHUR O God, that there were but a mote in yours,
A grain, a dust, a gnat, a wandering hair,
Any annoyance in that precious sense!
Then, feeling what small things are boisterous there,
Your vile intent must needs seem horrible.

HUBERT Is this your promise? Go to, hold your
   tongue!

ARTHUR Hubert, the utterance of a brace of
   tongues
Must needs want pleading for a pair of eyes.
Let me not hold my tongue, let me not, Hubert;
Or, Hubert, if you will, cut out my tongue,
So I may keep mine eyes. O, spare mine eyes,
Though to no use but still to look on you!
Lo, by my troth, the instrument is cold
And would not harm me.

HUBERT   I can heat it, boy.

ARTHUR No, in good sooth; the fire is dead
   with grief,
Being create for comfort, to be used
In undeserved extremes. See else yourself.
There is no malice in this burning coal;
The breath of heaven has blown his spirit out,
And strewed repentant ashes on his head.

HUBERT But with my breath I can revive it, boy.

ARTHUR An if you do, you will but make it blush
And glow with shame of your proceedings, Hubert.
Nay, it perchance will sparkle in your eyes,
And like a dog that is compelled to fight,
Snatch at his master that doth tarre him on.
All things that you should use to do me wrong
Deny their office; only you do lack
That mercy which fierce fire and iron extends,
Creatures of note for mercy-lacking uses.

HUBERT Well, see to live. I will not touch thine eye
For all the treasure that thine uncle owes.
Yet am I sworn, and I did purpose, boy,
With this same very iron to burn them out.

ARTHUR O, now you look like Hubert! All this while
You were disguisèd.

HUBERT   Peace, no more. Adieu.
Your uncle must not know but you are dead.
I'll fill these doggèd spies with false reports;
And, pretty child, sleep doubtless and secure
That Hubert, for the wealth of all the world,
Will not offend thee.

ARTHUR   O God! I thank you, Hubert.

HUBERT Silence, no more. Go closely in with me.
Much danger do I undergo for thee. [*Exeunt*]

The Merchant of Venice *c.1594-96*

ACT **3** | SCENE **2**

❝Let music sound while he doth make his choice.❞

In this play, Venice is a place where Christian men bond by laughing together at those they consider different from themselves: people of other cultures, depressives, women. In doing so, they raise the question of how one can trust any verbal agreement in a context where witticisms can spontaneously change a word's meaning; where jokes are invariably aggressive ones – cracked at the expense of some victim; and where male friendships override all rival bonds. A Jewish man and a Christian woman, Shylock and Portia, pose this question in different ways; and in doing so they bring out the similarities between their different situations. Our two scenes from the play illustrate their techniques of dealing with Shakespeare's Venice.

Portia inhabits a patriarchal culture, where a father's word controls his daughter's actions even from beyond the grave. Her dead father left her with solemn instructions to obey the rules of a silly game: she must marry the man who chooses the correct one of three caskets made of silver, lead, or gold. Portia elects to play by the rules, but does so in a way that suits herself; she allows the suitors she dislikes to be led by their weaknesses to the wrong caskets, and she does everything she can to help the man she fancies choose correctly. Each man she rejects is dull and self-obsessed, from the Neapolitan who idolizes his horse to the County Palatine who cannot laugh, from the Englishman who cannot speak her language to the boastful Moroccan prince, who cannot see Portia in any terms but of physical 'fairness'.

What distinguishes her preferred suitor Bassanio from the rest is his intelligence, his wit, and his willingness to be taught by Portia. At the beginning of our extract she tells him she could 'teach' him 'How to choose right', but will not break her promise to her father, while Bassanio says that she 'doth teach me answers' as they talk; and later, this is exactly what she does in the matter of the caskets. She commands that a song be sung whose first three lines rhyme with 'lead', and whose sense (that something more than visual attraction must underpin any lasting relationship) puts Bassanio on track to selecting the right casket. Afterwards, Bassanio justifies Portia's good opinion of him by turning to her for ratification of his success, 'As doubtful whether what I see be true / Until confirmed, signed, ratified by you'. Portia's father instructed Portia, Portia instructs Bassanio, and her tuition of him combined with his willingness to be taught suggests that he will never be the dominant partner in their marriage.

Portia ensures that this will remain the case even after she has 'given' herself to him completely. She draws up her own prenuptial contract in the form of the ring she also gives him, which he must never give away. When she later engineers a situation where he has to surrender the ring – adopting the disguise of a lawyer and demanding it from him as payment for saving his friend Antonio's life – she displays an unmatchable gift for laying down wayward laws of her own; rules designed to be broken, which appraise the faith of the witty Venetian men more accurately than any rule devised to be followed and rigorously policed.

OPPOSITE Bassanio assures Portia that he will never part with the ring she gave him in this 18th-century engraving by John and Josiah Boydell.

Portia's house in Belmont

[*Enter* BASSANIO, PORTIA, GRATIANO,
  NERISSA, *and* ATTENDANTS]

PORTIA I pray you tarry. Pause a day or two
Before you hazard, for in choosing wrong
I lose your company. Therefore forbear awhile.
There's something tells me – but it is not love –
I would not lose you; and you know yourself
Hate counsels not in such a quality.
But lest you should not understand me well –
And yet a maiden hath no tongue but thought –
I would detain you here some month or two
Before you venture for me. I could teach you
How to choose right, but then I am forsworn.
So will I never be; so may you miss me.
But if you do, you'll make me wish a sin,
That I had been forsworn. Beshrew your eyes,
They have o'erlooked me and divided me.
One half of me is yours, the other half yours –
Mine own, I would say; but if mine, then yours,
And so all yours. O, these naughty times
Put bars between the owners and their rights;
And so, though yours, not yours. Prove it so,
Let fortune go to hell for it, not I.
I speak too long, but 'tis to piece the time,
To eke it, and to draw it out in length
To stay you from election.

BASSANIO   Let me choose,
For as I am, I live upon the rack.

PORTIA Upon the rack, Bassanio? Then confess
What treason there is mingled with your love.

BASSANIO None but that ugly treason of mistrust
Which makes me fear th' enjoying of my love.
There may as well be amity and life
'Tween snow and fire as treason and my love.

PORTIA Ay, but I fear you speak upon the rack,
Where men enforcèd do speak anything.

BASSANIO Promise me life and I'll confess the truth.

PORTIA Well then, confess and live.

BASSANIO   'Confess and love'
Had been the very sum of my confession.
O happy torment, when my torturer
Doth teach me answers for deliverance!
But let me to my fortune and the caskets.

PORTIA Away, then; I am locked in one of them.
If you do love me, you will find me out.
Nerissa and the rest, stand all aloof.
Let music sound while he doth make his choice.
Then, if he lose, he makes a swan-like end,
Fading in music. That the comparison
May stand more proper, my eye shall be the stream
And wat'ry deathbed for him. He may win,

And what is music then? Then music is
Even as the flourish when true subjects bow
To a new-crownèd monarch. Such it is
As are those dulcet sounds in break of day
That creep into the dreaming bridegroom's ear
And summon him to marriage. Now he goes,
With no less presence, but with much more love,
Than young Alcides when he did redeem
The virgin tribute paid by howling Troy
To the sea-monster. I stand for sacrifice.
The rest aloof are the Dardanian wives,
With blearèd visages come forth to view
The issue of th' exploit. Go, Hercules.
Live thou, I live. With much much more dismay
I view the fight than thou that mak'st the fray.
[*Here music: a song, whilst* BASSANIO *comments
  on the caskets to himself*]

ONE FROM PORTIA'S TRAIN
  Tell me where is fancy bred,
  Or in the heart, or in the head?
  How begot, how nourishèd?

ALL Reply, reply.

ONE FROM PORTIA'S TRAIN
  It is engendered in the eyes,
  With gazing fed; and fancy dies
  In the cradle where it lies.
    Let us all ring fancy's knell.
    I'll begin it: Ding, dong, bell.

ALL Ding, dong, bell.

BASSANIO [*Aside*] So may the outward shows be
  least themselves;
The world is still deceived with ornament.
In law, what plea so tainted and corrupt
But, being seasoned with a gracious voice,
Obscures the show of evil? In religion,
What damnèd error but some sober brow
Will bless it and approve it with a text,
Hiding the grossness with fair ornament?
There is no vice so simple but assumes
Some mark of virtue on his outward parts.
How many cowards, whose hearts are all as false
As stairs of sand, wear yet upon their chins
The beards of Hercules and frowning Mars,
Who, inward searched, have livers white as milk!
And these assume but valour's excrement
To render them redoubted. Look on beauty
And you shall see 'tis purchased by the weight,
Which therein works a miracle in nature,
Making them lightest that wear most of it.
So are those crispèd snaky golden locks
Which makes such wanton gambols with the wind
Upon supposèd fairness, often known

'young Alcides … Go, Hercules.
Live thou, I live.'

Alcides is Hercules, who rescued the Trojan
Princess Hesione from a sea-monster. The
'Dardanian wives' are the weeping women of
Troy, who looked on. The Prince of Morocco
compared himself to Hercules in Act 2,
Scene 1; Bassanio, by contrast, is compared
to the Greek hero by Portia; but the
comparison is still a problematic one, given
Hercules's difficult relationship with women.

To be the dowry of a second head,
The skull that bred them in the sepulchre.
Thus ornament is but the guilèd shore
To a most dangerous sea, the beauteous scarf
Veiling an Indian beauty; in a word,
The seeming truth which cunning times put on
To entrap the wisest. [*Aloud*] Therefore, thou gaudy
   gold,
Hard food for Midas, I will none of thee.
[*To the silver casket*] Nor none of thee, thou pale
   and common drudge
'Tween man and man. But thou, thou meagre lead,
Which rather threaten'st than dost promise aught,
Thy paleness moves me more than eloquence,
And here choose I. Joy be the consequence!

PORTIA [*Aside*] How all the other passions fleet to air,
As doubtful thoughts, and rash-embraced despair,
And shudd'ring fear, and green-eyed jealousy!
O love, be moderate, allay thy ecstasy!
In measure rein thy joy; scant this excess.
I feel too much thy blessing. Make it less,
For fear I surfeit.

O love, be moderate, allay thy ecstasy!

BASSANIO [*Opening the leaden casket*]
            What find I here?
Fair Portia's counterfeit! What demi-god
Hath come so near creation? Move these eyes?
Or whether, riding on the balls of mine,
Seem they in motion? Here are severed lips
Parted with sugar breath; so sweet a bar
Should sunder such sweet friends. Here in her hairs
The painter plays the spider, and hath woven
A golden mesh t' entrap the hearts of men
Faster than gnats in cobwebs. But her eyes –

How could he see to do them? Having made one,
Methinks it should have power to steal both his
And leave itself unfurnished. Yet look how far
The substance of my praise doth wrong this shadow
In underprizing it, so far this shadow
Doth limp behind the substance. Here's the scroll,
The continent and summary of my fortune.
[*Reads*]
   You that choose not by the view
   Chance as fair and choose as true.
   Since this fortune falls to you,
   Be content and seek no new.
   If you be well pleased with this,
   And hold your fortune for your bliss,
   Turn you where your lady is
   And claim her with a loving kiss.
A gentle scroll. Fair lady, by your leave,
I come by note, to give and to receive.
Like one of two contending in a prize,
That thinks he hath done well in people's eyes,
Hearing applause and universal shout,
Giddy in spirit, still gazing in a doubt
Whether these peals of praise be his or no;
So, thrice-fair lady, stand I even so,
As doubtful whether what I see be true,
Until confirmed, signed, ratified by you.

PORTIA You see me, Lord Bassanio, where I stand,
Such as I am. Though for myself alone
I would not be ambitious in my wish
To wish myself much better, yet for you
I would be trebled twenty times myself,
A thousand times more fair, ten thousand times
   more rich,
That only to stand high in your account
I might in virtues, beauties, livings, friends,
Exceed account. But the full sum of me
Is sum of something which, to term in gross,
Is an unlessoned girl, unschooled, unpractisèd;
Happy in this, she is not yet so old
But she may learn; happier than this,
She is not bred so dull but she can learn;
Happiest of all is that her gentle spirit
Commits itself to yours to be directed,
As from her lord, her governor, her king.
Myself and what is mine to you and yours
Is now converted. But now I was the lord
Of this fair mansion, master of my servants,
Queen o'er myself; and even now, but now,
This house, these servants, and this same myself
Are yours, my lord's. I give them with this ring,
Which when you part from, lose, or give away,
Let it presage the ruin of your love,
And be my vantage to exclaim on you.

The Merchant of Venice *c.1594-96*

| ACT **4** | SCENE **1** |

> **An oath, an oath! I have an oath in heaven.
> Shall I lay perjury upon my soul?**

Portia shows a profound suspicion of words when drawing up her prenuptial agreement with Bassanio. The forms of expression she prefers are non-verbal ones: actions, such as keeping a ring safe; or music, such as the melody she has her musicians play as he chooses his casket. Shylock, by contrast, uses words to get his revenge on the Christians who have always verbally abused him. And words are what destroy him.

The Christian sense of humour is deadly to Shylock in a number of ways. Its punning ability to render words ambiguous threatens to disrupt the linguistic simplicity that is essential for financial transactions. Its delight in playful time-wasting runs counter to the merchant's need to take careful account of time, especially when calculating due interest on loans. And its racist invective dehumanizes him, threatening to place him outside the protection of the law, like a dog or a devil. So when an abusive Christian – Bassanio's friend Antonio – comes to ask him for a loan, which will fund Bassanio's expedition to win Portia, Shylock resorts to verbal humour as a means of avenging himself on his old enemy. He proposes what he calls a 'merry bond' – lending Antonio money with a pound of flesh as surety – in the hope of bringing home to Antonio's community a sense of the physical and psychological torment inflicted on Jews by Christian merry-making. Shylock's 'merry bond', in other words, teaches the Christians the lesson they have taught him; as he puts it: 'The villainy you teach me I will execute, and it shall go hard but I will better the instruction.'

But Shylock's contract with the Christians renders him vulnerable to their slipperiness, their ability to shift their verbal and moral ground whenever it suits them. When we first meet him, he refuses to eat with them on grounds of Jewish custom; but after drawing up the bond he accepts Bassanio's invitation to dinner, thus betraying his principles and giving Lorenzo the opportunity to elope with his daughter. The trial scene briefly puts an end to all clowning; but when Portia comes in disguised as a lawyer, just before our extract begins, she announces the return of Christian laughter from its temporary exile. Her famous speech on the 'quality of [Christian] mercy' indicates the extent to which Christianity itself is based on circumventing the letter of the law, since Christ took mankind's guilt upon himself. And when Shylock refuses to be merciful, he is forcefully shown the meaning of mercy through a series of legal tricks that are closely akin to jokes: the injunction that he shed no blood when he cuts his pound of flesh; the insistence that he take no more nor less than a pound; the revelation that he stands in imminent danger of execution for conspiring against a Venetian's life, and must therefore ask mercy for himself. The supreme comic teacher in this play is neither Shylock nor the men who despise him, but a woman who is almost equally despised. And it's she who controls Act 5, when she humbles Bassanio by asking for her ring back in the full knowledge that he doesn't have it. Portia has much to teach us on the subject of survival in a hostile environment.

OPPOSITE Al Pacino as Shylock in the 2004 film adaptation, directed by Michael Radford.

[*Enter the* DUKE, *the Magnificoes*, ANTONIO, BASSANIO, GRATIANO, SALERIO, SHYLOCK, NERISSA *appareled as a judge's clerk, and* PORTIA *as the young Doctor of Rome*, BALTHASAR]

PORTIA Is your name Shylock?

SHYLOCK   Shylock is my name.

PORTIA Of a strange nature is the suit you follow;
Yet in such rule that the Venetian law
Cannot impugn you as you do proceed.
You stand within his danger, do you not?

ANTONIO Ay, so he says.

PORTIA   Do you confess the bond?

ANTONIO I do.

PORTIA   Then must the Jew be merciful.

SHYLOCK On what compulsion must I? Tell me that.

PORTIA The quality of mercy is not strained.
It droppeth as the gentle rain from heaven
Upon the place beneath. It is twice blest:
It blesseth him that gives, and him that takes.
'Tis mightiest in the mightiest. It becomes
The thronèd monarch better than his crown.
His sceptre shows the force of temporal power,
The attribute to awe and majesty,
Wherein doth sit the dread and fear of kings;
But mercy is above this sceptred sway.
It is enthronèd in the hearts of kings,
It is an attribute to God himself,
And earthly power doth then show likest God's
When mercy seasons justice. Therefore, Jew,
Though justice be thy plea, consider this:
That in the course of justice none of us
Should see salvation. We do pray for mercy,
And that same prayer doth teach us all to render
The deeds of mercy. I have spoke thus much
To mitigate the justice of thy plea,
Which if thou follow, this strict court of Venice
Must needs give sentence 'gainst the merchant there.

SHYLOCK My deeds upon my head! I crave the law,
The penalty and forfeit of my bond.

PORTIA Is he not able to discharge the money?

BASSANIO Yes, here I tender it for him in the court,
Yea, twice the sum. If that will not suffice
I will be bound to pay it ten times o'er
On forfeit of my hands, my head, my heart.
If this will not suffice, it must appear
That malice bears down truth. And, I beseech you,
Wrest once the law to your authority.
To do a great right, do a little wrong,
And curb this cruel devil of his will.

PORTIA It must not be. There is no power in Venice
Can alter a decree establishèd.

'Twill be recorded for a precedent,
And many an error by the same example
Will rush into the state. It cannot be.

SHYLOCK A Daniel come to judgment, yea, a Daniel!
O wise young judge, how I do honour thee!

PORTIA I pray you, let me look upon the bond.

SHYLOCK Here 'tis, most reverend doctor, here it is.

PORTIA Shylock, there's thrice thy money offered thee.

SHYLOCK An oath, an oath! I have an oath in heaven.
Shall I lay perjury upon my soul?
No, not for Venice.

PORTIA   Why, this bond is forfeit,
And lawfully by this the Jew may claim
A pound of flesh, to be by him cut off
Nearest the merchant's heart. Be merciful.
Take thrice thy money. Bid me tear the bond.

SHYLOCK When it is paid according to the tenor.
It doth appear you are a worthy judge.
You know the law; your exposition
Hath been most sound. I charge you, by the law
Whereof you are a well-deserving pillar,
Proceed to judgment. By my soul I swear
There is no power in the tongue of man
To alter me. I stay here on my bond.

ANTONIO Most heartily I do beseech the court
To give the judgment.

PORTIA   Why then, thus it is:
You must prepare your bosom for his knife –

SHYLOCK O noble judge! O excellent young man!

PORTIA For the intent and purpose of the law
Hath full relation to the penalty
Which here appeareth due upon the bond.

> ### 'My deeds upon my head!'
> **One of several references in this scene to the trial of Jesus, this echoes the cry of the Jewish crowd: 'His blood be on us, and on our children' (Matthew 27:25). Later Shylock says he would rather 'any of the stock of Barabbas' had been his daughter's husband than a Christian. Barabbas was the thief whom the Jews asked Pilate to free instead of Jesus (Mark 15:6–15).**

SHYLOCK 'Tis very true. O wise and upright judge!
How much more elder art thou than thy looks!

PORTIA Therefore lay bare your bosom.

SHYLOCK   Ay, his breast.
So says the bond, doth it not, noble judge?
'Nearest his heart' – those are the very words.

PORTIA It is so. Are there balance here to weigh
The flesh?

SHYLOCK I have them ready.

PORTIA Have by some surgeon, Shylock, on your
charge,
To stop his wounds, lest he do bleed to death.

SHYLOCK Is it so nominated in the bond?

PORTIA It is not so expressed, but what of that?
'Twere good you do so much for charity.

SHYLOCK I cannot find it. 'Tis not in the bond.

PORTIA [*To* ANTONIO] You, merchant, have you
anything to say?

ANTONIO But little. I am armed and well prepared.
Give me your hand, Bassanio; fare you well.
Grieve not that I am fall'n to this for you,
For herein Fortune shows herself more kind
Than is her custom; it is still her use
To let the wretched man outlive his wealth
To view with hollow eye and wrinkled brow
An age of poverty, from which ling'ring penance
Of such misery doth she cut me off.
Commend me to your honourable wife.
Tell her the process of Antonio's end.
Say how I loved you. Speak me fair in death,
And, when the tale is told, bid her be judge
Whether Bassanio had not once a love.
Repent but you that you shall lose your friend,
And he repents not that he pays your debt;
For if the Jew do cut but deep enough,
I'll pay it instantly with all my heart.

BASSANIO Antonio, I am married to a wife
Which is as dear to me as life itself;
But life itself, my wife, and all the world,
Are not with me esteemed above thy life.
I would lose all, ay, sacrifice them all
Here to this devil, to deliver you.

PORTIA [*Aside*] Your wife would give you little
thanks for that
If she were by to hear you make the offer.

GRATIANO I have a wife who, I protest, I love.
I would she were in heaven, so she could
Entreat some power to change this currish Jew.

NERISSA [*Aside*] 'Tis well you offer it behind
her back;
The wish would make else an unquiet house.

SHYLOCK [*Aside*] These be the Christian
husbands. I have a daughter –
Would any of the stock of Barabbas
Had been her husband rather than a Christian! –
[*Aloud*]
We trifle time. I pray thee pursue sentence.

PORTIA A pound of that same merchant's flesh is thine.
The court awards it, and the law doth give it.

SHYLOCK Most rightful judge!

PORTIA And you must cut this flesh from off his breast.
The law allows it, and the court awards it.

SHYLOCK Most learnèd judge! A sentence! Come,
prepare!

PORTIA Tarry a little; there is something else.
This bond doth give thee here no jot of blood:
The words expressly are 'a pound of flesh'.
Take then thy bond, take thou thy pound of flesh;
But, in the cutting it, if thou dost shed
One drop of Christian blood, thy lands and goods
Are by the laws of Venice confiscate
Unto the state of Venice.

GRATIANO O upright judge! Mark, Jew! O learnèd
judge!

SHYLOCK Is that the law?

PORTIA   Thyself shalt see the act;
For as thou urgest justice, be assured
Thou shalt have justice, more than thou desir'st.

GRATIANO O learnèd judge! Mark, Jew. A learnèd
judge!

SHYLOCK I take this offer, then. Pay the bond thrice,
And let the Christian go.

BASSANIO   Here is the money.

PORTIA Soft, the Jew shall have all justice. Soft, no
haste.
He shall have nothing but the penalty.

GRATIANO O Jew, an upright judge, a learnèd judge!

PORTIA Therefore prepare thee to cut off the flesh.
Shed thou no blood, nor cut thou less nor more
But just a pound of flesh. If thou tak'st more
Or less than a just pound, be it but so much
As makes it light or heavy in the substance
Or the division of the twentieth part
Of one poor scruple – nay, if the scale do turn
But in the estimation of a hair,
Thou diest and all thy goods are confiscate.

GRATIANO A second Daniel, a Daniel, Jew!
Now, infidel, I have you on the hip.

The quality of mercy is not strained. It droppeth as the gentle rain from heaven Upon the place beneath.

Henry IV
Part I
c.1596-97

ACT **2** SCENE **4**

" There lives not three good men unhanged in England,
and one of them is fat and grows old. "

Shakespeare's splitting of the reign of Henry IV into two parts corresponds to the splitting apart of his kingdom, as insubordination spreads and rebellions break out. It reinforces, too, the astonishing multiplication of would-be kings that emerge as a result of Henry's illegal seizure of the crown in *Richard II*. Both parts are full of competing versions of the monarch. The rebels Worcester, Northumberland and Hotspur see him as their creation, since they helped to put him on the throne, and believe they can read his mind, assuming that he 'studies day and night' to pay his debt to them with their deaths – an assumption that leads them to mutiny.

In Act 2, Henry's son Prince Hal and his friend Falstaff take it in turns to play the role of king in a pub. In Act 3, Hotspur is christened 'the king of honour' by his ally Douglas. And in the final battle between Henry and the rebels at Shrewsbury, dozens of men play the king, 'marching in his coats' as decoys for the rebels' blades. As a result, the battlefield seems crowded with Henries, so that Douglas must 'murder' all the royal wardrobe 'piece by piece' if he wishes to kill the king himself. Henry, then, is not two parts but many, as if his expert performance of the previously forbidden role of king has inspired all ambitious men to think they can emulate his acting skills with impunity.

Prince Hal sees a way out of this threat to the royal supremacy through his relationship with Sir John Falstaff. Falstaff's swollen body stands both for England's sickness and its vitality: its expectation, like a pregnant mother's, of better times to come. And he is a master of comic improvisation, a skill he bequeaths to his princely apprentice.

In our scene, he teaches Hal the essential art of evading definition by others. Falstaff's opening performance in the extract, as a solitary reminder of the old chivalric virtues that struggle to survive in a wicked world, is wonderfully convincing even for an audience that knows his cowardice. Next he displays the rapid-fire verbal skills that are vital for defending reputations, brazenly rewriting the history of his recent encounter with the disguised prince at Gadshill, which he presents as an heroic fight against overwhelming odds, though in fact it consisted of his running away. And he instructs Hal, too, in the value of confounding people's expectations (in Act 1 Hal calls it 'falsifying men's hopes') – as when he finds an excuse, against all odds, for the outrageous fibs he has been telling. 'These lies are like their father that begets them,' Hal declares as he gives his own eyewitness account of Falstaff's flight, 'gross as a mountain, open, palpable.' But Sir John has an instant response. 'By the Lord,' he cries, 'I knew thee as well as he that made ye'; but 'Was it for me to kill the heir-apparent?' The evasion is so fast and so clever that there's nothing Hal can do but forgive him. Kings would pay good money, one suspects, to acquire Falstaff's ability to escape the consequences of his actions. It's an ability Hal cultivates throughout his time in the fat knight's company, and that stands him in good stead when he comes to the throne.

OPPOSITE Michael Gambon as Falstaff and Matthew Macfadyen as Hal in the National Theatre's 2005 production.

[*Enter* PRINCE HENRY *and* POINS. *To them enter* FALSTAFF, GADSHILL, BARDOLPH, *and* PETO, *followed by* FRANCIS *with sack (sherry)*]

POINS Welcome, Jack. Where hast thou been?

FALSTAFF A plague of all cowards, I say, and a vengeance too! Marry and amen! Give me a cup of sack, boy. Ere I lead this life long, I'll sew nether-stocks, and mend them and foot them too. A plague of all cowards! Give me a cup of sack, rogue. Is there no virtue extant? [*He drinks*]

PRINCE Didst thou never see Titan kiss a dish of butter, pitiful-hearted Titan, that melted at the sweet tale of the sun's? If thou didst, then behold that compound.

FALSTAFF You rogue, here's lime in this sack too! There is nothing but roguery to be found in villainous man; yet a coward is worse than a cup of sack with lime in it. A villainous coward! Go thy ways, old Jack, die when thou wilt. If manhood, good manhood, be not forgot upon the face of the earth, then am I a shotten herring. There lives not three good men unhanged in England, and one of them is fat and grows old. God help the while! A bad world, I say. I would I were a weaver; I could sing psalms, or anything. A plague of all cowards, I say still.

PRINCE How now, wool-sack! What mutter you?

FALSTAFF A king's son! If I do not beat thee out of thy kingdom with a dagger of lath, and drive all thy subjects afore thee like a flock of wild geese, I'll never wear hair on my face more. You Prince of Wales!

PRINCE Why, you whoreson round man, what's the matter?

FALSTAFF Are not you a coward? Answer me to that. And Poins there?

POINS 'Zounds, ye fat paunch, an ye call me coward, by the Lord I'll stab thee.

FALSTAFF I call thee coward! I'll see thee damned ere I call thee coward; but I would give a thousand pound I could run as fast as thou canst. You are straight enough in the shoulders – you care not who sees your back. Call you that backing of your friends? A plague upon such backing! Give me them that will face me. Give me a cup of sack. I am a rogue if I drunk today.

PRINCE O villain! Thy lips are scarce wiped since thou drunkest last.

FALSTAFF All is one for that. [*He drinks*] A plague of all cowards, still say I.

PRINCE What's the matter?

FALSTAFF What's the matter! There be four of us here have ta'en a thousand pound this day morning.

PRINCE Where is it, Jack? Where is it?

FALSTAFF Where is it! Taken from us it is; a hundred upon poor four of us.

PRINCE What, a hundred, man?

FALSTAFF I am a rogue if I were not at half-sword with a dozen of them two hours together. I have scap'd by miracle. I am eight times thrust through the doublet, four through the hose; my buckler cut through and through; my sword hacked like a hand-saw – *ecce signum!* [*He shows his sword*] I never dealt better since I was a man. All would not do. A plague of all cowards! [*Pointing to* GADSHILL, PETO, *and* BARDOLPH] Let them speak. If they speak more or less than truth, they are villains and the sons of darkness.

PRINCE Speak, sirs; how was it?

GADSHILL We four set upon some dozen –

FALSTAFF Sixteen at least, my lord.

GADSHILL And bound them.

> **'I would I were a weaver;
> I could sing psalms, or anything.'**
>
> Weavers were often Puritans, for whom singing psalms was an important form of worship. Falstaff here contrasts his own virtue with the world's wickedness – ironically enough, since he has just taken part in a robbery. His double standards are confirmed by his later claim that he could thrash Hal with 'a dagger of lath' – the weapon used by Vices or devils on the English stage.

PETO No, no, they were not bound.

FALSTAFF You rogue, they were bound, every man of them, or I am a Jew else, an Ebrew Jew.

GADSHILL As we were sharing, some six or seven fresh men set upon us –

FALSTAFF And unbound the rest, and then come in the other.

PRINCE What, fought you with them all?

FALSTAFF All! I know not what you call all, but if I fought not with fifty of them, I am a bunch of radish. If there were not two- or three-and-fifty upon poor old Jack, then am I no two-legged creature.

PRINCE Pray God you have not murdered some of them.

FALSTAFF Nay, that's past praying for. I have peppered two of them; two I am sure I have paid – two rogues in buckram suits. I tell thee what, Hal, if I tell thee a lie, spit in my face, call me horse. Thou knowest my old ward – [*He acts out the fight*] here I lay, and thus I bore my point. Four rogues in buckram let drive at me –

PRINCE What, four? Thou saidst but two even now.

FALSTAFF Four, Hal, I told thee four.

POINS Ay, ay, he said four.

FALSTAFF These four came all afront, and mainly thrust at me. I made me no more ado but took all their seven points in my target, thus.

PRINCE Seven? Why, there were but four even now.

FALSTAFF In buckram?

POINS Ay, four in buckram suits.

FALSTAFF Seven, by these hilts, or I am a villain else.

PRINCE [*Aside to* POINS] Prithee, let him alone. We shall have more anon.

PRINCE I'll be no longer guilty of this sin. This sanguine coward, this bed-presser, this horse-back-breaker, this huge hill of flesh –

FALSTAFF 'Sblood, you starveling, you elf-skin, you dried neat's tongue, you bull's pizzle, you stock-fish – O for breath to utter what is like thee! You tailor's-yard, you sheath, you bow-case, you vile standing tuck –

PRINCE Well, breathe awhile, and then to it again; and when thou hast tired thyself in base comparisons, hear me speak but this.

POINS Mark, Jack.

These lies are like their father that begets them – gross as a mountain, open, palpable.

FALSTAFF Dost thou hear me, Hal?

PRINCE Ay, and mark thee too, Jack.

FALSTAFF Do so, for it is worth the listening to. These nine in buckram that I told thee of –

PRINCE [*Aside to* POINS] So, two more already.

FALSTAFF Their points being broken –

POINS Down fell their hose.

FALSTAFF Began to give me ground. But I followed me close, came in foot and hand, and with a thought seven of the eleven I paid.

PRINCE [*Aside to* POINS] O monstrous! Eleven buckram men grown out of two!

FALSTAFF But, as the devil would have it, three misbegotten knaves in Kendal green came at my back and let drive at me; for it was so dark, Hal, that thou couldst not see thy hand.

PRINCE These lies are like their father that begets them – gross as a mountain, open, palpable. Why, thou clay-brained guts, thou knotty-pated fool, thou whoreson, obscene, greasy tallow-catch –

FALSTAFF What, art thou mad? Art thou mad? Is not the truth the truth?

PRINCE Why, how couldst thou know these men in Kendal green when it was so dark thou couldst not see thy hand? Come, tell us your reason. What sayest thou to this?

POINS Come, your reason, Jack, your reason.

FALSTAFF What, upon compulsion? Zounds, an I were at the strappado, or all the racks in the world, I would not tell you on compulsion. Give you a reason on compulsion! If reasons were as plentiful as blackberries, I would give no man a reason upon compulsion, I.

PRINCE We two saw you four set on four and bound them, and were masters of their wealth. Mark now, how a plain tale shall put you down. Then did we two set on you four; and, with a word, out-faced you from your prize, and have it; yea, and can show it you here in the house. And, Falstaff, you carried your guts away as nimbly, with as quick dexterity, and roared for mercy, and still run and roared, as ever I heard bull-calf. What a slave art thou, to hack thy sword as thou hast done, and then say it was in fight! What trick, what device, what starting-hole canst thou now find out to hide thee from this open and apparent shame?

POINS Come, let's hear, Jack; what trick hast thou now?

FALSTAFF By the Lord, I knew ye as well as he that made ye. Why, hear you, my masters: was it for me to kill the heir-apparent? Should I turn upon the true prince? Why, thou knowest I am as valiant as Hercules; but beware instinct – the lion will not touch the true prince. Instinct is a great matter; I was now a coward on instinct. I shall think the better of myself and thee during my life – I for a valiant lion, and thou for a true prince. But by the Lord, lads, I am glad you have the money. Hostess, clap to the doors. Watch tonight, pray tomorrow. Gallants, lads, boys, hearts of gold, all the titles of good fellowship come to you! What, shall we be merry? Shall we have a play extempore?

PRINCE Content, and the argument shall be thy running away.

FALSTAFF Ah, no more of that, Hal, an thou lovest me!

Henry IV
Part I

c. 1596-97

ACT **3** | SCENE **1**

**" I had rather live
With cheese and garlic in a windmill, far,
Than feed on cates and have him talk to me
In any summer house in Christendom. "**

Henry IV Part I

At each stage of *Henry IV* Part I, the scenes dominated by Falstaff mock the actions of the rebels against King Henry. Falstaff's ridiculous self-inflation exposes the subtler self-inflation of the rebels, whose claims to honour rest on an equally insubstantial basis. Falstaff is the master of the 'incomprehensible lie', which he can defend with astonishing agility; but the grossness of his lies alerts us to the far more dangerous grossness of the rebels' fabrication of their case against the monarch.

There are many specific echoes of the rebels' plot in the Falstaff scenes. In Act 1, the fat knight asks Prince Hal to change the designation of highwaymen when he is king to 'Diana's foresters … minions of the moon'. His efforts to mythologize lawlessness are no more absurd than the rebels' efforts to dignify their cause with resonant titles. Later, Falstaff looks forward to seeing the 'true prince … prove a false thief' when Hal takes part in a robbery with him. This anticipates the following scene, where the rebel Worcester accuses Henry of stealing the crown like a common criminal. Later still, Hal and Poins betray Falstaff after the robbery, robbing him of his ill-gotten booty so as to generate 'laughter for a month, and a good jest for ever'. Hotspur then enters reading a letter from a friend, which warns him: 'The purpose you undertake is dangerous; the friends you have named uncertain … and your whole plot too light for the counterpoise of so great an opposition.' Hal's plot to rob the robber Falstaff is no lighter than Hotspur's 'light' conspiracy against his sovereign. And Hal's betrayal of Falstaff (in Part I, at least) is harmless; whereas Hotspur's betrayal of his king has dreadful consequences, for his followers as well as for himself.

Hotspur's lightness is at its hilarious best in our extract, where he constantly undermines the bragging of the Welsh Prince Owen Glendower , his fellow rebel. Glendower claims that his birth was marked by omens: 'The frame and huge foundation of the earth / Shaked like a coward'; but Hotspur says the earth was suffering from 'a kind of colic' at the time. When Glendower claims to be able to call spirits from the 'vasty deep', Hotspur responds: 'Why, so can I, or so can any man; / But will they come when you do call for them?' Hotspur's stubborn pragmatism here springs from his lifelong refusal to let anyone put him down; and this becomes clear when he asserts soon afterwards that the portion of the kingdom he is to get after the king's defeat is marginally smaller than those of his co-conspirators. Within seconds this assertion sparks off another squabble with Glendower – but the threat of bloodshed is as suddenly averted when first the Welshman and then Hotspur backs down. As Hotspur says, 'I do not care', since the issue of the land means nothing to him; he is concerned only with his honour. But Hotspur's honour is as illusory as Glendower's magical powers. It's Falstaff who points this out in Act 5, where he dismisses the young man's 'honour' as a lot of hot air. Not long after, Hotspur and most of his troops are dead. The crucial difference between his kind of hot air and Falstaff's is that Hotspur's kills people.

OPPOSITE *The Dispute between Hotspur, Worcester, Mortimer and Glendower* – 18th-century painting by Henry Fuseli.

[*Enter* HOTSPUR, WORCESTER, MORTIMER,
and GLENDOWER]

MORTIMER These promises are fair, the parties sure,
And our induction full of prosperous hope.

HOTSPUR Lord Mortimer and cousin Glendower,
Will you sit down? And uncle Worcester?
A plague upon it, I have forgot the map!

GLENDOWER No, here it is. Sit, cousin Percy, sit,
Good cousin Hotspur, for by that name
As oft as Lancaster doth speak of you,
His cheek looks pale and with a rising sigh
He wisheth you in heaven.

HOTSPUR   And you in hell,
As oft as he hears Owen Glendower spoke of.

GLENDOWER I cannot blame him. At my nativity
The front of heaven was full of fiery shapes,
Of burning cressets; and at my birth
The frame and huge foundation of the earth
Shaked like a coward.

HOTSPUR Why, so it would have done at the
same season if your mother's cat had but kittened,
though yourself had never been born.

GLENDOWER I say the earth did shake when
   I was born.

HOTSPUR And I say the earth was not of my mind,
If you suppose as fearing you it shook.

GLENDOWER The heavens were all on fire, the
   earth did tremble –

HOTSPUR O, then the earth shook to see the
   heavens on fire,
And not in fear of your nativity.
Diseasèd nature oftentimes breaks forth
In strange eruptions; oft the teeming earth
Is with a kind of colic pinched and vexed
By the imprisoning of unruly wind
Within her womb; which, for enlargement striving,
Shakes the old beldam earth and topples down
Steeples and moss-grown towers. At your birth
Our grandam earth, having this distemp'rature,
In passion shook.

GLENDOWER   Cousin, of many men
I do not bear these crossings. Give me leave
To tell you once again that at my birth
The front of heaven was full of fiery shapes,
The goats ran from the mountains, and the herds
Were strangely clamorous to the frighted fields.
These signs have marked me extraordinary,
And all the courses of my life do show
I am not in the roll of common men.
Where is he living, clipped in with the sea
That chides the banks of England, Scotland, Wales,
Which calls me pupil or hath read to me?

And bring him out that is but woman's son
Can trace me in the tedious ways of art
And hold me pace in deep experiments.

HOTSPUR I think there's no man speaks better Welsh.
   I'll to dinner.

MORTIMER Peace, cousin Percy, you will make him mad.

GLENDOWER I can call spirits from the vasty deep.

HOTSPUR Why, so can I, or so can any man;
But will they come when you do call for them?

GLENDOWER Why, I can teach you, cousin, to
   command the devil.

HOTSPUR And I can teach thee, coz, to shame
   the devil
By telling truth. Tell truth, and shame the devil.
If thou have power to raise him, bring him hither,
And I'll be sworn I have power to shame him hence.
O, while you live, tell truth and shame the devil!

MORTIMER Come, come, no more of this unprofitable chat.

GLENDOWER Three times hath Henry Bolingbroke
   made head
Against my power; thrice from the banks of Wye
And sandy-bottomed Severn have I sent him
Bootless home and weather-beaten back.

HOTSPUR Home without boots, and in foul weather too!
How 'scapes he agues, in the devil's name?

GLENDOWER Come, here's the map. Shall we divide
   our right
According to our threefold order ta'en?

MORTIMER The archdeacon hath divided it
Into three limits very equally.
England, from Trent and Severn hitherto,
By south and east is to my part assigned;
All westward – Wales beyond the Severn shore
And all the fertile land within that bound –
To Owen Glendower; [*To* HOTSPUR] and, dear
   coz, to you
The remnant northward lying off from Trent.
And our indentures tripartite are drawn,
Which being sealèd interchangeably –
A business that this night may execute –
To-morrow, cousin Percy, you and I
And my good Lord of Worcester will set forth
To meet your father and the Scottish power,
As is appointed us, at Shrewsbury.
My father Glendower is not ready yet,
Not shall we need his help these fourteen days.
Within that space you may have drawn together
Your tenants, friends, and neighbouring gentlemen.

GLENDOWER A shorter time shall send me to you, lords;
And in my conduct shall your ladies come,
From whom you now must steal and take no leave;

For there will be a world of water shed
Upon the parting of your wives and you.

HOTSPUR Methinks my moiety, north from
    Burton here,
In quantity equals not one of yours.
See how this river comes me cranking in,
And cuts me from the best of all my land
A huge half-moon, a monstrous cantle out.
I'll have the current in this place dammed up,
And here the smug and silver Trent shall run
In a new channel, fair and evenly.
It shall not wind with such a deep indent
To rob me of so rich a bottom here.

GLENDOWER Not wind? It shall, it must; you
    see it doth.

MORTIMER Yea, but
Mark how he bears his course, and runs me up
With like advantage on the other side,
Gelding the opposèd continent as much
As on the other side it takes from you.

'Sometime he angers me …
a finless fish'

In this passage Hotspur mocks Glendower's
passion for prophecies. Prophecies –
sometimes attributed to the legendary Welsh
magician Merlin – often supported early modern
rebellions, which led to their banning by
successive governments. One of Shakespeare's
sources, Holinshed's *Chronicles*, records one
such prediction in which the 'moldwarp' (mole)
stood for Henry IV, who would be defeated by
a dragon, representing Glendower, and other
animals. Another source, *The Mirror for
Magistrates*, makes fun of Glendower's
esoteric learning, much as Hotspur does.

WORCESTER Yea, but a little charge will trench
    him here,
And on this north side win this cape of land,
And then he runs straight and even.

HOTSPUR I'll have it so; a little charge will do it.

GLENDOWER I'll not have it altered.

HOTSPUR   Will not you?

GLENDOWER No, nor you shall not.

HOTSPUR   Who shall say me nay?

GLENDOWER Why, that will I.

HOTSPUR Let me not understand you, then;
    speak it in Welsh.

GLENDOWER I can speak English, lord, as well as you,
For I was trained up in the English court,
Where, being but young, I framèd to the harp
Many an English ditty lovely well,
And gave the tongue a helpful ornament –

A virtue that was never seen in you.

HOTSPUR Marry,
And I am glad of it with all my heart!
I had rather be a kitten and cry mew
Than one of these same metre ballad-mongers;
I had rather hear a brazen canstick turned,
Or a dry wheel grate on the axle-tree;
And that would set my teeth nothing on edge,
Nothing so much as mincing poetry.
'Tis like the forced gait of a shuffling nag.

GLENDOWER Come, you shall have Trent turned.

HOTSPUR I do not care. I'll give thrice so much land
To any well-deserving friend;
But in the way of bargain – mark ye me –
I'll cavil on the ninth part of a hair.
Are the indentures drawn? Shall we be gone?

GLENDOWER The moon shines fair. You may
    away by night.
I'll haste the writer, and withal
Break with your wives of your departure hence.
I am afraid my daughter will run mad,
So much she doteth on her Mortimer. [*Exit*]

MORTIMER Fie, cousin Percy! How you cross
    my father!

HOTSPUR I cannot choose. Sometime he angers me
With telling me of the moldwarp and the ant,
Of the dreamer Merlin and his prophecies,
And of a dragon and a finless fish,
A clip-winged griffin and a moulten raven,
A couching lion and a ramping cat,
And such a deal of skimble-skamble stuff
As puts me from my faith. I tell you what:
He held me last night at the least nine hours
In reckoning up the several devils' names
That were his lackeys. I cried, 'Hum!' and 'Well, go to!'
But marked him not a word. O, he is as tedious
As a tired horse, a railing wife;
Worse than a smoky house. I had rather live
With cheese and garlic in a windmill, far,
Than feed on cates and have him talk to me
In any summer house in Christendom.

MORTIMER In faith, he is a worthy gentleman,
Exceedingly well read, and profited
In strange concealments, valiant as a lion,
And as wondrous affable, and as bountiful
As mines of India. Shall I tell you, cousin?
He holds your temper in a high respect,
And curbs himself even of his natural scope
When you come 'cross his humour; faith, he does.
I warrant you, that man is not alive
Might so have tempted him as you have done
Without the taste of danger and reproof.
But do not use it oft, let me entreat you.

The Merry Wives of Windsor

c. 1597-98

ACT **5** | SCENE **5**

'For me, I am here a Windsor stag,
and the fattest, I think, i' th' forest.'

The Merry Wives of Windsor

Legend has it that Elizabeth I commanded Shakespeare to write a play in which Falstaff, the fat knight from the *Henry IV* plays, falls in love – thus confirming the physical fruitfulness of his laughter-engendering body. If she did, Shakespeare did not quite comply with this request when he wrote the *Merry Wives*, since in it Falstaff courts two married women at once, with the aim of taking advantage of their wealth as well as their bodies to relieve his financial and sexual needs.

He is hardly, then, 'in love'. Interestingly, too, this is the only comedy Shakespeare wrote without a powerful member of the ruling classes in it, and the only play besides the histories that he chose to set entirely in England. One wonders if he wanted to teach his monarch a lesson about the way things were in her country, from the perspective of people of his own social status?

Here England is a kind of middle-class utopia, where the only character besides Falstaff with connections to royalty – an impoverished gentleman called Fenton, who once drank with 'the wild Prince and Poins' – is regarded with deep suspicion by the middle-class parents of the girl he wants to marry. Throughout Shakespeare's histories, the middle classes carefully exempt themselves from the epic narrative of the nation, paying their way out of military service and thus avoiding the slaughters and betrayals that bedevil the aristocracy; and in the *Merry Wives* they firmly decline to be dragged back into danger by a rash alliance. The events of ruling-class history are not just irrelevant to these people but obnoxious to them. Instead the play narrates the stories of ordinary men and women, history as it's purveyed in Tudor books of comic anecdotes, whose pranks are faithfully reproduced in the farcical situations it contains; situations based, as nowhere else in Shakespeare, on a mutual trust that never seems in any serious danger of breaking down.

The titular merry wives, Mistress Page and Mistress Ford, occupy an egalitarian rural space in which everyone can participate in plots to make or break, prevent or preserve one another's marriages. It's a space where women rule the roost, hatching stratagems designed to show, as Mistress Page insists, that 'Wives may be merry and yet honest too', in contrast to the dishonest merriment favoured by hereditary knights like Falstaff. And it's a space where jokes do no harm, as all the characters assure us. The wives' deception of Falstaff – which culminates in the scene quoted here, where he has been lured into Windsor forest in hopes of an assignation, disguised as the legendary hunter Herne, only to be laughed into humility by children and adults disguised as fairies – aims to prevent him hurting their husbands by committing adultery. And Fenton's tricking of Anne Page's parents, when he elopes with her while they are mocking Falstaff, proves that he has laid aside his aristocratic wildness and committed himself to the stability of middle-class matrimony. The egalitarianism of the comedy consists in the fact that nearly everyone in it not only plays pranks but has a prank played on them. This is a commonwealth of laughter, one of only 2 or 3 plays in Shakespeare's oeuvre that are unshadowed by the threat of death or the intimidating presence of monarchs. As such, it deserves to be better known.

OPPOSITE Falstaff with Mistress Ford and Mistress Page (the 'Merry Wives'), in an 18th-century engraving by William Sharpe.

[*Enter* FALSTAFF *disguised as Herne the Hunter, with antlers on his head*]

FALSTAFF The Windsor bell hath struck twelve; the minute draws on. Now, the hot-blooded gods assist me! Remember, Jove, thou wast a bull for thy Europa; love set on thy horns. O powerful love, that in some respects makes a beast a man; in some other, a man a beast! You were also, Jupiter, a swan for the love of Leda. O omnipotent love! How near the god drew to the complexion of a goose! A fault done first in the form of a beast – O Jove, a beastly fault! – and then another fault in the semblance of a fowl – think on 't, Jove, a foul fault! When gods have hot backs, what shall poor men do? For me, I am here a Windsor stag, and the fattest, I think, i' th' forest. Send me a cool rut-time, Jove, or who can blame me to piss my tallow? Who comes here? My doe?

[*Enter* MISTRESS FORD *and* MISTRESS PAGE]

M. FORD Sir John! Art thou there, my deer, my male deer?

FALSTAFF My doe with the black scut! Let the sky rain potatoes, let it thunder to the tune of Greensleeves, hail kissing-comfits, and snow eringoes; let there come a tempest of provocation, I will shelter me here.

> Mistress Quickly's speech as the Fairy Queen, together with the name of the inn where Falstaff stays – the Garter – has led scholars to suggest that this play was written for the Garter Feast, held in April 1597, at which new members of this aristocratic fraternity were elected. 'Chairs of order' are the stalls in St George's Chapel, Windsor, which have been set aside for members of the Order. 'Coat', 'crest' and 'blazon' refer to the aristocrats' coats of arms, their heraldic crests, and the emblems on their banners. *Honi soit qui mal y pense* – 'Shame to him who thinks ill of it' – is the Order's motto.

M. FORD Mistress Page is come with me, sweetheart.

FALSTAFF Divide me like a bribed buck, each a haunch. I will keep my sides to myself, my shoulders for the fellow of this walk, and my horns I bequeath your husbands. Am I a woodman, ha? Speak I like Herne the hunter? Why, now is Cupid a child of conscience; he makes restitution. As I am a true spirit, welcome!

[*A noise of horns*]

M. PAGE Alas, what noise?

M. FORD God forgive our sins!

FALSTAFF What should this be?

M. FORD, M. PAGE Away, away! [*They run off*]

FALSTAFF I think the devil will not have me damned, lest the oil that's in me should set hell on fire; he would never else cross me thus.

[*Enter* SIR HUGH EVANS *like a satyr;* ANNE PAGE *as a Fairy;* PISTOL *as Hobgoblin;* M. QUICKLY *as the Fairy Queen, and others as Fairies; all with tapers*]

M. QUICKLY Fairies black, grey, green, and white,
You moonshine revellers, and shades of night,
You orphan heirs of fixèd destiny,
Attend your office and your quality.
Crier Hobgoblin, make the fairy oyes.

PISTOL Elves, list your names. Silence, you airy toys.
Cricket, to Windsor chimneys shalt thou leap.
Where fires thou find'st unraked and hearths
      unswept,
There pinch the maids as blue as bilberry.
Our radiant Queen hates sluts and sluttery.

FALSTAFF They are fairies; he that speaks to them shall die.
I'll wink and couch; no man their works must eye.

[*Lies down upon his face*]

EVANS Where's Pede? Go you, and where you find a
      maid
That ere she sleep has thrice her prayers said,
Raise up the organs of her fantasy,
Sleep she as sound as careless infancy.
But those as sleep and think not on their sins,
Pinch them, arms, legs, backs, shoulders, sides, and shins.

M. QUICKLY About, about!
Search Windsor Castle, elves, within and out.
Strew good luck, oafs, on every sacred room,
That it may stand till the perpetual doom
In state as wholesome as in state 'tis fit,
Worthy the owner, and the owner it.
The several chairs of order look you scour
With juice of balm and every precious flower.
Each fair instalment, coat, and sev'ral crest
With loyal blazon evermore be blest!
And nightly, meadow-fairies, look you sing,
Like to the Garter's compass, in a ring.
Th' expressure that it bears, green let it be,
More fertile-fresh than all the field to see;
And '*Honi soit qui mal y pense*' write
In em'rald tufts, flowers purple, blue and white,
Like sapphire, pearl and rich embroidery,
Buckled below fair knighthood's bending knee.
Fairies use flowers for their charactery.
Away, disperse; but till 'tis one o'clock
Our dance of custom, round about the oak
Of Herne the Hunter, let us not forget.

EVANS Pray you, lock hand in hand; yourselves in
      order set;
And twenty glow-worms shall our lanterns be,
To guide our measure round about the tree.

But, stay. I smell a man of middle earth.

FALSTAFF God defend me from that Welsh fairy, lest he transform me to a piece of cheese!

PISTOL Vile worm, thou wast o'erlooked even in thy birth.

M. QUICKLY With trial-fire touch me his finger-end.
If he be chaste, the flame will back descend,
And turn him to no pain; but if he start,
It is the flesh of a corrupted heart.

PISTOL A trial, come!

EVANS Come, will this wood take fire?
[*They put their tapers to his fingers, and he starts*]

I do begin to perceive that I am made an ass.

FALSTAFF O, O, O!

M. QUICKLY Corrupt, corrupt, and tainted in desire!
About him, fairies; sing a scornful rhyme;
And, as you trip, still pinch him to your time.
[*They dance around Falstaff, pinching him
and singing*]
   Fie on sinful fantasy!
   Fie on lust and luxury!
   Lust is but a bloody fire,
   Kindled with unchaste desire,
   Fed in heart, whose flames aspire,
   As thoughts do blow them, higher and higher.
   Pinch him, fairies, mutually;
   Pinch him for his villainy.
Pinch him, and burn him, and turn him about,
Till candles and starlight and moonshine be out.
[*During the song, DOCTOR CAIUS comes one way and
steals away a boy in green; SLENDER another way and
takes off a boy in white; and FENTON comes and steals
away ANNE PAGE. A noise of hunting is heard within.
M. QUICKLY, PISTOL, EVANS, and all the Fairies
run away. FALSTAFF pulls off his buck's head, and rises
to run after them. Enter PAGE, FORD, M. PAGE, and
M. FORD*]

PAGE Nay, do not fly; I think we have watched you now.
Will none but Herne the Hunter serve your turn?

M. PAGE I pray you, come, hold up the jest no higher.
Now, good Sir John, how like you Windsor wives?
[*Pointing to FALSTAFF's horns*]
See you these, husband? Do not these fair yokes
Become the forest better than the town?

FORD Now, sir, who's a cuckold now? Master
Brook, Falstaff's a knave, a cuckoldly knave; here
are his horns, Master Brook; and, Master Brook, he
hath enjoyed nothing of Ford's but his buck-basket,
his cudgel, and twenty pounds of money, which
must be paid to Master Brook; his horses are
arrested for it, Master Brook.

M. FORD Sir John, we have had ill luck; we could
never mate. I will never take you for my love again,
but I will always count you my deer.

FALSTAFF I do begin to perceive that I am made
an ass.

FORD Ay, and an ox too. Both the proofs are extant.

FALSTAFF And these are not fairies? By the Lord,
I was three or four times in the thought they were
not fairies; and yet the guiltiness of my mind, the
sudden surprise of my powers, drove the grossness
of the foppery into a received belief, in despite of
the teeth of all rhyme and reason, that they were
fairies. See now how wit may be made a Jack-a-Lent
when 'tis upon ill employment!

EVANS Sir John Falstaff, serve Got, and leave your
desires, and fairies will not pinse you.

FORD Well said, Fairy Hugh.

EVANS And leave you your jealousies too, I pray you.

FORD I will never mistrust my wife again till thou
art able to woo her in good English.

FALSTAFF Have I laid my brain in the sun and
dried it, that it wants matter to prevent so gross
o'er-reaching as this? Am I ridden with a Welsh
goat too? Shall I have a coxcomb of frieze? 'Tis time
I were choked with a piece of toasted cheese.

EVANS Seese is not good to give putter; your belly
is all putter.

FALSTAFF 'Seese' and 'putter'! Have I lived to stand
at the taunt of one that makes fritters of English?
This is enough to be the decay of lust and late-
walking through the realm.

M. PAGE Why, Sir John, do you think, though we
would have thrust virtue out of our hearts by the
head and shoulders, and have given ourselves
without scruple to hell, that ever the devil could
have made you our delight?

FORD What, a hodge-pudding? A bag of flax?

M. PAGE A puffed man?

PAGE Old, cold, withered, and of intolerable entrails?

FORD And one that is as slanderous as Satan?

PAGE And as poor as Job?

FORD And as wicked as his wife?

EVANS And given to fornications, and to taverns,
and sack, and wine, and metheglins, and to drinkings,
and swearings, and starings, pribbles and prabbles?

FALSTAFF Well, I am your theme; you have the
start of me. I am dejected. I am not able to answer
the Welsh flannel. Ignorance itself is a plummet o'er
me. Use me as you will.

Henry IV Part II

c.1598-99

ACT 4 | SCENE 5

6 God knows, my son,
By what by-paths and indirect crook'd ways
I met this crown 9

Henry IV Part II

Henry IV Part I pulsates with the self-destructive energy of youth, as metaphors of air and fire accompany the clash between two young men, Hal and Hotspur, and even the elderly Falstaff lays claim to a spurious adolescence, shouting as he robs a group of merchants, 'young men must live.'

In Part II, by contrast, everyone including Falstaff is intensely mindful of old age. Metaphors of earth and water dominate, and the temperature of the play is cold, with superannuated rebels struggling to summon up the will to rise against what they perceive as the king's oppression, cramming their ancient joints into armour and marching to war with a chill in their hearts. The king himself is sick, and grows sicker as the action goes on, seeking vainly for the reassurance of company: 'O me,' he cries at one point, 'come near me now I am much ill!' Falstaff too feels his mortality, and waxes nostalgic with his old acquaintance Justice Shallow as they drink together in Shallow's orchards, waiting for the moment when Prince Hal comes into his inheritance as Henry's heir, and pays off Falstaff's debts.

But this moment never comes. Where Part I was full of professions of friendship, Part II is full of betrayals: from the betrayal of Hotspur by his father Northumberland, who failed to join him at the battle of Shrewsbury – a failure painfully recalled in the opening scene – to Northumberland's betrayal of a new set of rebels (led by the reluctant Archbishop of York), when he once again breaks his promise to support an insurrection; from the betrayal of the rebels by Hal's brother, Prince John – who promises to uphold their complaints if they will disperse their troops, then has the ringleaders summarily executed – to Hal's betrayal in Act 5 of the hopes of Falstaff, whom he banishes from his presence on pain of imprisonment. Many of the characters are isolated: Falstaff and Hal spend little time together, King Henry misses his absent son, and the rebels are left stranded by the bad faith of friends and enemies. There has never been a more touchingly elegiac portrait of a nation in decay than the one Shakespeare gives us here.

Before the opening of our extract, Hal enters his father's bedchamber to find him seemingly dead. Lifting the crown from his pillow, the prince wanders off with it, plunged in thought about the future. When King Henry wakes from his deathlike sleep he sees at once that the crown is missing, and a frantic search ensues; a search that ends with the finding of the prince, crown in hand, engaged (as Henry thinks) in the last and worst of a series of treacherous acts that began with Henry's own treachery in seizing the crown from Richard II. Henry's bitter accusation of his son and Hal's eloquent response to it are two of the richest fusions of family and state politics in Shakespeare's work. The scene ends with advice from Henry – for Hal to 'busy giddy minds with foreign quarrels' after his father's death – which offers the coldest of political motives for the wars waged by Henry V. There is something alarmingly topical about this scene, as we read it in the twenty-first century.

OPPOSITE Believing his father dead, Prince Hal removes Henry's crown in this late 19th-century illustration by Joseph N. Paton.

ACT 4 | SCENE 5
Westminster Palace, near London

[*Enter* KING HENRY IV *in his bed and* PRINCE
HENRY *(Hal, or Harry)*]

PRINCE I never thought to hear you speak again.

KING Thy wish was father, Harry, to that thought.
I stay too long by thee, I weary thee.
Dost thou so hunger for mine empty chair
That thou wilt needs invest thee with my honours
Before thy hour be ripe? O foolish youth,
Thou seek'st the greatness that will overwhelm thee!
Stay but a little, for my cloud of dignity
Is held from falling with so weak a wind
That it will quickly drop. My day is dim.
Thou hast stol'n that which after some few hours
Were thine without offence; and at my death
Thou hast sealed up my expectation.
Thy life did manifest thou loved'st me not,
And thou wilt have me die assured of it.
Thou hid'st a thousand daggers in thy thoughts,
Which thou hast whetted on thy stony heart
To stab at half an hour of my life.
What, canst thou not forbear me half an hour?
Then get thee gone and dig my grave thyself,
And bid the merry bells ring to thine ear
That thou art crownèd, not that I am dead.
Let all the tears that should bedew my hearse
Be drops of balm to sanctify thy head.
Only compound me with forgotten dust;
Give that which gave thee life unto the worms.
Pluck down my officers, break my decrees;
For now a time is come to mock at form –
Harry the Fifth is crowned. Up, vanity!
Down, royal state! All you sage counsellors, hence!
And to the English court assemble now,
From every region, apes of idleness.
Now, neighbour confines, purge you of your scum!
Have you a ruffian that will swear, drink, dance,
Revel the night, rob, murder, and commit

> **'Other, less fine in**
> **carat, is more precious,**
> **Preserving life in medicine potable'**
>
> **Low-carat, drinkable ('potable') gold was
> widely used as a medicine. The crown,
> which is regarded as more precious both
> because of its higher gold content and by
> virtue of what it stood for, is instead (says
> Hal) a poison, an infection, and its wearer's
> deadliest enemy.**

The oldest sins the newest kind of ways?
Be happy, he will trouble you no more.
England shall double gild his treble guilt,
England shall give him office, honour, might;
For the fifth Harry from curbed licence plucks
The muzzle of restraint, and the wild dog
Shall flesh his tooth on every innocent.
O my poor kingdom, sick with civil blows!
When that my care could not withhold thy riots,
What wilt thou do when riot is thy care?
O, thou wilt be a wilderness again,
Peopled with wolves, thy old inhabitants!

O foolish youth,
Thou seek'st the greatness
that will overwhelm thee!

PRINCE O, pardon me, my liege! But for my tears,
The moist impediments unto my speech,
I had forestalled this dear and deep rebuke
Ere you with grief had spoke and I had heard
The course of it so far. There is your crown,
And He that wears the crown immortally
Long guard it yours! If I affect it more
Than as your honour and as your renown,
Let me no more from this obedience rise,
Which my most true and inward duteous spirit
Teacheth this prostrate and exterior bending!
God witness with me, when I here came in
And found no course of breath within your
    majesty,
How cold it struck my heart! If I do feign,
O, let me in my present wildness die,
And never live to show th'incredulous world
The noble change that I have purposèd.
Coming to look on you, thinking you dead,
And dead almost, my liege, to think you were,
I spake unto this crown as having sense,
And thus upbraided it: 'The care on thee depending
Hath fed upon the body of my father;
Therefore thou best of gold art worst of gold.
Other, less fine in carat, is more precious,
Preserving life in medicine potable;
But thou, most fine, most honoured, most
    renowned,

Hast eat thy bearer up.' Thus, my most royal liege,
Accusing it, I put it on my head,
To try with it, as with an enemy
That had before my face murdered my father,
The quarrel of a true inheritor.
But if it did infect my blood with joy,
Or swell my thoughts to any strain of pride;
If any rebel or vain spirit of mine
Did with the least affection of a welcome
Give entertainment to the might of it,
Let God for ever keep it from my head,
And make me as the poorest vassal is
That doth with awe and terror kneel to it!

KING O my son,
God put it in thy mind to take it hence,
That thou mightst win the more thy father's love,
Pleading so wisely in excuse of it!
Come hither, Harry, sit thou by my bed,
And hear, I think, the very latest counsel
That ever I shall breathe. God knows, my son,
By what by-paths and indirect crook'd ways
I met this crown; and I myself know well
How troublesome it sat upon my head.
To thee it shall descend with better quiet,
Better opinion, better confirmation;
For all the soil of the achievement goes
With me into the earth. It seemed in me
But as an honour snatched with boist'rous hand;
And I had many living to upbraid
My gain of it by their assistances;
Which daily grew to quarrel and to bloodshed,
Wounding supposèd peace. All these bold fears
Thou seest with peril I have answerèd;
For all my reign hath been but as a scene
Acting that argument. And now my death
Changes the mood, for what in me was purchased
Falls upon thee in a more fairer sort,
So thou the garland wear'st successively.
Yet though thou stand'st more sure than I could do,
Thou art not firm enough, since griefs are green;
And all my friends, which thou must make thy friends,
Have but their stings and teeth newly ta'en out;
By whose fell working I was first advanced,
And by whose power I well might lodge a fear
To be again displaced; which to avoid,
I cut them off, and had a purpose now
To lead out many to the Holy Land,
Lest rest and lying still might make them look
Too near unto my state. Therefore, my Harry,
Be it thy course to busy giddy minds

With foreign quarrels, that action, hence borne out,
May waste the memory of the former days.
More would I, but my lungs are wasted so
That strength of speech is utterly denied me.
How I came by the crown, O God, forgive,
And grant it may with thee in true peace live!

PRINCE My gracious liege,
You won it, wore it, kept it, gave it me;
Then plain and right must my possession be,
Which I with more than with a common pain
'Gainst all the world will rightfully maintain.

[*Enter* PRINCE JOHN of LANCASTER,
WARWICK, *Lords, and others*]

KING Look, look, here comes my John of Lancaster.

PRINCE JOHN Health, peace, and happiness to my
royal father!

KING Thou bring'st me happiness and peace, son
John;
But health, alack, with youthful wings is flown
From this bare withered trunk. Upon thy sight
My worldly business makes a period.
Where is my Lord of Warwick?

PRINCE   My Lord of Warwick!

KING Doth any name particular belong
Unto the lodging where I first did swoon?

> *'And now my death …*
> *wear'st successively.'*
>
> **'Purchased' means obtained by action,
> not inherited. However Hal, by contrast,
> will wear the laurel garland of victory – that
> is, the crown – by right of succession, which
> is a 'fairer' or more attractive way of getting
> it, though not necessarily a juster one.**

WARWICK 'Tis called Jerusalem, my noble lord.

KING Laud be to God! Even there my life must end.
It hath been prophesied to me many years
I should not die but in Jerusalem,
Which vainly I supposed the Holy Land.
But bear me to that chamber; there I'll lie;
In that Jerusalem shall Harry die. [*Exeunt*]

Much Ado About Nothing

c. 1598

ACT **3** SCENE **1**

❝If I should speak
She would mock me into air. O, she would laugh me
Out of myself, press me to death with wit.❞

Much Ado About Nothing

Of all Shakespeare's plays, *Much Ado* has the most suggestive title. The play is about nothing – the trivial word games that take up the leisure time of the aristocracy in Messina – but it's also about how this 'nothing' can be blown up into something of substance, with potentially fatal results for those who get caught in the blast. This dangerous blurring of boundaries between substance and nothingness is evident from the start, when a group of noblemen return from a war that might as well have never happened, since it has no apparent consequences. When asked who died in action, a messenger replies: 'But few of any sort, and none of name'; and this introduces us into a world where the actions of ruling-class men can prove deadly to those beneath them.

The instigator of the conflict, Don John – bastard brother of the ruler of Messina, Don Pedro – has been forgiven and reinstated. And the war once ended, its participants turn for entertainment to a 'merry war' of words between the witty courtiers Benedick and Beatrice, which delights Don Pedro and his friend Count Claudio as much as bloodshed. Given the smooth transition between the war fought with swords and the war of words – and given that the same aristocrats take part in both – it should come as no surprise when the latter turns shockingly destructive.

This change of tone occurs as a result of 'noting' or eavesdropping – another element embedded in the title, since the terms 'nothing' and 'noting' sounded the same in Elizabethan English. Don Pedro and Claudio hatch a plot to make Benedick and Beatrice fall in love, despite the fact that the pair are always engaged in brilliant verbal sparring matches, with sometimes painful effects – especially for Benedick. The plot consists in having first Benedick, then Beatrice overhear conversations in which they learn that their sparring partner loves them – information that plants the seeds of affection in the eavesdropper. The intrigue is harmless enough; but linked with it is a more sinister scheme by Don John to drive a wedge between Count Claudio and his fiancée, Hero. Don John exploits a third Elizabethan meaning of 'nothing' – 'vagina' – by persuading Claudio first that his friend Don Pedro is courting Hero for himself, then that Hero has slept with a stranger on the eve of her wedding to the count. He substantiates the second accusation by staging an eavesdropping scene for Claudio, just like the ones arranged for Benedick and Beatrice, in which Don John's henchman Borachio makes love to a woman dressed in Hero's clothes. Claudio's easy trust of the traitor Don John, as against his friend and his fiancée, confirms the insubstantial nature of the young man's professions of attachment.

Our first scene is the one where Beatrice eavesdrops on a staged discussion between Hero and her maid concerning Benedick's love for Beatrice. Hero blames her witty cousin for her habit of 'mocking people into air', and proposes to put Benedick off her by devising 'honest slanders' to smear her name. These light remarks foreshadow the weighty accusations to which Hero herself will be subject in the following act – proof positive of how dangerous it can be to get involved in providing light entertainment for the powerful.

OPPOSITE Beatrice eavesdrops on the conversation between Hero and her maid in this 18th-century print by Rev. Matthew W. Peters.

[*Enter* HERO, MARGARET, *and* URSULA]

HERO

Good Margaret, run thee to the parlour;
There shalt thou find my cousin Beatrice
Proposing with the Prince and Claudio.
Whisper her ear, and tell her I and Ursula
Walk in the orchard, and our whole discourse
Is all of her; say that thou overheard'st us,
And bid her steal into the pleachèd bower,
Where honeysuckles, ripened by the sun,
Forbid the sun to enter – like favourites
Made proud by princes, that advance their pride

For look where Beatrice like a lapwing runs
Close by the ground to hear our conference.

Against that power that bred it. There will she
   hide her
To listen our propose. This is thy office;
Bear thee well in it, and leave us alone.

MARGARET

I'll make her come, I warrant you, presently. [*Exit*]

HERO

Now, Ursula, when Beatrice doth come,
As we do trace this alley up and down
Our talk must only be of Benedick.
When I do name him, let it be thy part
To praise him more than ever man did merit.
My talk to thee must be how Benedick
Is sick in love with Beatrice. Of this matter
Is little Cupid's crafty arrow made,
That only wounds by hearsay.
[*Enter* BEATRICE]
                      Now begin;
For look where Beatrice like a lapwing runs
Close by the ground to hear our conference.

URSULA

The pleasant'st angling is to see the fish
Cut with her golden oars the silver stream
And greedily devour the treacherous bait.
So angle we for Beatrice, who even now
Is couchèd in the woodbine coverture.
Fear you not my part of the dialogue.

HERO

Then go we near her, that her ear lose nothing
Of the false-sweet bait that we lay for it.
[*They approach* BEATRICE's *hiding-place*]

No, truly, Ursula, she is too disdainful.
I know her spirits are as coy and wild
As haggards of the rock.

URSULA

                      But are you sure
That Benedick loves Beatrice so entirely?

HERO

So says the Prince and my new-trothèd lord.

URSULA

And did they bid you tell her of it, madam?

'odd and from all fashions'

Antagonistic to ordinary behaviour. But
'fashion' could have its modern sense when
applied to clothing; and in this play Claudio
and Hero are fashion victims. Claudio starts
attending to his clothes after he is betrothed
to Hero, and Hero spends the night before
her wedding thinking about her wedding
gown ('a most rare fashion'). Hero is then
'fashioned' as an adulteress by Don John.

HERO

They did entreat me to acquaint her of it,
But I persuaded them, if they loved Benedick,
To wish him wrestle with affection,
And never to let Beatrice know of it.

URSULA

Why did you so? Doth not the gentleman
Deserve as full as fortunate a bed
As ever Beatrice shall couch upon?

HERO

O god of love! I know he doth deserve
As much as may be yielded to a man;
But nature never framed a woman's heart
Of prouder stuff than that of Beatrice.
Disdain and scorn ride sparkling in her eyes,
Misprising what they look on, and her wit
Values itself so highly that to her
All matter else seems weak. She cannot love,
Nor take no shape nor project of affection,
She is so self-endearèd.

URSULA

                    Sure, I think so.
And therefore certainly it were not good
She knew his love, lest she make sport at it.

HERO

Why, you speak truth. I never yet saw man,
How wise, how noble, young, how rarely featured,
But she would spell him backward. If fair-faced,
She would swear the gentleman should be her sister;
If black, why, Nature, drawing of an antic,
Made a foul blot; if tall, a lance ill-headed;
If low, an agate very vilely cut;
If speaking, why, a vane blown with all winds;
If silent, why, a block movèd with none.
So turns she every man the wrong side out,
And never gives to truth and virtue that
Which simpleness and merit purchaseth.

URSULA

Sure, sure, such carping is not commendable.

HERO

No, not to be so odd and from all fashions
As Beatrice is cannot be commendable.
But who dare tell her so? If I should speak
She would mock me into air. O, she would
   laugh me
Out of myself, press me to death with wit.
Therefore let Benedick, like covered fire,
Consume away in sighs, waste inwardly.
It were a better death than die with mocks,
Which is as bad as die with tickling.

URSULA

Yet tell her of it. Hear what she will say.

HERO

No; rather I will go to Benedick
And counsel him to fight against his passion.
And truly, I'll devise some honest slanders
To stain my cousin with. One doth not know
How much an ill word may empoison liking.

Contempt, farewell!

URSULA

O, do not do your cousin such a wrong.
She cannot be so much without true judgment –
Having so swift and excellent a wit
As she is prized to have – as to refuse
So rare a gentleman as Signior Benedick.

HERO

He is the only man of Italy –
Always excepted my dear Claudio.

URSULA

I pray you be not angry with me, madam,
Speaking my fancy. Signior Benedick,
For shape, for bearing, argument and valour,
Goes foremost in report through Italy.

HERO

Indeed, he hath an excellent good name.

URSULA

His excellence did earn it ere he had it.
When are you married, madam?

HERO

Why, every day – tomorrow. Come, go in.
I'll show thee some attires, and have thy counsel
Which is the best to furnish me tomorrow.

URSULA [*Aside*] She's limed, I warrant you. We
  have caught her, madam.

> ### 'press me to death with wit.'
> One of many phrases in the play that link
> wit with violence. Criminals were crushed to
> death with heavy weights if they refused to
> enter a plea. Hero means that Beatrice would
> silence her with mockery, then mock her for
> being silent. To avoid a similar fate, she
> adds, Benedick should die by sighing (it
> was believed that your life was shortened
> with every sigh).

HERO [*Aside*]
If it prove so, then loving goes by haps.
Some Cupid kills with arrows, some with traps.

[*Exeunt* **HERO** *and* **URSULA**]

BEATRICE [*Coming forward*]
What fire is in mine ears? Can this be true?
Stand I condemned for pride and scorn so much?
Contempt, farewell! And maiden pride, adieu!
No glory lives behind the back of such.
And, Benedick, love on; I will requite thee,
Taming my wild heart to thy loving hand.
If thou dost love, my kindness shall incite thee
To bind our loves up in a holy band.
For others say thou dost deserve, and I
Believe it better than reportingly. [*Exit*]

Much Ado About Nothing

c.1598

ACT **4** | SCENE **1**

❛men are only turned into tongue,
and trim ones too.❜

Hero is the ideal woman of the mindless Renaissance male: obedient, mostly silent, and willing to be moulded into whatever shape men care to make of her. In the first act of eavesdropping in the play, a servant thinks he has heard Don Pedro say he plans to court her, and her father Leonato urges her to accept the prince's courtship ('I trust you will be ruled by your father,' adds her uncle). But soon afterwards the prince reveals that he has been wooing her on Claudio's behalf; and when he hands her over to him at the end of Act 2, she gives no sign of disappointment at getting a count for a husband instead of a monarch.

In Act 3, she readily assents to Claudio's proposal that she trick her cousin Beatrice into thinking Benedick loves her; and her willingness to put on a performance may be what begins to turn Claudio against her, making him receptive to Don John's libels. If she could lie so glibly once, why shouldn't she do it again, with or without her fiancé's knowledge? In Act 4, Claudio denounces Hero on her wedding day for an infidelity he thinks he saw her commit; and as he does so, he reads her body as an index of dishonesty: 'Would you not swear, / All you that see her, that she were a maid, / By these exterior shows? But she is none … Her blush is guiltiness, not modesty.' Too late Hero discovers the disadvantages of proving too amenable to the ever-changing demands of the male imagination.

It seems fitting, then, that the friar's plan to reconcile her to Claudio involves an appeal to the count's erotic fantasies about her. In our extract the friar suggests that it be announced that Hero died when she was libelled. Once he thinks her dead, the friar contends, Claudio's memory will fabricate a new and better Hero, lovelier in every limb than the girl he lost. When this happens, it will be a simple matter to reunite the young couple, since Hero will have been restored to the status of Claudio's pornographic pin-up, the undisputed mistress of his dreams.

Hero's cousin Beatrice is quite different. In the first scene of the play she exposes the vapidity of men's attitude to war by offering to eat anyone Benedick has killed; an offer that forces him and his male companions to confront the material realities of combat, and the emptiness of the compliments for valour with which they shower one another (it seems evident that he has killed no one). Her verbal attacks hurt Benedick like 'poniards' (daggers); yet for all her love of aggressive wordplay, with its unmasking of the consequences of aggression – the pain it inflicts, the blood it draws – she never loses her loyalty to the men and women she trusts. She is the first to declare Hero's innocence when she's slandered, and the first to demand retribution for the slander, urging Benedick to 'Kill Claudio' as proof that he has a better sense of the substance of things – of what really matters – than his vapid friends. She is the shrew who won't be tamed, the woman who won't be reinvented – and the heroine who has no need to adopt a male disguise to speak her mind.

OPPOSITE Alex Jennings as Benedick restrains Siobhan Redmond as Beatrice in the Royal Shakespeare Company's 1996 production.

[*Enter* LEONATO, FRIAR, BENEDICK, HERO, *and* BEATRICE]

FRIAR There is some strange misprision in the princes.

BENEDICK Two of them have the very bent of honour,
And if their wisdoms be misled in this
The practice of it lives in John the bastard,
Whose spirits toil in frame of villainies.

LEONATO I know not. If they speak but truth of her
These hands shall tear her; if they wrong her honour
The proudest of them shall well hear of it.
Time hath not yet so dried this blood of mine,
Nor age so eat up my invention,
Nor fortune made such havoc of my means,
Nor my bad life reft me so much of friends,
But they shall find awaked in such a kind
Both strength of limb and policy of mind,
Ability in means and choice of friends,
To quit me of them throughly.

FRIAR   Pause awhile,
And let my counsel sway you in this case.
Your daughter here the princes left for dead;
Let her awhile be secretly kept in,
And publish it that she is dead indeed.
Maintain a mourning ostentation,
And on your family's old monument
Hang mournful epitaphs, and do all rites
That appertain unto a burial.

LEONATO What shall become of this? What will this do?

FRIAR Marry, this, well carried, shall on her behalf
Change slander to remorse. That is some good.
But not for that dream I on this strange course,
But on this travail look for greater birth.
She – dying, as it must so be maintained,
Upon the instant that she was accused –
Shall be lamented, pitied, and excused
Of every hearer. For it so falls out
That what we have we prize not to the worth
Whiles we enjoy it, but being lacked and lost,
Why, then we rack the value, then we find
The virtue that possession would not show us
Whiles it was ours. So will it fare with Claudio.
When he shall hear she died upon his words,
The idea of her life shall sweetly creep
Into his study of imagination,
And every lovely organ of her life
Shall come apparelled in more precious habit,
More moving-delicate and full of life,
Into the eye and prospect of his soul
Than when she lived indeed. Then shall he mourn,
If ever love had interest in his liver,
And wish he had not so accusèd her –
No, though he thought his accusation true.
Let this be so, and doubt not but success
Will fashion the event in better shape
Than I can lay it down in likelihood.
But if all aim but this be levelled false,
The supposition of the lady's death
Will quench the wonder of her infamy.
And if it sort not well, you may conceal her,
As best befits her wounded reputation,
In some reclusive and religious life,
Out of all eyes, tongues, minds, and injuries.

BENEDICK Signior Leonato, let the Friar advise you.
And though you know my inwardness and love
Is very much unto the Prince and Claudio,
Yet, by mine honour, I will deal in this
As secretly and justly as your soul
Should with your body.

Kill Claudio.

LEONATO Being that I flow in grief,
The smallest twine may lead me.

FRIAR 'Tis well consented. Presently away;
For to strange sores strangely they strain the cure.
Come, lady, die to live. This wedding day
Perhaps is but prolonged. Have patience and endure.

[*Exeunt all but* BENEDICK *and* BEATRICE]

BENEDICK Lady Beatrice, have you wept all this while?

BEATRICE Yea, and I will weep a while longer.

BENEDICK I will not desire that.

BEATRICE You have no reason; I do it freely.

BENEDICK Surely I do believe your fair cousin is wronged.

BEATRICE Ah, how much might the man deserve of me that would right her!

BENEDICK Is there any way to show such friendship?

BEATRICE A very even way, but no such friend.

BENEDICK May a man do it?

BEATRICE It is a man's office, but not yours.

BENEDICK I do love nothing in the world so well as you. Is not that strange?

BEATRICE As strange as the thing I know not. It were as possible for me to say I loved nothing so well as you; but believe me not, and yet I lie not. I confess nothing, nor I deny nothing. I am sorry for my cousin.

BENEDICK By my sword, Beatrice, thou lovest me.

BEATRICE Do not swear, and eat it.

BENEDICK I will swear by it that you love me; and I will make him eat it that says I love not you.

BEATRICE Will you not eat your word?

BENEDICK With no sauce that can be devised to it. I protest I love thee.

BEATRICE Why then, God forgive me!

BENEDICK What offence, sweet Beatrice?

BEATRICE You have stayed me in a happy hour. I was about to protest I loved you.

> ## 'a princely testimony
> ## … a sweet gallant, surely!'
>
> In her fury at the injustice done to her cousin – and in frustration at her own impotence – Beatrice assaults Hero's accusers with wordplay. Earlier she said that Claudio chose to 'bear [Hero] in hand' until they came to 'take hands' – meaning that he strung her along until they were due to be united in marriage. A 'princely testimony' refers to the fact that the witness who supported Claudio's accusation was a prince, Don Pedro. 'Count' means a story or a legal indictment, as well as alluding to Claudio's title. A comfit is a sugar-plum – an ironic allusion to Claudio's non-existent gallantry and sweetness.

BENEDICK And do it with all thy heart.

BEATRICE I love you with so much of my heart that none is left to protest.

BENEDICK Come, bid me do any thing for thee.

BEATRICE Kill Claudio.

BENEDICK Ha! Not for the wide world.

BEATRICE You kill me to deny it. Farewell.

BENEDICK Tarry, sweet Beatrice.

BEATRICE I am gone, though I am here. There is no love in you. Nay, I pray you, let me go.

BENEDICK Beatrice.

BEATRICE In faith, I will go.

BENEDICK We'll be friends first.

BEATRICE You dare easier be friends with me than fight with mine enemy.

BENEDICK Is Claudio thine enemy?

BEATRICE Is a not approved in the height a villain, that hath slandered, scorned, dishonoured my kinswoman? O that I were a man! What, bear her in hand until they come to take hands, and then, with public accusation, uncovered slander, unmitigated rancour – O God, that I were a man! I would eat his heart in the market-place.

BENEDICK Hear me, Beatrice.

BEATRICE Talk with a man out at a window! A proper saying!

BENEDICK Nay, but Beatrice –

BEATRICE Sweet Hero! She is wronged, she is slandered, she is undone.

BENEDICK Beat –

BEATRICE Princes and counties! Surely, a princely testimony, a goodly count, Count Comfit; a sweet gallant, surely! O that I were a man for his sake! Or that I had any friend would be a man for my sake! But manhood is melted into courtesies, valour into compliment, and men are only turned into tongue, and trim ones too. He is now as valiant as Hercules that only tells a lie and swears it. I cannot be a man with wishing, therefore I will die a woman with grieving.

BENEDICK Tarry, good Beatrice. By this hand, I love thee.

BEATRICE Use it for my love some other way than swearing by it.

BENEDICK Think you in your soul the Count Claudio hath wronged Hero?

BEATRICE Yea, as sure as I have a thought or a soul.

BENEDICK Enough, I am engaged; I will challenge him. I will kiss your hand, and so I leave you. By this hand, Claudio shall render me a dear account. As you hear of me, so think of me. Go, comfort your cousin. I must say she is dead. And so, farewell. [*Exeunt*]

Henry V *c.1599*

"Once more unto the breach, dear friends, once more,
Or close the wall up with our English dead."

Falstaff never appears in *Henry V*; but the lessons he taught Prince Hal, now King Henry, resonate throughout the play. Henry remains a humorist, and the cruelty of his humour recalls the sometimes cruel taunting to which he subjected his old friend. In Act 2, for instance, he uncovers a plot against him by two noblemen, and publicizes the discovery by handing them scrolls containing what they think are battle orders, but which instead hold proof of their treachery – a prank that does not feature in Shakespeare's sources (Shakespeare made it up himself). Far more disturbing is the gigantic jest that is Henry's invasion of France. It's one of a series of dazzling diversions designed to draw attention away from the problematic nature of his inheritance.

Since his claim to the English throne is poor, he claims the French one; since military action is in his interest, he presents it as God's will; since he is the aggressor in his continental war, he transfers the blame for it to his enemies, telling the citizens of besieged Harfleur: 'you yourselves are cause / If your pure maidens fall into the hand / Of hot and forcing violation'. It's the comic sleight of hand involved in these post-Falstaffian evasions that strikes us as chilling. His lies are not gross, as Falstaff's were, but breezy and scarcely visible. And their breeziness kills people.

The link between laughter and slaughter in Henry's reign is at its strongest in Act 1, when the Archbishop of Canterbury – eager to stave off royal plans to tax the church – describes England's former French campaigns as a grotesque spectator sport, in which the hero Edward III 'Stood smiling' to watch his son 'Forage in blood of French nobility'. Henry at once catches the archbishop's tone, and seizes the pretext of the Dauphin's gift of tennis balls (a mocking reference to Hal's wild youth) to depict his intended French campaign as a bloodier, better joke. The Frenchman's jest, he quips, will 'savour but of shallow wit / When thousands weep more than did laugh at it.' Henry's invasion is designed to show that the English king is the wittiest man in Europe, and that all his verbal and political debts will be repaid at once, with interest. Henry, in fact, must be the undisputed master of ceremonies in the play that bears his name.

But Falstaff leaves Hal another legacy besides the ability to forge brilliant ripostes and evasions. Though no commoner himself, the fat knight acted as a bridge between the prince and the common people, whose language Hal learned in his company. Familiarity with his people provides Henry with his most brilliant stratagem: that of rhetorically ennobling the English nation. As he storms the breach in our extract, Henry urges all his men, not just the aristocracy, to recall their glorious lineage: 'For there is none of you so mean and base / That hath not noble lustre in his eyes.' In saying so, he distracts his observers from the less than royal status of his own ancestry. When he calls his soldiers 'brothers, friends, and countrymen', he transforms them into aspects of himself, thus strengthening his power to the extent that it cannot be resisted in his lifetime. The skill with which he achieves this he owes to Falstaff.

OPPOSITE Kenneth Branagh as Henry V urges his troops to make one final assault on the walls of Harfleur in the Royal Shakespeare Company's 1984 production.

[*Enter* CHORUS]

CHORUS
Thus with imagined wing our swift scene flies
In motion of no less celerity
Than that of thought. Suppose that you have seen
The well-appointed king at Dover pier
Embark his royalty, and his brave fleet
With silken streamers the young Phoebus fanning.
Play with your fancies, and in them behold
Upon the hempen tackle ship-boys climbing;
Hear the shrill whistle which doth order give
To sounds confused; behold the threaden sails,
Borne with th'invisible and creeping wind,
Draw the huge bottoms through the furrowed sea,
Breasting the lofty surge. O do but think
You stand upon the rivage and behold
A city on th'inconstant billows dancing –

*Work, work
your thoughts*

For so appears this fleet majestical,
Holding due course to Harfleur. Follow, follow!
Grapple your minds to sternage of this navy,
And leave your England, as dead midnight still,
Guarded with grandsires, babies, and old women,
Either past or not arrived to pith and puissance.
For who is he whose chin is but enriched
With one appearing hair that will not follow
These culled and choice-drawn cavaliers to France?
Work, work your thoughts, and therein see a siege;
Behold the ordnance on their carriages,
With fatal mouths gaping on girded Harfleur.
Suppose th'ambassador from the French comes back,
Tells Harry that the King doth offer him
Katharine his daughter, and with her to dowry
Some petty and unprofitable dukedoms.
The offer likes not, and the nimble gunner
With linstock now the devilish cannon touches,
[*Alarum, and chambers go off*]
And down goes all before them. Still be kind,
And eke out our performance with your mind.
[*Exit*]

SCENE **1**

[*Alarum. Enter the* KING *and Soldiers, with
    scaling-ladders*]

KING
Once more unto the breach, dear friends,
    once more,
Or close the wall up with our English dead.
In peace there's nothing so becomes a man
As modest stillness and humility;
But when the blast of war blows in our ears,
Then imitate the action of the tiger:
Stiffen the sinews, summon up the blood,
Disguise fair nature with hard-favoured rage.
Then lend the eye a terrible aspect,
Let it pry through the portage of the head
Like the brass cannon; let the brow o'erwhelm it
As fearfully as doth a gallèd rock
O'erhang and jutty his confounded base,
Swilled with the wild and wasteful ocean.
Now set the teeth and stretch the nostril wide,
Hold hard the breath, and bend up every spirit
To his full height. On, on, you noblest English,
Whose blood is fet from fathers of war-proof –
Fathers that like so many Alexanders
Have in these parts from morn till even fought
And sheathed their swords for lack of argument.
Dishonour not your mothers; now attest
That those whom you called fathers did beget you.
Be copy now to men of grosser blood,
And teach them how to war. And you, good
    yeomen,
Whose limbs were made in England, show us here
The mettle of your pasture; let us swear
That you are worth your breeding – which I doubt
    not;
For there is none of you so mean and base
That hath not noble lustre in your eyes.
I see you stand like greyhounds in the slips,
Straining upon the start. The game's afoot.
Follow your spirit, and upon this charge
Cry, 'God for Harry, England, and Saint George!'
[*Exeunt. Alarum, and chambers go off*]

*I would give all my
fame for a pot of
ale, and safety.*

ACT 3 | SCENE 2
France – before Harfleur

[*Enter* NYM, BARDOLPH, PISTOL, *and* BOY]

BARDOLPH
On, on, on, on, on! To the breach, to the breach!

NYM
Pray thee corporal, stay. The knocks are too hot,
and for mine own part I have not a case of lives.
The humour of it is too hot, that is the very
plainsong of it.

PISTOL
'The plainsong' is most just, for humours do abound.
Knocks go and come; God's vassals drop and die,
        And sword and shield
        In bloody field,
    Doth win immortal fame.

BOY
Would I were in an alehouse in London! I would
give all my fame for a pot of ale, and safety.

PISTOL
And I.
        If wishes would prevail with me
        My purpose should not fail with me
        But thither would I hie.

BOY
        As duly
        But not as truly
        As bird doth sing on bough.

> *'I knew by that piece of service the men would carry coals. They would have me as familiar with men's pockets as their gloves or their handkerchiefs; which makes much against my manhood, if I should take from another's pocket to put into mine, for it is plain pocketing up of wrongs.'*
>
> **To 'carry coals' is to allow one's reputation to be smeared – to submit to insults. 'Pocketing up of wrongs' means the same thing: literally, it means to pocket stolen goods, but it also means to tamely accept insults, which is unmanly ('makes much against my manhood') – an amusing concept, since the phrase is uttered by a boy, who seeks to 'cast up' or vomit out his cowardly current employers.**

[*Enter* FLUELLEN]

FLUELLEN [*Driving them forward*]
Up to the breach, you dogs! Avaunt, you cullions!

PISTOL
Be merciful, great duke, to men of mould.
Abate thy rage, abate thy manly rage,
Abate thy rage, great duke.
Good bawcock, bate thy rage. Use lenity, sweet
   chuck.

NYM
These be good humours! Your honour runs bad
   humours.

[*Exeunt all but* BOY]

BOY
As young as I am, I have observed these three
swashers. I am boy to them all three, but all
they three, though they would serve me, could not
be man to me, for indeed three such antics do not
amount to a man. For Bardolph, he is white-livered
and red-faced; by the means whereof a faces it out,
but fights not. For Pistol, he hath a killing tongue
and a quiet sword; by the means whereof a breaks
words, and keeps whole weapons. For Nym, he hath
heard that men of few words are the best men, and
therefore he scorns to say his prayers, lest a should
be thought a coward. But his few bad words are
matched with as few good deeds; for a never broke
any man's head but his own, and that was against a
post when he was drunk. They will steal anything
and call it 'purchase'. Bardolph stole a lute-case,
bore it twelve leagues, and sold it for three
halfpence. Nym and Bardolph are sworn brothers
in filching, and in Calais they stole a fire shovel.
I knew by that piece of service the men would carry
coals. They would have me as familiar with men's
pockets as their gloves or their handkerchiefs;
which makes much against my manhood, if I
should take from another's pocket to put into mine,
for it is plain pocketing up of wrongs. I must leave
them, and seek some better service. Their villainy
goes against my weak stomach, and therefore I
must cast it up. [*Exit*]

Julius Caesar

c.1599

ACT **3** | SCENE **2**

6 **If you have tears,
prepare to shed them now.** 9

The power of this play lies in the fallibility of the people in it, as compared to the durability of the many myths of ancient Rome. Shakespeare represents the Roman commoners, the plebeians, as comically fickle; in our extract they are persuaded by Mark Antony to execute a sudden *volte-face* and turn against the faction they supported, the patriots who murdered Caesar to prevent him taking absolute power in the republic. But the Roman ruling classes – the patricians – are as fickle as the commoners.

Caesar – who likes to think himself as 'constant as the northern star' – twice changes his mind about whether he should attend the Senate on the day he is assassinated. Brutus, who plans to assassinate Caesar, is persuaded to reveal the details of his conspiracy to his wife Portia, despite his determination to conceal them. Portia insists that her courage is unshakeable, but cracks up when her husband's plot comes to a head. Brutus later falls out with his friend Cassius, only to fall into his arms again with an erotically charged exchange of compliments. Everyone in the play is full of doubts; and when omens occur – when 'fiery warriors fight upon the clouds' and 'ghosts … shriek and squeal about the streets' – nobody knows for certain how to read them.

Yet somehow, in our extract, Caesar's friend Mark Antony succeeds in constructing a myth of Caesar that has endured throughout the centuries since his death. Before this scene we knew of the great man's weaknesses: his deafness, his epileptic fits, his overbearing arrogance. But afterwards he is immortal – as we discover in Act 4, when his ghost appears to Brutus on the eve of his defeat. Antony's construction of Caesar's immortality is a masterpiece of propaganda, worthy of study by any aspiring politician.

He begins by stressing his mortality: 'But yesterday the word of Caesar might / Have stood against the world. Now lies he there.' But he adds that if the Romans knew the contents of his will they would revere him like a holy martyr, 'And dip their napkins in his sacred blood'. Caesar's prospective sainthood, then, depends on his bequests to the citizens – a solid enough basis for adulation. And Antony finds an equally solid basis for the indignation he wishes to wake on his friend's behalf. His account of the great man's death is simply an extended description of his mantle. It's this garment, not the body beneath it, that feels the pain of Brutus's betrayal as he stabs his former ally. When Antony says 'This was the most unkindest cut of all', he means the cutting of Caesar's clothes, not Caesar; and Caesar's grief at Brutus's unkindness is powerfully conveyed when Antony describes him muffling his face in his mantle before collapsing. So effective is this strategy for arousing the citizens' emotions that Antony even dares to mock them for crying over fabric: 'Kind souls, what, weep you when you but behold / Our Caesar's vesture wounded? Look you here. / Here is himself, marred, as you see, with traitors.' Caesar's posthumous fame, then, is shaped by Antony as an expert tailor shapes a piece of cloth. And Antony's success in making him a lasting celebrity is confirmed by the fact that emperors have donned Caesar's surname like a robe of office ever since.

OPPOSITE Mark Antony addresses the crowd in *Mark Antony's Oration* by George Edward Robertson.

Rome – the Forum

[*Enter* BRUTUS *and the* PLEBEIANS. *To them enter* MARK ANTONY *with Attendants bearing* CAESAR's *body*]

BRUTUS Good countrymen, let me depart alone,
And for my sake stay here with Antony.
Do grace to Caesar's corpse, and grace his speech
Tending to Caesar's glories, which Mark Antony
By our permission is allowed to make.
I do entreat you, not a man depart
Save I alone till Antony have spoke. [*Exit*]

FIRST PLEBEIAN Stay, ho! And let us hear
Mark Antony.

THIRD PLEBEIAN Let him go up into the
public chair.
We'll hear him. Noble Antony, go up.

ANTONY For Brutus' sake, I am beholden to you.
[*Goes into the pulpit*]

FOURTH PLEBEIAN What does he say of Brutus?

THIRD PLEBEIAN He says, for Brutus' sake
He finds himself beholden to us all.

FOURTH PLEBEIAN 'Twere best he speak no
harm of Brutus here.

FIRST PLEBEIAN This Caesar was a tyrant.

THIRD PLEBEIAN Nay, that's certain.
We are blest that Rome is rid of him.

SECOND PLEBEIAN Peace! Let us hear what
Antony can say.

ANTONY You gentle Romans –

ALL Peace, ho! Let us hear him.

ANTONY Friends, Romans, countrymen, lend
me your ears.
I come to bury Caesar, not to praise him.
The evil that men do lives after them;
The good is oft interrèd with their bones.
So let it be with Caesar. The noble Brutus
Hath told you Caesar was ambitious.
If it were so, it was a grievous fault,
And grievously hath Caesar answered it.
Here, under leave of Brutus and the rest –
For Brutus is an honourable man,
So are they all, all honourable men –
Come I to speak in Caesar's funeral.
He was my friend, faithful and just to me;
But Brutus says he was ambitious,
And Brutus is an honourable man.
He hath brought many captives home to Rome,
Whose ransoms did the general coffers fill.

Did this in Caesar seem ambitious?
When that the poor have cried, Caesar hath wept;
Ambition should be made of sterner stuff.
Yet Brutus says he was ambitious,
And Brutus is an honourable man.
You all did see that on the Lupercal
I thrice presented him a kingly crown,
Which he did thrice refuse. Was this ambition?
Yet Brutus says he was ambitious,
And sure he is an honourable man.
I speak not to disprove what Brutus spoke,
But here I am to speak what I do know.
You all did love him once, not without cause;
What cause withholds you then to mourn for him?
O judgment, thou art fled to brutish beasts,
And men have lost their reason! [*He weeps*] Bear
with me;
My heart is in the coffin there with Caesar,
And I must pause till it come back to me.

FIRST PLEBEIAN Methinks there is much reason
in his sayings.

SECOND PLEBEIAN If thou consider rightly of
the matter,
Caesar has had great wrong.

THIRD PLEBEIAN Has he not, masters?
I fear there will a worse come in his place.

FOURTH PLEBEIAN Marked ye his words? He
would not take the crown,
Therefore 'tis certain he was not ambitious.

FIRST PLEBEIAN If it be found so, some will
dear abide it.

SECOND PLEBEIAN Poor soul! His eyes are red
as fire with weeping.

THIRD PLEBEIAN There's not a nobler man in
Rome than Antony.

FOURTH PLEBEIAN Now mark him, he begins
again to speak.

ANTONY But yesterday the word of Caesar might
Have stood against the world. Now lies he there,
And none so poor to do him reverence.
O masters, if I were disposed to stir
Your hearts and minds to mutiny and rage,
I should do Brutus wrong, and Cassius wrong,
Who, you all know, are honourable men.
I will not do them wrong; I rather choose
To wrong the dead, to wrong myself and you,
Than I will wrong such honourable men.
But here's a parchment with the seal of Caesar;

Friends, Romans, countrymen, lend me your ears.

I found it in his closet – 'tis his will.
Let but the commons hear this testament,
Which, pardon me, I do not mean to read,
And they would go and kiss dead Caesar's wounds
And dip their napkins in his sacred blood,
Yea, beg a hair of him for memory
And, dying, mention it within their wills,
Bequeathing it as a rich legacy
Unto their issue.

FOURTH PLEBEIAN We'll hear the will. Read it,
Mark Antony.

ALL The will, the will! We will hear Caesar's will.

ANTONY Have patience, gentle friends, I must not
read it.
It is not meet you know how Caesar loved you.
You are not wood, you are not stones, but men;
And being men, hearing the will of Caesar,
It will inflame you, it will make you mad.
'Tis good you know not that you are his heirs,
For, if you should, O what would come of it!

FOURTH PLEBEIAN Read the will; we'll hear it,
Antony!
You shall read us the will – Caesar's will.

ANTONY Will you be patient? Will you stay awhile?
I have o'ershot myself to tell you of it.
I fear I wrong the honourable men
Whose daggers have stabbed Caesar; I do fear it.

FOURTH PLEBEIAN They were traitors.
Honourable men!

ALL The will! The testament!

SECOND PLEBEIAN They were villains,
murderers. The will! Read the will!

ANTONY You will compel me then to read the will?
Then make a ring about the corpse of Caesar,
And let me show you him that made the will.
Shall I descend? And will you give me leave?

SECOND PLEBEIAN Come down.

FOURTH PLEBEIAN Descend.

THIRD PLEBEIAN You shall have leave.

[**ANTONY** *comes down*]

FOURTH PLEBEIAN A ring! Stand round.

FIRST PLEBEIAN Stand from the hearse, stand
from the body.

SECOND PLEBEIAN Room for Antony, most
noble Antony!

ANTONY Nay, press not so upon me; stand far off.

ALL Stand back! Room! Bear back!

ANTONY If you have tears, prepare to shed them now.
You all do know this mantle. I remember

> ## 'they would go and kiss … his sacred blood'
>
> At the beginning of this speech Antony says that now Caesar is dead there is 'none so poor to do him reverence' – that is, nobody lowly enough to owe him obeisance. Here he suggests that if the commoners knew the contents of Caesar's will they would treat him like a martyr, dipping their handkerchiefs in his blood to take home as holy relics. This is part of the process of making Caesar live on, godlike, after his death, which his followers set in motion. Their success can be measured by the fact that another Caesar – Octavius Caesar, Julius's adopted son – was later crowned as Rome's first emperor.

The first time ever Caesar put it on.
'Twas on a summer's evening, in his tent,
That day he overcame the Nervii.
Look, in this place ran Cassius' dagger through;
See what a rent the envious Casca made;
Through this the well-belovèd Brutus stabbed,
And as he plucked his cursèd steel away,
Mark how the blood of Caesar followed it,
As rushing out of doors to be resolved
If Brutus so unkindly knocked or no.
For Brutus, as you know, was Caesar's angel –
Judge, O you gods, how dearly Caesar loved him!
This was the most unkindest cut of all;
For when the noble Caesar saw him stab,
Ingratitude, more strong than traitors' arms,
Quite vanquished him. Then burst his mighty heart,
And in his mantle muffling up his face,
Even at the base of Pompey's statue,
Which all the while ran blood, great Caesar fell.
O, what a fall was there, my countrymen!
Then I, and you, and all of us fell down,
Whilst bloody treason flourished over us.
O now you weep, and I perceive you feel
The dint of pity. These are gracious drops.
Kind souls, what, weep you when you but behold
Our Caesar's vesture wounded? Look you here.
Here is himself, marred, as you see, with traitors.
[*He uncovers* **CAESAR**'s *body*]

FIRST PLEBEIAN O piteous spectacle!

SECOND PLEBEIAN O noble Caesar!

THIRD PLEBEIAN O woeful day!

FOURTH PLEBEIAN O traitors, villains!

FIRST PLEBEIAN O most bloody sight!

SECOND PLEBEIAN We will be revenged.

ALL Revenge! About! Seek! Burn! Fire! Kill! Slay!
Let not a traitor live!

As You Like It

c.1598–1600

ACT **2** | SCENE **7**

‘ **All the world's a stage,
And all the men and women
merely players.** ’

As You Like It begins with tyranny, in a land ruled by a usurper where the strong are corrupt and the weak oppressed. Here violence is endemic in relations between men, who hatch murderous plots and break each other's necks with casual cruelty.

Paranoia, too, is endemic among the powerful: Duke Frederick banishes Rosalind for being the daughter of the duke he ousted, and takes against Orlando for being the son of a knight he loathed. And language is the weapon of tyrants, used by the bully Oliver to insult his servant Adam and his brother Orlando, and to persuade the wrestler Charles to kill his sibling. The weak, meanwhile, are denied the use of speech: Duke Frederick forbids Rosalind to defend herself against his suspicions, and the courtier Le Beau feels unable to criticize him when he warns Orlando to escape his malice: 'What he is … more suits you to conceive than I to speak of.' But when Orlando and old Adam flee to the forest of Arden – hot on the heels of Rosalind and her friend Celia – they find themselves in a place of unexpected liberty, which has much to teach the 'civilized' lands they have left behind them.

Rosalind's banished father, Duke Senior, lives in the forest like the legendary Robin Hood, and there seeks to reconstruct the 'golden world' of classical mythology, where justice, equality and free speech reigned. 'Arden' sounds like 'Eden', and in it the Duke feels himself exempt from 'the penalty of Adam, / The seasons' difference'. Later Adam returns there, in the shape of Orlando's elderly retainer, who brings with him the values of the distant past, 'The constant service of the antique world, / When service sweat for duty, not for meed'. In Arden the old servant no longer has to sweat at all: it's his master Orlando who brings him food in our extract, like a doe to its fawn. And instead of Adam owing duty to his master, Orlando owes an incalculable debt of gratitude to Adam, for giving him all his savings when he had nothing. The roles of master and servant, then, seem here to be interchangeable, a property of the 'wild wood' that finds its most amazing manifestation in Act 5, when Adam's former master Oliver repents and becomes a shepherd, and Duke Frederick is suddenly converted at the forest's edge from tyranny to a life of religious service.

Free speech is personified in Arden by Duke Senior's mournful companion Jaques, whose status as a traveller means that he serves no master, and who is granted licence by the duke to speak his mind – the licence usually granted to jesters like Touchstone. In our scene, he uses this liberty to utter the most famous speech in any Shakespeare comedy, 'All the world's a stage', where he compares the life of man to a theatre performance. Each man, he claims, takes on a range of roles in his journey from first to second childhood. From this point of view, the positions of Orlando and old Adam, Duke Senior and the boy Ganymede whom he befriends in later scenes, could easily find themselves reversed as they travel through their lives. It's a philosophy that neatly justifies Duke Senior's egalitarianism, and which has always recommended itself to Shakespeare's audiences.

OPPOSITE Orlando (Richard Johnson) and Jaques (Robert Harris) in the Royal Shakespeare Company's 1957 production.

❦ | ACT 2 | SCENE 7
France – the Forest of Arden

[DUKE SENIOR, JAQUES, AMIENS, *and Lords dressed like outlaws. To them enter* ORLANDO, *with sword drawn*]

ORLANDO
Forbear, and eat no more!

JAQUES
              Why, I have eat none yet.

ORLANDO
Nor shalt not, till necessity be served.

JAQUES
Of what kind should this cock come of?

DUKE SENIOR
Art thou thus boldened, man, by thy distress?
Or else a rude despiser of good manners,
That in civility thou seem'st so empty?

ORLANDO
You touched my vein at first. The thorny point
Of bare distress hath ta'en from me the show
Of smooth civility. Yet am I inland bred,
And know some nurture. But forbear, I say.
He dies that touches any of this fruit
Till I and my affairs are answerèd.

JAQUES
An you will not be answered with reason, I must die.

DUKE SENIOR
What would you have? Your gentleness shall force
More than your force move us to gentleness.

ORLANDO
I almost die for food, and let me have it.

DUKE SENIOR
Sit down and feed, and welcome to our table.

ORLANDO
Speak you so gently? Pardon me, I pray you.
I thought that all things had been savage here,
And therefore put I on the countenance
Of stern commandment. But whate'er you are
That in this desert inaccessible,
Under the shade of melancholy boughs,
Lose and neglect the creeping hours of time;
If ever you have looked on better days,
If ever been where bells have knolled to church,
If ever sat at any good man's feast,

If ever from your eyelids wiped a tear,
And know what 'tis to pity and be pitied,
Let gentleness my strong enforcement be;
In the which hope I blush, and hide my sword.

DUKE SENIOR
True is it that we have seen better days,
And have with holy bell been knolled to church,
And sat at good men's feasts, and wiped our eyes
Of drops that sacred pity hath engendered;
And therefore sit you down in gentleness,
And take upon command what help we have
That to your wanting may be ministered.

ORLANDO
Then but forbear your food a little while,
Whiles, like a doe, I go to find my fawn
And give it food. There is an old poor man,
Who after me hath many a weary step

> ### 'Yet am I inland bred, And know some nurture.'
>
> Orlando means he was brought up in the civilized interior region of the country, far from its wild borders. This initiates a discussion of the relationship between 'gentleness' (gentle behaviour, the state of being a gentleman) and the brute 'force' traditionally associated with living in the wilderness, which culminates in Orlando's words: 'let gentleness my strong enforcement be' – that is, let his own or Duke Senior's kindness or gentlemanly status be the force that compels the duke to show pity on Orlando's predicament. The discussion is continued in the song of Amiens, which makes the wilderness seem gentle in comparison with 'civilization'.

Limped in pure love. Till he be first sufficed,
Oppressed with two weak evils, age and hunger,
I will not touch a bit.

DUKE SENIOR
             Go find him out,
And we will nothing waste till you return.

ORLANDO
I thank ye, and be blest for your good comfort! [*Exit*]

DUKE SENIOR
Thou seest we are not all alone unhappy.
This wide and universal theatre
Presents more woeful pageants than the scene
Wherein we play in.

This wide and universal theatre Presents more woeful pageants than the scene Wherein we play in.

JAQUES
                    All the world's a stage,
And all the men and women merely players.
They have their exits and their entrances,
And one man in his time plays many parts,
His acts being seven ages. At first the infant,
Mewling and puking in the nurse's arms.
Then the whining schoolboy, with his satchel
And shining morning face, creeping like snail
Unwillingly to school. And then the lover,
Sighing like furnace, with a woeful ballad
Made to his mistress' eyebrow. Then a soldier,
Full of strange oaths, and bearded like the pard,
Jealous in honour, sudden and quick in quarrel,
Seeking the bubble reputation
Even in the cannon's mouth. And then the justice,
In fair round belly with good capon lined,
With eyes severe and beard of formal cut,
Full of wise saws and modern instances;
And so he plays his part. The sixth age shifts
Into the lean and slippered pantaloon,
With spectacles on nose and pouch on side,
His youthful hose, well saved, a world too wide
For his shrunk shank; and his big manly voice,
Turning again toward childish treble, pipes
And whistles in his sound. Last scene of all,
That ends this strange eventful history,
Is second childishness and mere oblivion;
Sans teeth, sans eyes, sans taste, sans everything.

[*Re-enter* ORLANDO, *with* ADAM]

DUKE SENIOR
Welcome. Set down your venerable burden
And let him feed.

ORLANDO
                    I thank you most for him.

ADAM
So had you need;
I scarce can speak to thank you for myself.

DUKE SENIOR
Welcome; fall to. I will not trouble you
As yet to question you about your fortunes.
Give us some music; and, good cousin, sing.

AMIENS [*Sings*]
                    Blow, blow, thou winter wind.
                    Thou art not so unkind
                            As man's ingratitude.
                    Thy tooth is not so keen,
                    Because thou art not seen,
                            Although thy breath be rude.
          Hey-ho, sing hey-ho unto the green holly.
          Most friendship is feigning, most loving mere folly.
                    Then hey-ho, the holly!
                    This life is most jolly.

                    Freeze, freeze, thou bitter sky,
                    That dost not bite so nigh
                            As benefits forgot.
                    Though thou the waters warp,
                    Thy sting is not so sharp
                            As friend remembered not.
          Hey-ho, sing hey-ho unto the green holly.
          Most friendship is feigning, most loving mere folly.
                    Then hey-ho, the holly!
                    This life is most jolly.

DUKE SENIOR
If that you were the good Sir Rowland's son,
As you have whispered faithfully you were,
And as mine eye doth his effigies witness
Most truly limned and living in your face,
Be truly welcome hither. I am the Duke
That loved your father. The residue of your fortune,
Go to my cave and tell me. Good old man,
Thou art right welcome, as thy master is.
Support him by the arm. Give me your hand,
And let me all your fortunes understand.   [*Exeunt*]

As You Like It

c.1598–1600

ACT 4 SCENE 1

❝ Men have died from time to time, and worms
have eaten them, but not for love. ❞

Of all Shakespeare's heroines, Rosalind seems to find greatest freedom in the act of cross-dressing. Her reinvention of herself as a boy protects her from men's predatory imaginations, and helps her to learn about their bodies, minds and habits, good and bad. It teaches her too about the extent to which sexual conventions are social constructs, capable of being remodelled or reinvented at the desire of the community that frames them.

This is a potentially revolutionary discovery, transforming the human body into a miniature stage within which an almost infinite range of roles may be acted out. More disturbingly, it exposes the extent to which both genders consent to their own entrapment within ridiculously narrow parameters. *As You Like It* provides a specifically theatrical escape route from this entrapment.

When she flees into the forest, Rosalind disguises herself as Ganymede, a youth who stands somewhere between the second and third of Jaques' seven ages of a man's development. Thanks to his age, poised at the entry to adulthood but not yet furnished with the signs of 'ripe' masculinity – a deep voice and a beard – Ganymede lacks a recognized place in Elizabethan society, so that he exemplifies better than anyone else the fact that thought is free in Arden, where your time of life and social function are not traps but themes on which variations may be playfully improvised, limited only by a boy's imagination.

If Ganymede's age exempts him from set social roles, it also exempts him from set notions of gender. He is 'pretty', his appearance conforming to male conventions of feminine beauty; his sparkling repartee resembles a woman's; and the ease with which he acts a female role for Orlando's benefit – performing the part of the 'absent' Rosalind, as in our extract – arises, Ganymede claims, from the fact that his emotions are governed by the ever-changing moon. As a 'moonish youth' he can 'grieve, be effeminate, changeable … proud, fantastical, apish, shallow, inconstant … as boys and women are for the most part cattle of this colour'. In this fickle state he is equally attractive to either sex, and can apply his wit with equal skill to debunking male and female efforts to impose tyrannical limits on desire.

In our second scene, for instance, he regards the conventional role of the literary lover as a set of absurdities that deserves to be derided: 'Men have died from time to time,' he tells Orlando, 'and worms have eaten them, but not for love.' These are words Orlando should remember, since he fell in love with Rosalind when he first saw her, yet doesn't have the wit to recognize her in Ganymede. Orlando's failure of recognition springs from his tendency to fantasize; he imagines Rosalind as impossibly 'virtuous', and cannot bear to be told by Ganymede that her most intriguing characteristic may not be her goodness or her beauty but her 'wit' – the capacity for rapid improvisation that refuses to be confined by someone else's script. Nevertheless, it's Rosalind's wit that keeps her close to Orlando throughout the play, and that conjures up a happy ending for them in the final act. And since Rosalind became Ganymede, men have never again had any real excuse to cling to the hackneyed notions of femininity she explodes in Act 4, Scene 1.

OPPOSITE A Victorian engraving of Rosalind disguised as Ganymede. Orlando's love-poem is pinned to the tree behind her.

[*Enter* ROSALIND *disguised as Ganymede and* CELIA. *To them enter* ORLANDO]

ROSALIND Why, how now, Orlando! Where have you been all this while? You a lover! An you serve me such another trick, never come in my sight more.

ORLANDO My fair Rosalind, I come within an hour of my promise.

ROSALIND Break an hour's promise in love! He that will divide a minute into a thousand parts, and break but a part of the thousandth part of a minute in the affairs of love, it may be said of him that Cupid hath clapped him o' th' shoulder, but I'll warrant him heart-whole.

ORLANDO Pardon me, dear Rosalind.

ROSALIND Nay, an you be so tardy, come no more in my sight. I had as lief be wooed of a snail.

ORLANDO Of a snail?

ROSALIND Ay, of a snail; for though he comes slowly, he carries his house on his head – a better jointure, I think, than you make a woman. Besides, he brings his destiny with him.

ORLANDO What's that?

ROSALIND Why, horns, which such as you are fain to be beholden to your wives for. But he comes armed in his fortune, and prevents the slander of his wife.

ORLANDO Virtue is no horn-maker, and my Rosalind is virtuous.

ROSALIND And I am your Rosalind.

CELIA It pleases him to call you so; but he hath a Rosalind of a better leer than you.

ROSALIND Come, woo me, woo me, for now I am in a holiday humour, and like enough to consent. What would you say to me now, an I were your very very Rosalind?

ORLANDO I would kiss before I spoke.

ROSALIND Nay, you were better speak first, and when you were gravelled for lack of matter you might take occasion to kiss. Very good orators, when they are out, they will spit; and for lovers lacking – God warn us! – matter, the cleanliest shift is to kiss.

ORLANDO How if the kiss be denied?

ROSALIND Then she puts you to entreaty, and there begins new matter.

ORLANDO Who could be out, being before his beloved mistress?

ROSALIND Marry, that should you, if I were your mistress, or I should think my honesty ranker than my wit.

ORLANDO What, of my suit?

ROSALIND Not out of your apparel, and yet out of your suit. Am not I your Rosalind?

ORLANDO I take some joy to say you are, because I would be talking of her.

ROSALIND Well, in her person I say I will not have you.

ORLANDO Then in mine own person I die.

ROSALIND No, faith, die by attorney. The poor world is almost six thousand years old, and in all this time there was not any man died in his own person, videlicet, in a love-cause. Troilus had his brains dashed out with a Grecian club; yet he did what he could to die before, and he is one of the patterns of love. Leander, he would have lived many a fair year, though Hero had turned nun, if it had not been for a hot midsummer night; for, good youth, he went but forth to wash him in the Hellespont, and being taken with the cramp was drowned; and the foolish chroniclers of that age found it was Hero of Sestos. But these are all lies. Men have died from time to time, and worms have eaten them, but not for love.

ORLANDO I would not have my right Rosalind of this mind, for, I protest, her frown might kill me.

ROSALIND By this hand, it will not kill a fly. But come, now I will be your Rosalind in a more coming-on disposition; and ask me what you will, I will grant it.

ORLANDO Then love me, Rosalind.

ROSALIND Yes, faith, will I, Fridays and Saturdays and all.

ORLANDO And wilt thou have me?

ROSALIND Ay, and twenty such.

ORLANDO What sayest thou?

ROSALIND Are you not good?

ORLANDO I hope so.

ROSALIND Why then, can one desire too much of a good thing? Come, sister, you shall be the priest and marry us. Give me your hand, Orlando. What do you say, sister?

> ### 'Who could be out, being before his beloved mistress?'
>
> 'Out' here means at a loss for words in his courtship or 'suit'. Rosalind goes on to interpret 'out' as meaning 'denied entrance to her body'. If he were not denied entrance, she says, this would besmirch her chastity, or make her 'honesty ranker than her wit'. She then takes 'suit', meaning courtship, to mean a suit of clothes.

ORLANDO Pray thee, marry us.

CELIA I cannot say the words.

ROSALIND You must begin, 'Will you, Orlando' –

CELIA Go to. Will you, Orlando, have to wife this Rosalind?

ORLANDO I will.

ROSALIND Ay, but when?

> ### 'Troilus had his brains dashed out ... Hero of Sestos.'
>
> **Rosalind refers here to the most famous of classical lovers: the Trojan Troilus, who was betrayed by Cressida and thought he would die of it – though in fact he was killed by Achilles (his story was told by Chaucer); and Leander, who swam the Hellespont every night to visit her and was drowned (his story was told by Shakespeare's great predecessor, Marlowe).**

ORLANDO Why now, as fast as she can marry us.

ROSALIND Then you must say: 'I take thee, Rosalind, for wife.'

ORLANDO I take thee, Rosalind, for wife.

ROSALIND I might ask you for your commission; but I do take thee, Orlando, for my husband. There's a girl goes before the priest; and certainly a woman's thought runs before her actions.

ORLANDO So do all thoughts; they are winged.

ROSALIND Now tell me how long you would have her, after you have possessed her.

ORLANDO For ever and a day.

ROSALIND Say 'a day' without the 'ever'. No, no, Orlando; men are April when they woo, December when they wed; maids are May when they are maids, but the sky changes when they are wives. I will be more jealous of thee than a Barbary cock-pigeon over his hen, more clamorous than a parrot against rain, more new-fangled than an ape, more giddy in my desires than a monkey. I will weep for nothing, like Diana in the fountain, and I will do that when you are disposed to be merry; I will laugh like a hyena, and that when thou art inclined to sleep.

ORLANDO But will my Rosalind do so?

ROSALIND By my life, she will do as I do.

ORLANDO O, but she is wise.

ROSALIND Or else she could not have the wit to do this. The wiser, the waywarder. Make the doors upon a woman's wit, and it will out at the casement; shut that and 'twill out at the key-hole; stop that, 'twill fly with the smoke out at the chimney.

ORLANDO A man that had a wife with such a wit, he might say 'Wit, whither wilt?'

ROSALIND Nay, you might keep that check for it till you met your wife's wit going to your neighbour's bed.

ORLANDO And what wit could wit have to excuse that?

ROSALIND Marry, to say she came to seek you there. You shall never take her without her answer, unless you take her without her tongue. O, that woman that cannot make her fault her husband's occasion, let her never nurse her child herself, for she will breed it like a fool!

ORLANDO For these two hours, Rosalind, I will leave thee.

ROSALIND Alas, dear love, I cannot lack thee two hours!

ORLANDO I must attend the Duke at dinner. By two o'clock I will be with thee again.

ROSALIND Ay, go your ways, go your ways. I knew what you would prove; my friends told me as much, and I thought no less. That flattering tongue of yours won me. 'Tis but one cast away, and so, come death! Two o'clock is your hour?

ORLANDO Ay, sweet Rosalind.

ROSALIND By my troth, and in good earnest, and so God mend me, and by all pretty oaths that are not dangerous, if you break one jot of your promise or come one minute behind your hour, I will think you the most pathetical break-promise, and the most hollow lover, and the most unworthy of her you call Rosalind that may be chosen out of the gross band of the unfaithful. Therefore beware my censure, and keep your promise.

ORLANDO With no less religion than if thou wert indeed my Rosalind. So, adieu.

ROSALIND Well, Time is the old justice that examines all such offenders, and let Time try. Adieu.
[*Exit* ORLANDO]

Come, woo me, woo me, for now I am in a holiday humour, and like enough to consent.

Hamlet

c.1600

ACT **3** | SCENE **1**

‘ To be, or not to be –
that is the question ,

The opening scene of *Hamlet* sets the tone of the play. Nervous sentries bellow challenges in the dark, uncertain of who is present, fearful of hidden danger. As the action unfolds, the play's full title, *Hamlet Prince of Denmark*, comes to encapsulate the problems of identity that trouble the sentries. Each of its terms is a contested site.

'Hamlet' shares his name with his dead father, whose ghost starts him on the tortuous path to avenging its murder at the hands of his uncle Claudius, now King of Denmark. Claudius's kingship renders Hamlet's status as 'Prince' problematic; his inheritance of the crown is by no means certain, and as a prince he has a duty to act for the good of his country, not in his private interest, which complicates his revenge. Even 'Denmark' is contested, its borders disputed by its neighbour Norway, whose Prince Fortinbras marches about the play's periphery, eager to reclaim land taken by the Danes in years gone by.

But this is only the beginning of Hamlet's struggle with problems of identity. As he knows from his studies at Wittenberg, human beings are made up of a number of conflicting elements – body and soul, family relationships (father, son), social functions (king, prince, clown) – whose demands may clash with one another. Hamlet's duty to Claudius as king collides with his duty to his father; his assassination of Claudius's mortal body would endanger his own immortal soul. Worse still, people sometimes seem to be what they are not. Hamlet is clearly aware of this before he meets the ghost, since he dresses in black at Claudius's wedding feast to show his disapproval of the marriage, and informs his mother Gertrude that his clothes are no formal gesture, because 'I have that within which passeth show; / These but the trappings and the suits of woe'.

Nevertheless, the appearance of the ghost raises all Hamlet's cogitations on identity to fever pitch. The ghost itself is a problem. Is it the spirit of Hamlet's father, or an evil spirit that has taken old Hamlet's form in order to damn his son? Its claims about Claudius intensify the disjunction between 'seeming' and 'being', since the king seems to be an effective governor – Hamlet spends much of the play trying to simplify his uncle's character by turning him into a 'villain'. The impossibility of doing so is demonstrated by the opening of our extract, where Claudius laments the 'heavy burden' of his guilt; this is no hardened criminal rejoicing in his ill-gotten gains. Hamlet's madness, then – which Claudius suspects may conceal a very rational agenda – perfectly suits his sense of having lost all co-ordinates by which to measure his position in Denmark. In our extract, after giving vent to his most celebrated speech, 'To be, or not to be' – a contemplation of suicide which concludes that it is no simpler than to go on living – he advises his former fiancée Ophelia to escape from a corrupt society by retiring to a convent. Doing so will free her from the calumnies and misogynistic platitudes that are the courtier's stock-in-trade, and which Hamlet himself repeats in his guise as a madman. But even this advice isn't straightforward: 'nunnery' was Elizabethan slang for a brothel. In *Hamlet* there is no escape into simplicity, even for the innocent.

OPPOSITE Laurence Olivier plays the title role of Hamlet in the classic 1948 film production.

[**KING CLAUDIUS**, **POLONIUS**, *and* **OPHELIA**
are on stage]

POLONIUS Ophelia, walk you here. – Gracious, so
please you,
We will bestow ourselves. –
[*To* **OPHELIA**]
Read on this book,
That show of such an exercise may colour
Your loneliness. We are oft to blame in this:
'Tis too much proved that with devotion's visage
And pious action we do sugar o'er
The devil himself.

KING O, 'tis too true!
[*Aside*] How smart a lash that speech doth give
my conscience!
The harlot's cheek, beautied with plast'ring art,
Is not more ugly to the thing that helps it
Than is my deed to my most painted word.
O heavy burden!

POLONIUS I hear him coming. Let's withdraw,
my lord.

[*Exeunt* **KING** *and* **POLONIUS**. *Enter* **HAMLET**]

O what a noble mind is here o'erthrown!

HAMLET To be, or not to be – that is the question:
Whether 'tis nobler in the mind to suffer
The slings and arrows of outrageous fortune,
Or to take arms against a sea of troubles,
And by opposing end them? To die, to sleep –
No more; and by a sleep to say we end
The heartache and the thousand natural shocks
That flesh is heir to – 'tis a consummation
Devoutly to be wished. To die, to sleep.
To sleep, perchance to dream. Ay, there's the rub,
For in that sleep of death what dreams may come
When we have shuffled off this mortal coil
Must give us pause. There's the respect
That makes calamity of so long life;
For who would bear the whips and scorns of time,
Th' oppressor's wrong, the proud man's contumely,
The pangs of disprized love, the law's delay,
The insolence of office, and the spurns
That patient merit of th' unworthy takes,
When he himself might his quietus make
With a bare bodkin? Who would these fardels bear,
To grunt and sweat under a weary life,

But that the dread of something after death –
The undiscovered country from whose bourn
No traveller returns – puzzles the will,
And makes us rather bear those ills we have
Than fly to others that we know not of?
Thus conscience does make cowards of us all,
And thus the native hue of resolution
Is sicklied o'er with the pale cast of thought,
And enterprises of great pith and moment
With this regard their currents turn awry,
And lose the name of action. Soft you now,
The fair Ophelia! – Nymph, in thy orisons
Be all my sins remembered.

OPHELIA Good my lord,
How does your honour for this many a day?

HAMLET I humbly thank you, well, well, well.

OPHELIA My lord, I have remembrances of yours
That I have longèd long to redeliver;
I pray you now receive them.

HAMLET No, not I.
I never gave you aught.

OPHELIA My honoured lord, you know right well
you did,
And with them, words of so sweet breath
composed
As made the things more rich. Their perfume lost,
Take these again; for to the noble mind
Rich gifts wax poor when givers prove unkind.
There, my lord.

HAMLET Ha, ha! Are you honest?

OPHELIA My lord?

HAMLET Are you fair?

> ### *'Ay, there's the rub'*
> This speech is full of unfamiliar words.
> The 'rub' is an obstacle in a game of bowls,
> designed to stop or divert the ball. A 'coil' is a
> brawl or fight, and also means flesh. 'Makes
> calamity of so long life' means 'makes bad
> experiences last so long'. 'Spurns' are kicks;
> 'quietus' an end; a 'bodkin' a dagger; 'fardels'
> burdens; and 'cast' means 'tint'.

OPHELIA What means your lordship?

HAMLET That if you be honest and fair, your
honesty should admit no discourse to your beauty.

OPHELIA Could beauty, my lord, have better
commerce than with honesty?

HAMLET Ay, truly, for the power of beauty will sooner transform honesty from what it is to a bawd than the force of honesty can translate beauty into his likeness. This was sometime a paradox, but now the time gives it proof. I did love you once.

OPHELIA Indeed, my lord, you made me believe so.

HAMLET You should not have believed me; for virtue cannot so inoculate our old stock but we shall relish of it. I loved you not.

OPHELIA I was the more deceived.

HAMLET Get thee to a nunnery. Why wouldst thou be a breeder of sinners? I am myself indifferent honest, but yet I could accuse me of such things that it were better my mother had not borne me. I am very proud, revengeful, ambitious, with more offences at my beck than I have thoughts to put them in, imagination to give them shape, or time to act them in. What should such fellows as I do crawling between earth and heaven? We are arrant knaves, all; believe none of us. Go thy ways to a nunnery. Where's your father?

OPHELIA At home, my lord.

HAMLET Let the doors be shut upon him, that he may play the fool nowhere but in 's own house. Farewell.

OPHELIA O help him, you sweet heavens!

HAMLET If thou dost marry, I'll give thee this plague for thy dowry: be thou as chaste as ice, as pure as snow, thou shalt not escape calumny. Get thee to a nunnery, go, farewell. Or, if thou wilt needs marry, marry a fool; for wise men know well enough what monsters you make of them. To a nunnery, go, and quickly too. Farewell.

OPHELIA O heavenly powers, restore him!

HAMLET I have heard of your paintings too, well enough. God has given you one face, and you make yourselves another. You jig, you amble, and you lisp, and nickname God's creatures, and make your wantonness your ignorance. Go to, I'll no more on't; it hath made me mad. I say we will have no more marriages. Those that are married already, all but one, shall live; the rest shall keep as they are. To a nunnery, go. [*Exit*]

OPHELIA O what a noble mind is here o'erthrown! The courtier's, soldier's, scholar's eye, tongue, sword, The expectancy and rose of the fair state,

The glass of fashion and the mould of form, Th' observed of all observers, quite, quite down! And I, of ladies most deject and wretched, That sucked the honey of his music vows, Now see that noble and most sovereign reason, Like sweet bells jangled, out of tune and harsh; That unmatched form and feature of blown youth Blasted with ecstasy. O woe is me, To have seen what I have seen, see what I see!

[*Re-enter* **KING CLAUDIUS** *and* **POLONIUS**]

KING Love! His affections do not that way tend, Nor what he spake, though it lacked form a little, Was not like madness. There's something in his soul O'er which his melancholy sits on brood, And I do doubt the hatch and the disclose Will be some danger; which to prevent I have in quick determination Thus set it down: he shall with speed to England For the demand of our neglected tribute. Haply the seas and countries different, With variable objects, shall expel This something-settled matter in his heart Whereon his brains still beating puts him thus From fashion of himself. What think you on't?

POLONIUS It shall do well. But yet do I believe The origin and commencement of his grief Sprung from neglected love. How now, Ophelia! You need not tell us what Lord Hamlet said; We heard it all. My lord, do as you please; But, if you hold it fit, after the play Let his queen mother all alone entreat him

> ### 'I have heard of your paintings … make your wantonness your ignorance.'
>
> **Typical Elizabethan misogyny: 'Paintings' refers to make-up, which was frowned on by moralists. A 'jig' is a dance or song, to 'amble' is to walk seductively, to 'lisp' is to speak in an affected manner. To 'make your wantonness your ignorance' is to act dumb so as to seem sexy ('wanton').**

To show his griefs. Let her be round with him; And I'll be placed, so please you, in the ear Of all their conference. If she find him not, To England send him, or confine him where Your wisdom best shall think.

KING   It shall be so. Madness in great ones must not unwatched go. [*Exeunt*]

Hamlet

c.1600

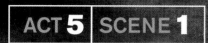

> **Alas, poor Yorick!**
> **I knew him, Horatio.**

The appearance of the ghost lets loose a parade of ghosts in *Hamlet*. Afterwards, the dawn resembles a russet-mantled spirit walking in the dew, and Hamlet himself looks to Ophelia like a phantom 'loosèd out of hell / To speak of horrors'. When Rosencrantz and Guildenstern are summoned to Elsinore to act as the king's informers, their mission is to find out why the prince has been acting so strangely since the wedding, but they learn only that he can no longer reconcile the disparate aspects of humanity – that for him the material and spiritual elements of mankind have become somehow disengaged.

A human being, Hamlet thinks, is 'infinite in faculties', yet remains no more than a 'quintessence of dust' – perhaps because of the ghost's revelation that the noblest-seeming exterior may conceal some dreadful secret, some grotesque abuse of its infinite potential. Characters circle warily, trying to probe each other's thoughts; yet the human mind, as Hamlet tells the informers, is not to be played on like an instrument. Hamlet's own attempts to probe Claudius's thoughts fail utterly. His best chance to kill him comes when the king is at prayer, his body vulnerable to assassination but his mind, Hamlet assumes, in heaven – which would render the killing pointless ('hire and salary, not revenge'). Ironically, it turns out that Hamlet has misread the situation: Claudius cannot pray, and his thoughts remain earthbound even though his hands are clasped in apparent devotion.

Many commentators see the gravedigger scene, when Hamlet addresses the skull of Yorick the jester, as marking a radical change in the prince's state of mind. Jesters were employed by monarchs to keep their feet firmly on the ground by reminding them of their humanity; and if the ghost of a king caused Hamlet's thoughts to spiral out of control, there could be no better way to anchor them again than to find the skull of a clown, whose very memory can make its finder laugh.

In our extract, the gravedigger (First Clown), acts as presenter for Yorick's act, swapping jokes with Hamlet like an equal. As they talk, Hamlet finds that human beings are getting simpler. He learns that the language of court compliment is rendered meaningless when a courtier is buried; and that the obscure language of the lawyer – designed to protect the profession from the scrutiny of non-specialists – is useless in the graveyard. There is a different hierarchy underground, where the corpses of tanners last longer than the syphilitic bodies of the rich. There, Alexander the Great – a conqueror, alcoholic and murderer, like Claudius – finds a new function as the clay bung for a beer-barrel. The only person who can communicate after death is Yorick, because his skull can still make us laugh at the desperate attempts of mortals to avert their mortality. Having learned all this, Hamlet finds his task of avenging his father less awe-inspiring. Soon after meeting Yorick in our extract, he talks calmly about the future for the first time: 'If it be now, 'tis not to come; if it be not to come, it will be now; if it be not now, yet it will come – the readiness is all.' Hamlet is finally ready to do what he must, when the moment presents itself.

OPPOSITE Horatio offers Hamlet the skull of 'poor Yorick' in this 19th-century painting by Eugéne Delacroix.

[*Enter* FIRST CLOWN. *He digs and sings. Enter* HAMLET *and* HORATIO *behind*]

FIRST CLOWN [*Sings*]
  In youth, when I did love, did love,
      Methought it was very sweet
  To contract-O-the time for-a-my behove,
      O methought there-a-was nothing-a meet.

HAMLET Has this fellow no feeling of his business, that a sings at grave-making?

HORATIO Custom hath made it in him a property of easiness.

HAMLET 'Tis e'en so; the hand of little employment hath the daintier sense.

FIRST CLOWN [*Sings*]
  But age with his stealing steps
      Hath clawed me in his clutch,
  And hath shipped me intil the land
      As if I had never been such.

[*Throws up a skull*]

HAMLET That skull had a tongue in it and could sing once. How the knave jowls it to the ground as if it were Cain's jawbone, that did the first murder! This might be the pate of a politician which this ass now o'er-reaches; one that would circumvent God, might it not?

HORATIO It might, my lord.

HAMLET Or of a courtier, which could say 'Good morrow, sweet lord! How dost thou, good lord?' This might be my Lord Such-a-one, that praised my Lord Such-a-one's horse when a meant to beg it, might it not?

HORATIO Ay, my lord.

HAMLET Why, e'en so. And now my Lady Worm's, chapless, and knocked about the mazard with a sexton's spade. Here's fine revolution, an we had the trick to see't. Did these bones cost no more the breeding but to play at loggats with 'em? Mine ache to think on't.

FIRST CLOWN [*Sings*]
  A pickaxe and a spade, a spade,
      For and a shrouding-sheet;
  O, a pit of clay for to be made
      For such a guest is meet.

[*Throws up another skull*]

HAMLET There's another. Why may not that be the skull of a lawyer? Where be his quiddities now, his quillets, his cases, his tenures, and his tricks? Why does he suffer this rude knave now to knock him about the sconce with a dirty shovel, and will not tell him of his action of battery? Hum! This fellow might be in's time a great buyer of land, with his

statutes, his recognizances, his fines, his double vouchers, his recoveries. Is this the fine of his fines, and the recovery of his recoveries, to have his fine pate full of fine dirt? Will his vouchers vouch him no more of his purchases, and double ones too, than the length and breadth of a pair of indentures? The very conveyances of his lands will hardly lie in this box; and must th'inheritor himself have no more, ha?

> ### 'Custom hath made it in him a property of easiness.'
>
> **Horatio means that the gravedigger has grown so accustomed to his trade that it comes easily to him. Hamlet agrees, pointing out that hands unused to manual labour have a more delicate sense of touch ('the daintier sense'), since they have not been hardened by calluses.**

HORATIO Not a jot more, my lord.

HAMLET Is not parchment made of sheepskins?

HORATIO Ay, my lord, and of calves' skins too.

HAMLET They are sheep and calves which seek out assurance in that. I will speak to this fellow. Whose grave's this, sirrah?

FIRST CLOWN Mine, sir.
[*Sings*] O, a pit of clay for to be made
              For such a guest is meet.

HAMLET I think it be thine indeed, for thou liest in't.

FIRST CLOWN You lie out on't, sir, and therefore it is not yours. For my part, I do not lie in't, yet it is mine.

HAMLET Thou dost lie in't, to be in't and say it is thine. 'Tis for the dead, not for the quick; therefore thou liest.

FIRST CLOWN 'Tis a quick lie, sir; 'twill away again from me to you.

HAMLET What man dost thou dig it for?

> ### 'Where be his quiddities now, ... full of fine dirt?'
>
> **Hamlet's legal terms hardly need comprehensive glossing. 'Quiddities': subtle distinctions; 'quillets': quibbles; 'tenures': property titles; 'action of battery': prosecution for assault; 'fines and recoveries': lawsuits over the transference of land; a 'double voucher' summons a pair of witnesses to attest to the ownership of land; 'statutes': mortgages on land; 'recognizances': bonds acknowledging a specific debt. 'Fine of his fines' puns on 'fine' meaning 'end'.**

FIRST CLOWN For no man, sir.

HAMLET What woman, then?

FIRST CLOWN For none neither.

HAMLET Who is to be buried in't?

FIRST CLOWN One that was a woman, sir; but, rest her soul, she's dead.

HAMLET How absolute the knave is! We must speak by the card, or equivocation will undo us. By the Lord, Horatio, these three years I have took note of it: the age is grown so picked that the toe of the peasant comes so near the heel of the courtier, he galls his kibe. How long hast thou been a grave-maker?

FIRST CLOWN Of all the days i'th' year, I came to't that day that our last King Hamlet overcame Fortinbras.

HAMLET How long is that since?

HAMLET Whose was it?

FIRST CLOWN A whoreson mad fellow's it was. Whose do you think it was?

HAMLET Nay, I know not.

FIRST CLOWN A pestilence on him for a mad rogue! A poured a flagon of Rhenish on my head once. This same skull, sir, was Yorick's skull, the King's jester.

HAMLET This?

FIRST CLOWN E'en that.

HAMLET Let me see. [*Takes the skull*] Alas, poor Yorick! I knew him, Horatio. A fellow of infinite jest, of most excellent fancy. He hath borne me on his back a thousand times; and now, how abhorred my imagination is! My gorge rises at it. Here hung those lips that I have kissed I know not how oft. Where be your gibes now, your gambols, your

That skull had a tongue in it and could sing once.

FIRST CLOWN Cannot you tell that? Every fool can tell that. It was the very day that young Hamlet was born – he that was mad and sent into England.

HAMLET Ay, marry, why was he sent into England?

FIRST CLOWN Why, because a was mad. A shall recover his wits there; or if a do not, 'tis no great matter there.

HAMLET Why?

FIRST CLOWN 'Twill not be seen in him there. There the men are as mad as he.

HAMLET How came he mad?

FIRST CLOWN Very strangely, they say.

HAMLET How strangely?

FIRST CLOWN Faith, e'en with losing his wits.

HAMLET Upon what ground?

FIRST CLOWN Why, here in Denmark. I have been sexton here, man and boy, thirty years.

HAMLET How long will a man lie i'th' earth ere he rot?

FIRST CLOWN I' faith, if a be not rotten before a die – as we have many pocky corses nowadays that will scarce hold the laying in – a will last you some eight year or nine year. A tanner will last you nine year.

HAMLET Why he more than another?

FIRST CLOWN Why, sir, his hide is so tanned with his trade that a will keep out water a great while; and your water is a sore decayer of your whoreson dead body. Here's a skull now; this skull has lain in the earth three-and-twenty years.

songs, your flashes of merriment that were wont to set the table on a roar? Not one now to mock your own grinning? Quite chap-fallen? Now get you to my lady's chamber, and tell her, let her paint an inch thick, to this favour she must come; make her laugh at that. Prithee, Horatio, tell me one thing.

HORATIO What's that, my lord?

HAMLET Dost thou think Alexander looked o' this fashion i'th' earth?

HORATIO E'en so.

HAMLET And smelt so? Pah! [*He throws down the skull*]

HORATIO E'en so, my lord.

HAMLET To what base uses we may return, Horatio! Why may not imagination trace the noble dust of Alexander till a find it stopping a bung-hole?

HORATIO 'Twere to consider too curiously to consider so.

HAMLET No faith, not a jot; but to follow him thither with modesty enough, and likelihood to lead it, as thus: Alexander died, Alexander was buried, Alexander returneth into dust; the dust is earth; of earth we make loam; and why of that loam whereto he was converted might they not stop a beer-barrel?
  Imperial Caesar, dead and turned to clay,
  Might stop a hole to keep the wind away.
  O, that that earth which kept the world in awe
  Should patch a wall t'expel the winter's flaw!
But soft, but soft; aside. Here comes the King.

Twelfth Night *c.1601*

ACT **2** | SCENE **4**

"She sat like Patience on a monument,
Smiling at grief."

Twelfth Night

Twelfth Night begins in stasis. Duke Orsino of Illyria thinks himself in love with Olivia; but he articulates this love in such general terms, and shows so little interest in Olivia's point of view, that he seems more obsessed with a private fantasy than any actual woman. Not surprisingly, Countess Olivia seeks to protect herself from his obsession.

Her brother having died, she swears an oath to abjure the company of men for seven years as she mourns his loss. More even than in Shakespeare's earlier plays, men and women are divided from one another by a rooted incompatibility between the genders: men are forceful and self-assertive, women silent, chaste, obedient, and never the twain, it seems, will meet. Orsino's dream is to see Olivia as devoted to him as she is to her dead brother, her body and brain possessed by 'one self king' – the duke. Meanwhile Olivia acts the part of the chaste, silent woman to the outside world, but her home is full of laughter: the jokes told by her jester Feste, the comic schemes of her riotous uncle Toby, the amusement she gets from the diplomatic games she plays by messenger with Orsino. In this play, men remain convinced of their own stable identities – despite their radical inconsistency – while women seek every available means to avoid being trapped by the limitations of the male imagination.

Into this situation bursts Viola, who is shipwrecked in Illyria, and resolves to disguise herself as the boy Cesario and seek employment with the duke. This gives her privileged access to the world of men, whose intimate friendships are forged in hours (within three days Orsino has unlocked to Cesario the 'book' of his 'secret soul'), and whose views on women are so absurd as to make any real relationship with them impossible. In our first scene, Orsino begins by saying that men are more fickle than women ('Our fancies are more giddy and unfirm … Than women's are'), and ends by insisting that no woman can love as constantly as he does, since 'they lack retention'. Naturally Cesario/Viola disagrees with Orsino about women, but can only articulate his disagreement by telling the tale of a chaste, silent woman – his imaginary sister, a pastiche of the male ideal of femininity – who 'never told her love' and whose history is therefore a disappointing 'blank'. But Cesario's relationship with Orsino is more promising, since the duke has no restrictive expectations of the boy who loves him, and allows him to speak freely, if obliquely, in his company.

Meanwhile Cesario attracts Olivia by his unmanliness: his courtesy, his timidity, his understanding of what women like in a courtship (which he expresses in a celebrated description of how he would woo the countess if he were Orsino). As a result, Cesario breaks the stasis in Illyria. A man and a woman fall for him, and change becomes possible, precipitated by Cesario's changing adolescent body, which is neither conventionally masculine nor fixedly feminine, but shares elements of both. And when Viola's twin brother Sebastian turns up later in the play, the stage is set for a double wedding (Viola's to Orsino, Sebastian's to Olivia), and the promise of better relations between men and women than anyone might have expected from the hackneyed views on gender trotted out by Orsino in our extract.

OPPOSITE Orsino (Keith Michell) and Vivien Leigh (Viola) in the Royal Shakespeare Company's 1955 production.

[*Enter* DUKE ORSINO, VIOLA *disguised as Cesario,*
  CURIO, *and others*]

DUKE Give me some music. Now good morrow,
  friends.
Now, good Cesario, but that piece of song,
That old and antique song we heard last night.
Methought it did relieve my passion much,
More than light airs and recollected terms
Of these most brisk and giddy-pacèd times.
Come, but one verse.

> '*so wears she to him,*
> *So sways she level in her husband's heart.*'
>
> **'So wears she to him':** in this way she
> adapts herself to him, as clothes adapt
> themselves to the wearer. 'So sways she
> level' could mean 'thus she will rule [sway]
> equally'. In the Duke's next speech, 'thy
> affection cannot hold the bent' means your
> love cannot remain taut (like a bow-string
> before the arrow is loosed – with an
> obvious sexual application).

CURIO He is not here, so please your lordship, that
  should sing it.

DUKE Who was it?

CURIO Feste the jester, my lord; a fool that the
lady Olivia's father took much delight in. He is
about the house.

DUKE Seek him out, and play the tune the while.
[*Exit* CURIO. *Music plays*]
Come hither, boy. If ever thou shalt love,
In the sweet pangs of it remember me;
For such as I am all true lovers are,
Unstaid and skittish in all motions else
Save in the constant image of the creature
That is beloved. How dost thou like this tune?

VIOLA It gives a very echo to the seat
Where Love is throned.

DUKE   Thou dost speak masterly.
My life upon't, young though thou art, thine eye
Hath stayed upon some favour that it loves;
Hath it not, boy?

VIOLA   A little, by your favour.

DUKE What kind of woman is't?

VIOLA   Of your complexion.

DUKE She is not worth thee, then. What years, i' faith?

VIOLA About your years, my lord.

DUKE Too old, by heaven! Let still the woman take
An elder than herself; so wears she to him,
So sways she level in her husband's heart.
For, boy, however we do praise ourselves,
Our fancies are more giddy and unfirm,
More longing, wavering, sooner lost and won
Than women's are.

VIOLA   I think it well, my lord.

DUKE Then let thy love be younger than thyself,
Or thy affection cannot hold the bent;
For women are as roses, whose fair flower
Being once displayed, doth fall that very hour.

VIOLA And so they are. Alas, that they are so!
To die, even when they to perfection grow!

[*Re-enter* CURIO *and* FESTE]

DUKE O fellow, come, the song we had last night.
Mark it, Cesario; it is old and plain.
The spinsters and the knitters in the sun
And the free maids that weave their thread with
  bones
Do use to chant it. It is silly sooth,
And dallies with the innocence of love,
Like the old age.

FESTE Are you ready, sir?

DUKE Ay. Prithee, sing.

There is no woman's sides
Can bide the beating of so strong a passion
As love doth give my heart

FESTE [*Sings*]

    Come away, come away death,
And in sad cypress let me be laid;
    Fly away, fly away breath,
I am slain by a fair cruel maid.
My shroud of white, stuck all with yew,
      O prepare it.
My part of death, no one so true
      Did share it.

    Not a flower, not a flower sweet
On my black coffin let there be strown;
    Not a friend, not a friend greet
My poor corpse, where my bones shall be
    thrown.
A thousand thousand sighs to save,
      Lay me O where
Sad true lover never find my grave,
      To weep there.

DUKE There's for thy pains.

FESTE No pains, sir. I take pleasure in singing, sir.

DUKE I'll pay thy pleasure then.

FESTE Truly, sir, and pleasure will be paid, one time or another.

DUKE Give me now leave to leave thee.

FESTE Now the melancholy god protect thee, and the tailor make thy doublet of changeable taffeta, for thy mind is a very opal. I would have men of such constancy put to sea, that their business might be everything and their intent everywhere; for that's it that always makes a good voyage of nothing. Farewell. [*Exit*]

> **'Our shows are more than will … in our love.'**
>
> 'Our shows are more than will' – our displays of affection are greater than our desire, or than our will to put true love into action. This contrasts with the woman Viola describes – Cesario's imaginary sister – who also puts on a display, but as an allegorical statue or 'monument' of patience, keeping the cause of her grief – hopeless love – to herself.

DUKE Let all the rest give place.
[**CURIO** *and Attendants retire*]
      Once more, Cesario,
Get thee to yon same sovereign cruelty.
Tell her my love, more noble than the world,
Prizes not quantity of dirty lands;

The parts that fortune hath bestowed upon her
Tell her I hold as giddily as fortune;
But 'tis that miracle and queen of gems
That nature pranks her in attracts my soul.

VIOLA But if she cannot love you, sir?

DUKE I cannot be so answered.

VIOLA   Sooth, but you must.
Say that some lady, as perhaps there is,
Hath for your love as great a pang of heart
As you have for Olivia. You cannot love her;
You tell her so. Must she not then be answered?

DUKE There is no woman's sides
Can bide the beating of so strong a passion
As love doth give my heart; no woman's heart
So big, to hold so much. They lack retention.
Alas, their love may be called appetite –
No motion of the liver, but the palate –
That suffer surfeit, cloyment and revolt;
But mine is all as hungry as the sea,
And can digest as much. Make no compare
Between that love a woman can bear me
And that I owe Olivia.

VIOLA   Ay, but I know –

DUKE What dost thou know?

VIOLA Too well what love women to men may owe.
In faith, they are as true of heart as we.
My father had a daughter loved a man,
As it might be, perhaps, were I a woman,
I should your lordship.

DUKE   And what's her history?

VIOLA A blank, my lord. She never told her love,
But let concealment, like a worm i' th' bud,
Feed on her damask cheek. She pined in thought,
And with a green and yellow melancholy
She sat like Patience on a monument,
Smiling at grief. Was not this love indeed?
We men may say more, swear more, but indeed
Our shows are more than will; for still we prove
Much in our vows, but little in our love.

DUKE But died thy sister of her love, my boy?

VIOLA I am all the daughters of my father's house,
And all the brothers too – and yet I know not.
Sir, shall I to this lady?

DUKE   Ay, that's the theme.
To her in haste. Give her this jewel. Say
My love can give no place, bide no denay. [*Exeunt*]

Twelfth Night *c.1601*

ACT **2** | SCENE **5**

❝ Some are born great,
some achieve greatness,
and some have greatness
thrust upon 'em. ❞

Alongside the story of Viola runs a second plot, which like *Hamlet* has revenge at its core. From one point of view, comic repartee is a form of revenge – a way of getting instant retribution for an insult; and the rivalry between Olivia's steward Malvolio and her jester Feste develops into a comic quest for vengeance, triggered by Feste's initial failure to find a prompt response to Malvolio's taunts.

The profession of jester is a hazardous one, as Cesario observes: 'He must observe their mood on whom he jests, / The quality of persons, and the time'; and failure to get a laugh may result in redundancy. When Malvolio attacks him, Feste is particularly vulnerable – he's out of favour with his mistress – and the steward aims to capitalize on her disfavour to get him sacked. He tells her how he saw Feste 'put down' by a village idiot; and when the jester doesn't react to his gibes, adds: 'Look you now, he's out of his guard already. Unless you laugh and minister occasion to him, he is gagged.' Here the steward mocks the clown's reliance on the community, his need for a sympathetic audience to sustain his performances. Men like Malvolio, by contrast – Malvolio implies – are self-reliant, capable of maintaining their dignity without assistance. Feste's eventual response is to collaborate with a community of jokers – Olivia's uncle Toby, Maria, Fabian and the doltish Sir Andrew Aguecheek – to show the steward how completely he relies on other people, and how precarious is his own position in Illyria.

Malvolio's weakness is his conviction that he knows exactly where he stands. Reacting angrily to the midnight revelry of Sir Toby, he asks him, 'Is there no respect of place, persons, nor time in you?' His sense of his own place makes him averse to those whose position is ambiguous, like Cesario, who cannot be easily categorized ('Not yet old enough for a man, nor young enough for a boy …'), or the punning jester. Secretly, however, Malvolio longs for a change in situation, as we learn in our extract. He dreams of marrying his mistress, a fantasy as foolish as Orsino's – and as indifferent to Olivia's feelings. When he pictures their married life together he focuses on himself acting as head of the household, while the countess dozes idly on a sofa. Sir Toby and his fellow conspirators have only to play on this dream of upward mobility by presenting him with a forged love-letter, purportedly from Olivia but actually written by her maid, and the stage is set for our second scene, the funniest Shakespeare wrote.

But their plot has a darker side. Malvolio's loss of control over his fantasies leads to dismissal from his job, imprisonment as a madman, and an interrogation by Feste – disguised as a priest – on suspicion of heresy, a capital offence. In our extract, Sir Toby and his friends use the language of hunting as they eavesdrop on the steward; and by the end of the play their treatment of him resembles a blood sport. Malvolio's dislike of jokes is based on his conviction that they can lead to the destruction of order and sanity; and *Twelfth Night* suggests that this conviction may even be justified.

OPPOSITE Laurence Olivier as Malvolio, reading the forged love-letter, in the Royal Shakespeare Company's 1955 production, watched by Fabian (Lee Montague), Maria (Angela Baddeley), Sir Toby (Alan Webb) and Sir Andrew (Michael Denison).

[*Enter* SIR TOBY BELCH, SIR ANDREW AGUECHEEK, *and* FABIAN, *hiding.*
Enter MALVOLIO]

MALVOLIO 'Tis but fortune; all is fortune. Maria once told me she did affect me, and I have heard herself come thus near, that should she fancy it should be one of my complexion. Besides, she uses me with a more exalted respect than anyone else that follows her. What should I think on't?

SIR TOBY Here's an overweening rogue!

FABIAN O, peace! Contemplation makes a rare turkey-cock of him. How he jets under his advanced plumes!

SIR ANDREW 'Slight, I could so beat the rogue!

SIR TOBY Peace, I say.

MALVOLIO To be Count Malvolio!

SIR TOBY Ah, rogue!

SIR ANDREW Pistol him, pistol him.

SIR TOBY Peace, peace!

MALVOLIO There is example for't: the lady of the Strachy married the yeoman of the wardrobe.

SIR ANDREW Fie on him, Jezebel!

FABIAN O peace! Now he's deeply in. Look how imagination blows him.

MALVOLIO Having been three months married to her, sitting in my state –

SIR TOBY O for a stone-bow to hit him in the eye!

MALVOLIO Calling my officers about me, in my branched velvet gown; having come from a day-bed – where I have left Olivia sleeping –

SIR TOBY Fire and brimstone!

FABIAN O peace, peace!

MALVOLIO And then to have the humour of state, and – after a demure travel of regard, telling them I know my place as I would they should do theirs – to ask for my kinsman Toby –

SIR TOBY Bolts and shackles!

FABIAN O peace, peace, peace, now, now.

MALVOLIO Seven of my people, with an obedient start, make out for him. I frown the while, and perchance wind up my watch, or play with my – [*Touching his steward's chain*] some rich jewel. Toby approaches; curtsies there to me.

SIR TOBY Shall this fellow live?

FABIAN Though our silence be drawn from us with cars, yet peace.

> **'Contemplation makes a rare turkey-cock of him.'**
>
> This is one in a series of comparisons between Malvolio and birds, beasts or fishes (earlier the steward was a 'trout'), often associated with hunting. The cock turkey represents pride, since it displays its feathers like a peacock. When Malvolio finds the forged letter, Fabian says, 'Now is the woodcock near the gin' – the woodcock being a proverbially foolish bird, and 'gin' meaning snare. As the steward reads, Sir Toby likens him to a 'brock' (badger); a 'staniel' (sparrowhawk); and a hunting hound that has lost the scent (Fabian gives the hound a name, 'Sowter', and says that it will bay again as soon as it picks up a fresh scent).

MALVOLIO I extend my hand to him thus, quenching my familiar smile with an austere regard of control –

SIR TOBY And does not Toby take you a blow o' the lips then?

MALVOLIO Saying, 'Cousin Toby, my fortunes having cast me on your niece give me this prerogative of speech' –

SIR TOBY What, what?

MALVOLIO 'You must amend your drunkenness.'

SIR TOBY Out, scab!

FABIAN Nay, patience, or we break the sinews of our plot.

MALVOLIO 'Besides, you waste the treasure of your time with a foolish knight,' –

SIR ANDREW That's me, I warrant you.

MALVOLIO 'One Sir Andrew.'

SIR ANDREW I knew 'twas I, for many do call me fool.

MALVOLIO What employment have we here? [*Taking up the letter*]

FABIAN Now is the woodcock near the gin.

SIR TOBY O peace! And the spirit of humours intimate reading aloud to him!

MALVOLIO By my life, this is my lady's hand. These be her very c's, her u's, and her t's, and thus makes she her great P's. It is, in contempt of question, her hand.

SIR ANDREW Her c's, her u's, and her t's? Why that?

MALVOLIO [*Reads*] 'To the unknown beloved, this, and my good wishes.' Her very phrases! [*Opening the letter*] By your leave, wax. Soft! And the impressure her Lucrece, with which she uses to seal – 'tis my lady. To whom should this be?

FABIAN This wins him, liver and all.

MALVOLIO [*Reads*]
> 'Jove knows I love,
>   But who?
> Lips, do not move,
>   No man must know.'

'No man must know.' What follows? The numbers altered. 'No man must know.' If this should be thee, Malvolio?

SIR TOBY Marry, hang thee, brock!

MALVOLIO [*Reads*]
> 'I may command where I adore,
>   But silence like a Lucrece knife
> With bloodless stroke my heart doth gore.
>   M. O. A. I. doth sway my life.'

FABIAN A fustian riddle!

SIR TOBY Excellent wench, say I.

MALVOLIO 'M. O. A. I. doth sway my life.' Nay, but first let me see, let me see, let me see.

FABIAN What dish o' poison has she dressed him!

SIR TOBY And with what wing the staniel checks at it!

To be Count Malvolio!

MALVOLIO 'I may command where I adore.' Why, she may command me! I serve her, she is my lady. Why, this is evident to any formal capacity. There is no obstruction in this. And the end – what should that alphabetical position portend? If I could make that resemble something in me. Softly – 'M. O. A. I.'

SIR TOBY O ay, make up that, he is now at a cold scent.

FABIAN Sowter will cry upon't for all this, though it be as rank as a fox.

MALVOLIO 'M.' Malvolio – 'M' – why, that begins my name.

FABIAN Did not I say he would work it out? The cur is excellent at faults.

MALVOLIO 'M.' But then there is no consonancy in the sequel. That suffers under probation. 'A' should follow, but 'O' does.

FABIAN And 'O' shall end, I hope.

SIR TOBY Ay, or I'll cudgel him, and make him cry 'O!'

MALVOLIO And then 'I' comes behind.

FABIAN Ay, an you had any eye behind you, you might see more detraction at your heels than fortunes before you.

MALVOLIO 'M. O. A. I.' This simulation is not as the former; and yet to crush this a little, it would bow to me, for every one of these letters are in my name. Soft, here follows prose: 'If this fall into thy hand, revolve. In my stars I am above thee, but be not afraid of greatness. Some are born great, some achieve greatness, and some have greatness thrust upon 'em. Thy fates open their hands; let thy blood and spirit embrace them; and, to inure thyself to what thou art like to be, cast thy humble slough and appear fresh. Be opposite with a kinsman, surly with servants. Let thy tongue tang arguments of state; put thyself into the trick of singularity. She thus advises thee that sighs for thee. Remember who commended thy yellow stockings, and wished to see thee ever cross-gartered. I say, remember. Go to, thou art made if thou desirest to be so; if not, let me see thee a steward still, the fellow of servants, and not worthy to touch Fortune's fingers. Farewell. She that would alter services with thee,
>   The Fortunate-Unhappy.'

Daylight and champaign discovers not more. This is open. I will be proud, I will read politic authors, I will baffle Sir Toby, I will wash off gross acquaintance, I will be point-device the very man. I do not now fool myself, to let imagination jade me; for every reason excites to this, that my lady loves me. She did commend my yellow stockings of late, she did praise my leg being cross-gartered, and in this she manifests herself to my love, and with a kind of injunction drives me to these habits of her liking. I thank my stars, I am happy. I will be strange, stout, in yellow stockings, and cross-gartered, even with the swiftness of putting on. Jove and my stars be praised! Here is yet a postscript. 'Thou canst not choose but know who I am. If thou entertainest my love, let it appear in thy smiling; thy smiles become thee well. Therefore in my presence still smile, dear my sweet, I prithee.' Jove, I thank thee. I will smile; I will do everything that thou wilt have me. [*Exit*]

Troilus and Cressida *c.1601-2*

ACT **1** | SCENE **3**

 Take but degree away, untune that string,
And hark what discord follows.

For the Elizabethans, the Greeks and Trojans were exemplary. 'As true as Troilus' and 'as false as Cressida' were catchphrases; Helen was the loveliest of women; Achilles the greatest of warriors. When George Chapman published his partial translation of Homer's *Iliad* in 1597, he dedicated it to Shakespeare's patron, the Earl of Essex, as the epitome of 'Achillean virtues'. Four years later Essex had been executed for treason; the English Helen, Elizabeth, was old and ill; and Shakespeare turned to the tale of Troy in a mood of unprecedented pessimism.

The play opens with a prologue that parodies the prologue of *Henry V*, which established an imaginative partnership between actors and audience in restoring Henry to life. After an equally grandiloquent opening, the *Troilus* prologue collapses into bathos: 'Like or find fault; do as your pleasures are; / Now good or bad, 'tis but the chance of war.' The war it announces concerns definitions of good and bad, and which side will bequeath their definitions to posterity. The Trojans claim absolute consistency in their values. As they argue over whether to give Helen back to the Greeks from whom they stole her, Troilus contends that they should stick by their initial assessment of her value: if she was once worth fighting for, she must always remain so. But the Trojans are not consistent. Hector argues that stealing Helen was wrong, but that giving her up would make them look like idiots; and he ends by announcing his arrangements for a duel with the best Greek warrior. When we meet Helen later, she's an empty-headed puppet who sings a duet with a pimp. Troy has founded its self-image on a vacuum, and burns for a whim.

The Greeks, meanwhile, are pragmatic, keen to convey the best image of themselves to the history books and not caring how they do it. In our extract, Ulysses delivers a famous speech in defence of order or 'degree', but he speaks in the knowledge that the Greek camp is in disarray: Achilles is on strike, his insubordination spreading like syphilis. Even Ulysses is infected. As he describes Achilles's boyfriend Patroclus doing outrageous impressions of the Greek generals, he re-enacts those impressions, reducing audiences to helpless giggles with his mimicry of Agamemnon's 'wooden dialogue' (a fine example of which opens the extract), or of the aged warrior Nestor shaking the rivets of his armour in and out of their sockets as he struggles to put it on. Ulysses has no illusions as to the nobility of his superiors or their cause; nevertheless, he schemes to represent them as heroes to future generations.

The Greek technique of self-promotion is horribly exemplified in the death of Hector in Act 5. Achilles sends his ant-like Myrmidons to murder him, after which they raise the shout: 'Achilles hath the mighty Hector slain' – a lie that goes down in history. The proverbial heroism of the Greeks is based on nothing. Their respect for 'degree' may be profound, but it does not govern their actions – any more than Troilus's love for Cressida makes him stay by her side after he has slept with her. The glory that was ancient Greece or Troy, Shakespeare implies, was as full of 'faint defects' as England in the declining years of Elizabeth I.

OPPOSITE The Greek Achilles duels with the Trojan Hector in the Royal Shakespeare Company's 1996 production.

The Greek camp outside Troy

[*Enter* AGAMEMNON, NESTOR, ULYSSES,
    DIOMEDES, MENELAUS, *and others*]

AGAMEMNON

Speak, Prince of Ithaca; and be't of less expect
That matter needless, of importless burden,
Divide thy lips, than we are confident,
When rank Thersites opes his mastic jaws,
We shall hear music, wit and oracle.

ULYSSES

Troy, yet upon his basis, had been down,
And the great Hector's sword had lacked a master,
But for these instances:
The specialty of rule hath been neglected;
And look how many Grecian tents do stand
Hollow upon this plain, so many hollow factions.
When that the general is not like the hive
To whom the foragers shall all repair,
What honey is expected? Degree being vizarded,
Th' unworthiest shows as fairly in the masque.
The heavens themselves, the planets, and this centre
Observe degree, priority, and place,
Infixture, course, proportion, season, form,
Office and custom, in all line of order;
And therefore is the glorious planet Sol
In noble eminence enthroned and sphered
Amidst the other, whose med'cinable eye
Corrects the ill aspects of planets evil,
And posts like the commandment of a king,
Sans check, to good and bad. But when the planets
In evil mixture to disorder wander,
What plagues and what portents, what mutiny,
What raging of the sea, shaking of earth,
Commotion in the winds, frights, changes, horrors,
Divert and crack, rend and deracinate
The unity and married calm of states
Quite from their fixture! O when degree is shaked,
Which is the ladder to all high designs,
The enterprise is sick. How could communities,
Degrees in schools and brotherhoods in cities,
Peaceful commerce from dividable shores,
The primogenity and due of birth,
Prerogative of age, crowns, sceptres, laurels,
But by degree, stand in authentic place?
Take but degree away, untune that string,
And hark what discord follows. Each thing meets
In mere oppugnancy. The bounded waters
Should lift their bosoms higher than the shores
And make a sop of all this solid globe;
Strength should be lord of imbecility,

> **'When rank Thersites opes his mastic jaws,**
> **We shall hear music, wit and oracle.'**
>
> Thersites serves as a cynical commentator on the play, a companion to the foolish warrior Ajax. He delights in satirizing the Greek leadership (Ulysses describes him in action later). Agamemnon's speech here is convoluted, as always: he means that he expects Ulysses to say something relevant, just as he would expect the 'mastic' (abusive) Thersites to say nothing pleasant or useful at all.

And the rude son should strike his father dead.
Force should be right; or rather, right and wrong –
Between whose endless jar justice resides –
Should lose their names, and so should justice too.
Then everything includes itself in power,
Power into will, will into appetite;

> **'And therefore is ... to disorder wander'**
>
> Sol (the sun) was thought to be a planet circling the earth. The rays of his 'med'cinable eye' are curative (human eyes were thought to emit rays, too). A planet's 'aspect' is its astrological influence – the sun is described as correcting the bad influence of other planets, unless they 'wander' off course and join together in malign conjunctions ('evil mixture').

And appetite, an universal wolf,
So doubly seconded with will and power,
Must make perforce an universal prey,
And last eat up himself. Great Agamemnon,
This chaos, when degree is suffocate,
Follows the choking.
And this neglection of degree it is
That by a pace goes backward, with a purpose
It hath to climb. The general's disdained
By him one step below, he by the next,
That next by him beneath; so every step,
Exampled by the first pace that is sick
Of his superior, grows to an envious fever
Of pale and bloodless emulation.
And 'tis this fever that keeps Troy on foot,
Not her own sinews. To end a tale of length,
Troy in our weakness stands, not in her strength.

NESTOR

Most wisely hath Ulysses here discovered
The fever whereof all our power is sick.

AGAMEMNON

The nature of the sickness found, Ulysses,
What is the remedy?

ULYSSES

The great Achilles, whom opinion crowns
The sinew and the forehand of our host,
Having his ear full of his airy fame,
Grows dainty of his worth, and in his tent
Lies mocking our designs. With him Patroclus
Upon a lazy bed the livelong day
Breaks scurril jests;
And with ridiculous and awkward action,
Which, slanderer, he 'imitation' calls,
He pageants us. Sometime, great Agamemnon,
Thy topless deputation he puts on,
And like a strutting player, whose conceit
Lies in his hamstring, and doth think it rich
To hear the wooden dialogue and sound
'Twixt his stretched footing and the scaffoldage –
Such to-be-pitied and o'er-wrested seeming
He acts thy greatness in. And when he speaks
'Tis like a chime a-mending; with terms unsquared,
Which from the tongue of roaring Typhon dropped
Would seem hyperboles. At this fusty stuff
The large Achilles, on his pressed bed lolling,
From his deep chest laughs out a loud applause;
Cries, 'Excellent! 'Tis Agamemnon just.
Now play me Nestor; hem, and stroke thy beard,
As he being drest to some oration.'
That's done, as near as the extremest ends
Of parallels, as like as Vulcan and his wife.
Yet god Achilles still cries 'Excellent!
'Tis Nestor right. Now play him me, Patroclus,
Arming to answer in a night alarm.'
And then forsooth the faint defects of age
Must be the scene of mirth: to cough and spit,
And with a palsy, fumbling on his gorget,
Shake in and out the rivet. And at this sport
Sir Valour dies; cries, 'O enough, Patroclus,
Or give me ribs of steel! I shall split all
In pleasure of my spleen.' And in this fashion
All our abilities, gifts, natures, shapes,
Severals and generals of grace exact,
Achievements, plots, orders, preventions,
Excitements to the field or speech for truce,
Success or loss, what is or is not, serves
As stuff for these two to make paradoxes.

NESTOR

And in the imitation of these twain –
Who, as Ulysses says, opinion crowns
With an imperial voice – many are infect.
Ajax is grown self-willed and bears his head
In such a rein, in full as proud a place
As broad Achilles; keeps his tent like him;
Makes factious feasts; rails on our state of war
Bold as an oracle, and sets Thersites,
A slave whose gall coins slanders like a mint,
To match us in comparisons with dirt,
To weaken and discredit our exposure,
How rank soever rounded in with danger.

appetite, an universal
wolf ...
Must make perforce an
universal prey,
And last eat up himself.

ULYSSES

They tax our policy and call it cowardice,
Count wisdom as no member of the war,
Forestall prescience, and esteem no act
But that of hand. The still and mental parts
That do contrive how many hands shall strike
When fitness calls them on, and know by measure
Of their observant toil the enemies' weight –
Why, this hath not a finger's dignity.
They call this bed-work, mapp'ry, closet-war;
So that the ram that batters down the wall,
For the great swinge and rudeness of his poise,
They place before his hand that made the engine,
Or those that with the fineness of their souls
By reason guide his execution.

NESTOR

Let this be granted, and Achilles' horse
Makes many Thetis' sons.

Measure for Measure

ACT 2 | SCENE 2

‘ **The tempter or the tempted, who sins most?** ’

c.1604

Measure for Measure

Measure for Measure tells the story of three absolutists: people who pride themselves on their staunch resistance to compromise. When Duke Vincentio of Vienna hands over his dukedom to his deputy Angelo – intending both to test the man's integrity and to have him sort out the country after a period of bad government – he gives him 'My *absolute* power … here in Vienna', a statement that implies disdain for any partner in the business of ruling.

His advice to a condemned prisoner is similarly uncompromising: 'Be *absolute* for death,' he says, and recommends extinction as a release from the messy business of living. Angelo shares his single-mindedness, presenting himself as a man in total command of his senses: he 'scarce confesses / That his blood flows', as the duke unkindly puts it. And these men are more than matched in their self-discipline by the postulant nun Isabella, who wants to give up all male company in favour of a life of silent contemplation. Slowly, these three absolutists learn that in a community there can be no exclusiveness. Everyone, no matter how dignified or aloof, gets drawn into the web of wordplay, and everyone must in the end confess their common humanity.

The duke, for instance, spies on Angelo's activities disguised in the robes of a friar, as if to signal his detachment from earthly interests. But he gets caught up in the case of Claudio: a prisoner condemned to death by Angelo under the terms of a forgotten law that forbids sex outside marriage. Acknowledging his responsibility for Claudio's condemnation, the duke involves himself in increasingly harebrained schemes to save his life, including a desperate search for heads he can substitute for Claudio's – a tacit admission that human beings are not so different from one another after all. Meanwhile Angelo finds himself susceptible to a sin more deadly than fornication. He plans to commit a rape, then cover up the evidence so as to preserve his reputation as an angel, untouched by the temptations of the flesh.

Isabella's situation is worse. Her efforts to disengage herself from men are foiled by a message from her brother Claudio, delivered by the licentious Lucio, past master of the *double entendre*. Claudio begs her to persuade Angelo to spare him. Our extract comes from her first interview with the deputy, where Lucio spurs her on in her brother's defence like a frantic pimp ('He's coming, I perceive't'), while Isabella asks Angelo to imagine himself into the situation of others: of God, for instance, who pardons all mankind ('How would you be / If He which is the top of judgement should / But judge you as you are?'); or Claudio, whose temptations he must have experienced in his youth ('ask your heart what it doth know / That's like my brother's fault'). Her rhetoric proves all too persuasive. Seduced by her goodness, Angelo makes it a motive for evil in the following scene, where he proposes to spare her brother if she will sleep with him. Every aspect of human life, we conclude, is interconnected; every person in some way linked with the crimes of their neighbours. It's appropriate, then, that the play should end in a series of weddings, each a miniature model of the compromised Vienna where they take place.

OPPOSITE A 1797 engraving of Angelo and Isabella by W.C. Wilson.

[*Enter* ANGELO, ISABELLA, LUCIO, *and* PROVOST]

ANGELO He's sentenced; 'tis too late.

LUCIO [*Aside to* ISABELLA]   You are too cold.

ISABELLA Too late? Why, no; I that do speak a word
May call it back again. Well, believe this:
No ceremony that to great ones 'longs,
Not the king's crown nor the deputed sword,
The marshal's truncheon nor the judge's robe,
Become them with one half so good a grace
As mercy does.
If he had been as you and you as he,
You would have slipped like him, but he like you
Would not have been so stern.

ANGELO   Pray you be gone.

ISABELLA I would to heaven I had your potency,
And you were Isabel! Should it then be thus?
No, I would tell what 'twere to be a judge,
And what a prisoner.

LUCIO [*Aside to* ISABELLA] Ay, touch him; there's
the vein.

ANGELO Your brother is a forfeit of the law,
And you but waste your words.

ISABELLA   Alas, alas!
Why, all the souls that were were forfeit once,
And He that might the vantage best have took
Found out the remedy. How would you be
If He which is the top of judgment should
But judge you as you are? O think on that,
And mercy then will breathe within your lips
Like man new made.

ANGELO   Be you content, fair maid.
It is the law, not I, condemn your brother.
Were he my kinsman, brother, or my son,
It should be thus with him. He must die tomorrow.

ISABELLA Tomorrow! O, that's sudden! Spare him,
spare him!
He's not prepared for death. Even for our kitchens
We kill the fowl of season. Shall we serve heaven

O, it is excellent
To have a giant's strength,
but it is tyrannous
To use it like a giant.

With less respect than we do minister
To our gross selves? Good, good my lord, bethink you:
Who is it that hath died for this offence?
There's many have committed it.

LUCIO [*Aside to* ISABELLA]   Ay, well said.

ANGELO The law hath not been dead, though
it hath slept.

> **'We cannot weigh … less foul profanation.'**
>
> 'We cannot weigh our brother with ourself': we're unable to judge ourselves by the same standards with which we judge others. Isabella goes on to say that great men can get away with behaviour (such as treating religion lightly, or swearing) for which lesser mortals would be punished. Later still she claims a great man's authority serves as a protective skin to conceal his vices.

Those many had not dared to do that evil
If the first that did th' edict infringe
Had answered for his deed. Now 'tis awake,
Takes note of what is done, and, like a prophet,
Looks in a glass that shows what future evils –
Either raw, or by remissness new conceived,
And so in progress to be hatched and born –
Are now to have no successive degrees,
But ere they live, to end.

ISABELLA   Yet show some pity.

ANGELO I show it most of all when I show justice,
For then I pity those I do not know,
Which a dismissed offence would after gall,
And do him right that, answering one foul wrong,
Lives not to act another. Be satisfied.
Your brother dies tomorrow. Be content.

ISABELLA So you must be the first that gives this
sentence,
And he that suffers. O, it is excellent
To have a giant's strength, but it is tyrannous
To use it like a giant.

LUCIO [*Aside to* ISABELLA] That's well said.

ISABELLA Could great men thunder
As Jove himself does, Jove would never be quiet,
For every pelting petty officer
Would use his heaven for thunder, nothing but
thunder.
Merciful heaven,
Thou rather with thy sharp and sulphurous bolt
Split'st the unwedgeable and gnarlèd oak
Than the soft myrtle. But man, proud man,

Dressed in a little brief authority,
Most ignorant of what he's most assured,
His glassy essence, like an angry ape
Plays such fantastic tricks before high heaven
As makes the angels weep, who, with our spleens,
Would all themselves laugh mortal.

LUCIO [*Aside to* **ISABELLA**] O, to him, to him,
wench! He will relent.
He's coming; I perceive 't.

PROVOST [*Aside*]   Pray heaven she win him!

ISABELLA We cannot weigh our brother with
ourself.
Great men may jest with saints; 'tis wit in them,
But in the less foul profanation.

LUCIO [*Aside to* **ISABELLA**] Thou'rt i' th' right,
girl. More o' that.

ISABELLA That in the captain's but a choleric word,
Which in the soldier is flat blasphemy.

LUCIO [*Aside to* **ISABELLA**] Art advised o' that?
More on 't.

ANGELO Why do you put these sayings upon me?

ISABELLA Because authority, though it err like
others,
Hath yet a kind of medicine in itself
That skins the vice o' th' top. Go to your bosom;
Knock there, and ask your heart what it doth know
That's like my brother's fault. If it confess
A natural guiltiness such as is his,
Let it not sound a thought upon your tongue
Against my brother's life.

ANGELO [*Aside*]   She speaks, and 'tis
Such sense that my sense breeds with it. [*Aloud*]
Fare you well.

ISABELLA Gentle my lord, turn back.

ANGELO I will bethink me. Come again tomorrow.

ISABELLA Hark how I'll bribe you; good my lord,
turn back.

ANGELO How, bribe me?

'O cunning enemy … bait thy hook!'

The 'enemy' here is Satan. Notice that Angelo
is here 'jesting with saints', as Isabella put it
earlier: assuming *himself* to be saintly, which
is laughable (we later discover that his past
was very far from virtuous). The idea that
virtue can tempt people to corruption – or
that corrupted saints make the worst of
criminals – is central to this play.

ISABELLA Ay, with such gifts that heaven shall
share with you.

LUCIO [*Aside to* **ISABELLA**] You had marred all else.

ISABELLA Not with fond shekels of the tested gold,
Or stones, whose rate are either rich or poor
As fancy values them; but with true prayers
That shall be up at heaven and enter there
Ere sunrise, prayers from preservèd souls,
From fasting maids whose minds are dedicate
To nothing temporal.

ANGELO Well, come to me tomorrow.

LUCIO [*Aside to* **ISABELLA**] Go to; 'tis well; away.

ISABELLA Heaven keep your honour safe!

ANGELO [*Aside*]   Amen; for I
Am that way going to temptation,
Where prayer is crossed.

ISABELLA   At what hour tomorrow
Shall I attend your lordship?

ANGELO   At any time fore noon.

ISABELLA God save your honour!

[*Exeunt* **ISABELLA**, **LUCIO**, *and* **PROVOST**]

ANGELO   From thee; even from thy virtue!
What's this, what's this? Is this her fault or mine?
The tempter or the tempted, who sins most?
Ha!
Not she; nor doth she tempt; but it is I
That, lying by the violet in the sun,
Do as the carrion does, not as the flower,
Corrupt with virtuous season. Can it be
That modesty may more betray our sense
Than woman's lightness? Having waste ground
enough,
Shall we desire to raze the sanctuary
And pitch our evils there? O, fie, fie, fie!
What dost thou, or what art thou, Angelo?
Dost thou desire her foully for those things
That make her good? O, let her brother live!
Thieves for their robbery have authority
When judges steal themselves. What, do I love her,
That I desire to hear her speak again,
And feast upon her eyes? What is't I dream on?
O cunning enemy, that, to catch a saint,
With saints dost bait thy hook! Most dangerous
Is that temptation that doth goad us on
To sin in loving virtue. Never could the strumpet,
With all her double vigour, art and nature,
Once stir my temper; but this virtuous maid
Subdues me quite. Ever till now
When men were fond, I smiled and wondered how.
[*Exit*]

Othello *c.1603-4*

ACT **1** | SCENE **3**

❝ She loved me for the dangers I had passed,
And I loved her that she did pity them. ❞

Othello has the plot of a classical comedy. A pair of lovers run away together, against the wishes of the girl's father and with the collusion of a clever servant (Iago makes much of his self-interested 'service' to Othello). The elderly husband then becomes jealous of his younger wife, and is mercilessly mocked for his jealousy. But the story ends in murder and suicide — a consequence of Othello's precarious status as a foreigner in Venice, which means that, like Shylock, he sees mockery as aggression, jeopardizing his hard-won eminence as a Venetian general.

It's a consequence, too, of the unmotivated hatred Iago feels for his African master, which he conceals beneath a veneer of popular wisdom, trotting out a barrage of proverbial 'common sense' that is indistinguishable from prejudice: Moors are 'changeable in their wills'; Venetian women 'must have change'. What's shocking about *Othello* is how such simple ingredients, such a harmless old story, such commonplace sayings, can be a vehicle for so much cruelty, and generate such intensity of suffering.

Prejudice in *Othello*, as in *The Merchant of Venice*, is connected to a breakdown in the law. The lovers' elopement in Act 1 should have led to a trial, to determine whether there is a case against them for conspiracy or kidnap. Instead the Duke of Venice invites Othello, in our extract, to explain his actions informally, then brushes aside the objections of Desdemona's father Brabantio, placating him with a series of silly sayings or 'sentences' in rhyme. The duke wishes to procure Othello's service as general against the Turks, and cannot afford to waste time on a petty domestic dispute. Brabantio points out that he would feel differently if the Turks had occupied Venetian territory such as Cypress; under these conditions the duke would find placatory proverbs as offensive as Brabantio does. But Othello's trial is merely postponed, not waived. His own prejudices against Desdemona as a Venetian woman — widely thought at the time to be the most promiscuous women in Europe — are played upon by Iago, until Othello appoints himself her judge, jury and executioner in the final scene, denying her the right to defend herself against his accusations, and excusing his murder of her with a spurious 'cause' which is no more substantial than a handkerchief. The play's denouement would be funny if it were not so horrible.

Yet the lovers' relationship had a glorious beginning. In our extract, Othello describes Desdemona spurning prejudice and showing sympathy with a stranger's sufferings as she listens to his life story. As he speaks, she forgets not only his foreignness but her own culture's expectations of her gender. To Desdemona, Othello's narrative is both 'passing strange' and also 'pitiful' — worth weeping over. It makes her wish 'That heaven had made her such a man' — that is, that Othello had been created for her benefit, or that she had been created male. And it leads her actively to court him, in direct contravention of early modern rules concerning courtship. Her disobedience of her father, then, is a sign of her freedom from the petty assumptions that feed racism; which makes it all the more tragic that it should later be used as evidence for her disloyalty to her lover.

OPPOSITE Othello tells his life story to Desdemona – 19th-century painting by Henri J. Fradelle.

ACT **1** SCENE **3**
A council room in Venice

[*Enter* DUKE *and* SENATORS, BRABANTIO, OTHELLO, IAGO, RODERIGO, *and others*]

OTHELLO Most potent, grave, and reverend signors,
My very noble and approved good masters,
That I have ta'en away this old man's daughter,
It is most true; true, I have married her.
The very head and front of my offending
Hath this extent, no more. Rude am I in my speech,
And little blessed with the soft phrase of peace,
For since these arms of mine had seven years' pith
Till now some nine moons wasted, they have used
Their dearest action in the tented field,
And little of this great world can I speak
More than pertains to feats of broil and battle;
And therefore little shall I grace my cause
In speaking for myself. Yet, by your gracious patience,
I will a round unvarnished tale deliver
Of my whole course of love: what drugs, what charms,
What conjuration and what mighty magic –
For such proceeding I am charged withal –
I won his daughter.

BRABANTIO   A maiden never bold,
Of spirit so still and quiet that her motion
Blushed at herself – and she in spite of nature,
Of years, of country, credit, everything,
To fall in love with what she feared to look on!
It is a judgement maimed and most imperfect

'deadly breach'

'Deadly breach' means a dangerous gap in a fortification. Later, 'antres' are caverns; 'Anthropophagi' are cannibals; and men who had their faces in their chests were known to Elizabethans from Sir John Mandeville's *Travels*, a fantastic narrative popular throughout Europe in the Middle Ages. Some of these terms and concepts might have been as unfamiliar to Desdemona as they are to modern readers.

That will confess perfection so could err
Against all rules of nature, and must be driven
To find out practices of cunning hell
Why this should be. I therefore vouch again
That with some mixtures powerful o'er the blood,
Or with some dram conjured to this effect,
He wrought upon her.

DUKE   To vouch this is no proof
Without more wider and more overt test
Than these thin habits and poor likelihoods
Of modern seeming do prefer against him.

FIRST SENATOR But Othello, speak.
Did you by indirect and forcèd courses
Subdue and poison this young maid's affections?
Or came it by request, and such fair question
As soul to soul affordeth?

OTHELLO   I do beseech you,
Send for the lady to the Sagittary,
And let her speak of me before her father.
If you do find me foul in her report,
The trust, the office I do hold of you
Not only take away, but let your sentence
Even fall upon my life.

DUKE   Fetch Desdemona hither.

OTHELLO Ensign, conduct them. You best
   know the place.
[*Exeunt* IAGO *and Attendants*]
And till she come, as truly as to heaven
I do confess the vices of my blood,
So justly to your grave ears I'll present
How I did thrive in this fair lady's love,
And she in mine.

DUKE   Say it, Othello.

OTHELLO Her father loved me, oft invited me,
Still questioned me the story of my life
From year to year, the battles, sieges, fortunes
That I have passed.
I ran it through even from my boyish days
To th' very moment that he bade me tell it;
Wherein I spake of most disastrous chances,
Of moving accidents by flood and field,
Of hair-breadth scapes i'th' imminent deadly breach,
Of being taken by the insolent foe
And sold to slavery, of my redemption thence,
And portance in my traveller's history,
Wherein of antres vast and deserts idle,
Rough quarries, rocks, and hills whose heads touch
   heaven,
It was my hint to speak. Such was my process;
And of the cannibals that each other eat,
The Anthropophagi, and men whose heads
Do grow beneath their shoulders. This to hear
Would Desdemona seriously incline,
But still the house affairs would draw her thence,
Which ever as she could with haste dispatch
She'd come again, and with a greedy ear
Devour up my discourse; which I observing,
Took once a pliant hour, and found good means
To draw from her a prayer of earnest heart
That I would all my pilgrimage dilate,

Whereof by parcels she had something heard,
But not intentively. I did consent,
And often did beguile her of her tears
When I did speak of some distressful stroke
That my youth suffered. My story being done,
She gave me for my pains a world of kisses.
She swore in faith 'twas strange, 'twas passing strange,
'Twas pitiful, 'twas wondrous pitiful.
She wished she had not heard it, yet she wished
That heaven had made her such a man. She
    thanked me,
And bade me, if I had a friend that loved her,
I should but teach him how to tell my story,
And that would woo her. Upon this hint I spake.
She loved me for the dangers I had passed,
And I loved her that she did pity them.
This only is the witchcraft I have used.
Here comes the lady. Let her witness it.

[*Enter* **DESDEMONA**, **IAGO**, *and Attendants*]

> ### 'Let me speak like yourself … bootless grief.'
>
> 'Sentences' are proverbs, which the duke plans to use as a 'grece' or step to elevate the lovers to Brabantio's favour. He adds: one ceases to worry ('griefs are ended') when the worst thing you anticipated actually happens ('hopes' are anticipations). 'Patience her injury a mockery makes' means that being patient helps you to laugh at your problems, instead of indulging in 'bootless' (useless) grief.

DESDEMONA   My noble father,
I do perceive here a divided duty.
To you I am bound for life and education;
My life and education both do learn me
How to respect you; you are the lord of duty –
I am hitherto your daughter. But here's my husband,
And so much duty as my mother showed
To you, preferring you before her father,
So much I challenge that I may profess
Due to the Moor my lord.

BRABANTIO   God b'wi'you, I ha' done.
Please it your grace, on to the state affairs.
I had rather to adopt a child than get it.
Come hither, Moor.
I here do give thee that with all my heart
Which, but thou hast already, with all my heart
I would keep from thee. [*To* **DESDEMONA**] For
    your sake, jewel,
I am glad at soul I have no other child,
For thy escape would teach me tyranny,
To hang clogs on 'em. I have done, my lord.

DUKE Let me speak like yourself, and lay a sentence
Which, as a grece or step, may help these lovers
Into your favour.
When remedies are past, the griefs are ended
By seeing the worst which late on hopes depended.
To mourn a mischief that is past and gone
Is the next way to draw new mischief on.
What cannot be preserved when fortune takes,
Patience her injury a mockery makes.
The robbed that smiles steals something from the thief;
He robs himself that spends a bootless grief.

I will a round unvarnished tale deliver Of my whole course of love

DUKE I think this tale would win my daughter too.
Good Brabantio,
Take up this mangled matter at the best.
Men do their broken weapons rather use
Than their bare hands.

BRABANTIO   I pray you hear her speak.
If she confess that she was half the wooer,
Destruction on my head if my bad blame
Light on the man! Come hither, gentle mistress.
Do you perceive in all this noble company
Where most you owe obedience?

BRABANTIO So let the Turk of Cyprus us beguile,
We lose it not so long as we can smile.
He bears the sentence well that nothing bears
But the free comfort which from thence he hears,
But he bears both the sentence and the sorrow
That, to pay grief, must of poor patience borrow.
These sentences, to sugar or to gall,
Being strong on both sides, are equivocal.
But words are words. I never yet did hear
That the bruised heart was piercèd through the ear.
I humbly beseech you proceed to th'affairs of state.

Othello *c.1603-4*

ACT **3** | SCENE **3**

❝ **O, beware, my lord, of jealousy.**
It is the green-eyed monster which doth mock
The meat it feeds on. ❞

Iago's technique in stirring up Othello's jealousy is simple: he is 'honest'. By openly voicing his prejudices, by sharing his willingness to suspect even his friends, by advising Othello on his best course of action, he succeeds in making the Moor see everything as he does – including Othello. It's a technique that would be highly entertaining in another context, and Iago takes an infectious delight in it.

At the end of Act 2 he asks, 'what's he … that says I play the villain?' – then proceeds to give his honest opinion of Desdemona. She's 'easy … to subdue / In any honest suit' – in other words, easily persuaded to any good deed; but it's also easy for Iago to transform the word 'easy' into criticism – as in the phrase 'a woman of easy virtue'; or to turn the phrase 'She's framed as fruitful / As the free elements', a compliment on her generosity, into an insinuation that she is *sexually* 'free'. Thus Iago turns 'her virtue into pitch' – a sticky substance used in snares; and the phrase emphasizes the role that colour plays in his imagination, since pitch is as black as Desdemona's skin is white. Iago plans to turn white into black, metaphorically speaking – the ultimate achievement in false logic. And he does it in the name of honesty.

Our extract comes from the scene in which Iago first plants the seeds of suspicion in Othello's mind – one of the greatest Shakespeare wrote. Othello has a rich imagination, as we know from his account of his adventures, and the extract begins just after Iago has made some non-committal comment about Desdemona and Lieutenant Cassio; a remark that triggers Othello's strenuous efforts to imagine what Iago may be thinking. The general tells Iago that he looks 'As if there were some monster in thy thought / Too hideous to be shown' – and soon the monster has transferred itself to the mind of Othello, becoming the 'green-eyed monster', jealousy.

The funny thing is that this imaginative transference takes place despite Iago's open admission that he will give Othello no access to his thoughts, since even slaves are free to keep their cogitations to themselves. Meanwhile, the ensign keeps trotting out hackneyed popular wisdom, which insinuates a lot but says nothing directly. When he asks: 'where's that palace whereinto foul things / Sometimes intrude not', he implies not only that his thoughts are ugly, but that a beautiful woman may harbour unpleasant secrets, or that Othello's palatial residence in Cyprus may conceal something vile. Iago's virtuous-sounding invective against jealousy implies that Othello has good reason to be jealous. And when he says, 'I know our country disposition well', he turns Desdemona into a stereotypically promiscuous Venetian woman. The misogynistic undercurrent here is brought out by a nasty little pun: 'country' often stood for the female genitals in Elizabethan English. By the end of the extract, Iago has even persuaded Othello that Desdemona's willingness to defy prejudice and marry a Moor is a reason to distrust her. The poison of his racism and misogyny is so virulent that it warps Othello's view of himself as well as of his wife – a process that makes this the most painful of Shakespeare's tragedies to watch or read.

OPPOSITE Laurence Fishburne as Othello and Kenneth Branagh as Iago in the 1995 film adaptation.

[*Enter* IAGO *and* OTHELLO]

OTHELLO I prithee speak to me as to thy thinkings,
As thou dost ruminate, and give thy worst of
    thoughts
The worst of words.

IAGO   Good my lord, pardon me.
Though I am bound to every act of duty,
I am not bound to that all slaves are free to.
Utter my thoughts? Why, say they are vile and false,
As where's that palace whereinto foul things
Sometimes intrude not? Who has that breast so pure
But some uncleanly apprehensions
Keep leets and law-days, and in sessions sit
With meditations lawful?

OTHELLO Thou dost conspire against thy friend, Iago,
If thou but think'st him wronged and mak'st his ear
A stranger to thy thoughts.

IAGO   I do beseech you,
Though I perchance am vicious in my guess –
As, I confess, it is my nature's plague
To spy into abuses, and oft my jealousy
Shapes faults that are not – that your wisdom then,
From one that so imperfectly conceits,
Would take no notice, nor build yourself a trouble
Out of his scattering and unsure observance.
It were not for your quiet nor your good,
Nor for my manhood, honesty, and wisdom,
To let you know my thoughts.

OTHELLO   What dost thou mean?

IAGO Good name in man and woman, dear my lord,
Is the immediate jewel of their souls.
Who steals my purse steals trash; 'tis something,
    nothing;
'Twas mine, 'tis his, and has been slave to thousands.
But he that filches from me my good name
Robs me of that which not enriches him
And makes me poor indeed.

OTHELLO   By heaven, I'll know thy thoughts.

IAGO You cannot, if my heart were in your hand;
Nor shall not whilst 'tis in my custody.

OTHELLO Ha!

IAGO   O, beware, my lord, of jealousy.
It is the green-eyed monster which doth mock
The meat it feeds on. That cuckold lives in bliss
Who, certain of his fate, loves not his wronger.
But O, what damnèd minutes tells he o'er
Who dotes yet doubts, suspects yet fondly loves!

OTHELLO O misery!

IAGO Poor and content is rich, and rich enough,
But riches fineless is as poor as winter

To him that ever fears he shall be poor.
Good God the souls of all my tribe defend
From jealousy!

OTHELLO   Why, why is this?
Think'st thou I'd make a life of jealousy,
To follow still the changes of the moon
With fresh suspicions? No, to be once in doubt

> **'Who has that breast
> … meditations lawful?'**
>
> **Corrupt thoughts ('uncleanly
> apprehensions'), like corrupt judges, may
> attend law-courts ('leets') on days set aside
> for legal purposes ('law-days'), and discuss
> legal matters in session with legitimate
> thoughts – or just judges. This speech feeds
> into the play's many references to justice
> and the law, as discussed in the introduction.**

Is once to be resolved. Exchange me for a goat
When I shall turn the business of my soul
To such exsufflicate and blowed surmises
Matching thy inference. 'Tis not to make me jealous
To say my wife is fair, feeds well, loves company,
Is free of speech, sings, plays, and dances well;
Where virtue is, these are more virtuous.
Nor from mine own weak merits will I draw
The smallest fear or doubt of her revolt;
For she had eyes and chose me. No, Iago;
I'll see before I doubt; when I doubt, prove;
And on the proof, there is no more but this:
Away at once with love or jealousy.

*give thy worst of thoughts
The worst of words.*

IAGO I am glad of this, for now I shall have reason
To show the love and duty that I bear you
With franker spirit. Therefore, as I am bound,
Receive it from me. I speak not yet of proof.
Look to your wife; observe her well with Cassio;
Wear your eye thus, not jealous nor secure.
I would not have your free and noble nature
Out of self-bounty be abused. Look to't.
I know our country disposition well:
In Venice they do let God see the pranks
They dare not show their husbands; their best
    conscience
Is not to leave't undone, but keep't unknown.

OTHELLO Dost thou say so?

IAGO She did deceive her father, marrying you,
And when she seemed to shake and fear your looks
She loved them most.

OTHELLO   And so she did.

IAGO   Why, go to, then.
She that so young could give out such a seeming,
To seel her father's eyes up close as oak –
He thought 'twas witchcraft. But I am much to blame;
I humbly do beseech you of your pardon
For too much loving you.

OTHELLO   I am bound to thee for ever.

IAGO I see this hath a little dashed your spirits.

OTHELLO Not a jot, not a jot.

IAGO   I'faith, I fear it has.
I hope you will consider what is spoke
Comes from my love. But I do see you're moved.
I am to pray you not to strain my speech
To grosser issues, nor to larger reach
Than to suspicion.

OTHELLO   I will not.

> ### 'If I do prove her haggard
> ### … at fortune.'
>
> **Othello's metaphors here refer to the
> training of a hawk in falconry, and make a
> connection between wife and bird which is
> much used by Petruchio in *The Taming of
> the Shrew*. A 'haggard' is a wild hawk;
> 'jesses' are leg straps used to control a
> trained bird of prey; 'whistle her off' is to set
> her free to hunt at random ('prey at fortune').**

IAGO Should you do so, my lord,
My speech should fall into such vile success
Which my thoughts aimed not. Cassio's my worthy
   friend.
My lord, I see you're moved.

OTHELLO   No, not much moved.
I do not think but Desdemona's honest.

IAGO Long live she so, and long live you to think so!

OTHELLO And yet, how nature erring from itself –

IAGO Ay, there's the point; as, to be bold with you,
Not to affect many proposèd matches
Of her own clime, complexion, and degree,
Whereto we see in all things nature tends –
Foh! One may smell in such a will most rank,
Foul disproportions, thoughts unnatural.
But pardon me. I do not in position
Distinctly speak of her, though I may fear

Her will, recoiling to her better judgment,
May fall to match you with her country forms
And happily repent.

OTHELLO   Farewell, farewell.
If more thou dost perceive, let me know more.
Set on thy wife to observe. Leave me, Iago.

IAGO [*Going*] My lord, I take my leave.

OTHELLO Why did I marry? This honest creature
   doubtless
Sees and knows more, much more, than he unfolds.

IAGO [*Returning*] My lord, I would I might entreat
   your honour
To scan this thing no further. Leave it to time.
Although 'tis fit that Cassio have his place –
For sure, he fills it up with great ability –
Yet, if you please to hold him off awhile,
You shall by that perceive him and his means.
Note if your lady strain his entertainment
With any strong or vehement importunity;
Much will be seen in that. In the mean time,
Let me be thought too busy in my fears –
As worthy cause I have to fear I am –
And hold her free, I do beseech your honour.

OTHELLO Fear not my government.

IAGO   I once more take my leave. [*Exit*]

OTHELLO This fellow's of exceeding honesty,
And knows all qualities with a learned spirit
Of human dealings. If I do prove her haggard,
Though that her jesses were my dear heart-strings
I'd whistle her off and let her down the wind
To prey at fortune. Haply for I am black
And have not those soft parts of conversation
That chamberers have, or for I am declined
Into the vale of years – yet that's not much –
She's gone. I am abused, and my relief
Must be to loathe her. O curse of marriage,
That we can call these delicate creatures ours
And not their appetites! I had rather be a toad
And live upon the vapour of a dungeon
Than keep a corner in the thing I love
For others' uses. Yet 'tis the plague of great ones;
Prerogatived are they less than the base.
'Tis destiny unshunnable, like death.
Even then this forkèd plague is fated to us
When we do quicken.
[*Enter* DESDEMONA *and* EMILIA]
                         Look where she comes.
If she be false, O then heaven mocks itself!
I'll not believe't.

All's Well that Ends Well

c.1602-6

> I am a simple maid, and therein wealthiest
> That I protest I simply am a maid.

All's Well that Ends Well

As its title suggests, this play deals with happy endings, though it includes the recognition that all happiness has an ending. Its characters are conscious that they must deal with a flawed world on its own terms, and that they might not be able to protect themselves from being compromised by these dealings. This is another implication of the title: that happy endings justify the means used to reach them, and that not all of these means may be good. But it also invites us to consider the question of what it means to be 'well', physically or morally speaking. There's a sense, then, of resignation and doubt about the title that perfectly suits the troubled comedy it accompanies.

Verse is the play's chief medium, and much of that verse is rhymed. The protagonist Helena uses rhyme often, which gives her lines a proverbial feel, as if she is quoting ancient wisdom, a positive counterpart to the proverbs of Iago. She draws on ancient wisdom when she cures the elderly king of France of a terminal illness; and the bond thus forged between girl and monarch is reinforced by the fact that the king, too, uses rhyme, so that his and Helena's exchanges sound as if they are singing to the same tune. There's a sympathy between them that unites genders and generations through melodic utterance. Here, then, is another meaning of the title: that a conversation goes well when its metrical units end in rhyme. There's clearly something contrived about this claim; it's not true in any obvious sense. But its very contrivedness stresses the extent to which this play is preoccupied with engineering eventual happiness by all means necessary, regardless of improbabilities.

All's Well is full of elderly people who lament the passing of old-time excellence and the rise of a new, self-centred generation. In our extract, the king and the elderly courtier Lafeu are disgusted by the arrogance of young aristocrats like Count Bertram, who refuse to recognize Helena's qualities – despite her miraculous healing of the king – as a kind of nobility superior to theirs. When the king forces Bertram to marry her, the count is horrified, thinking the union will 'bring [him] down' from the social eminence he enjoys. The king is forced to point out how far Bertram's position is an artificial one: Helena can be 'built up' to a social status as high as his; the count can be 'thrown down' to a disease-ridden poverty. Bertram admits that the king is a master of 'great creation' – he can make or break his subjects – and consents to the marriage; but as soon as he has done so he flees to Italy with his friend Parolles, whose name allies him with the false words that govern the younger generation in France. Helena must follow him and resort to trickery to win him back. Their eventual reunion in the final act ought to signal the reconciliation of generations – the young represented by Bertram, the old by Helena, who is the king's 'great creation' – along with the miraculous healing of Bertram's 'dropsied honour' (as the king calls it in our extract). But the play has opened too many fissures between its characters to convince us that such 'wellness' can ever be more than a fading fancy.

OPPOSITE Helena tells the king that she is a 'simple maid' in this 1791 engraving by John and Josiah Boydell.

[*Enter* KING, BERTRAM, LAFEU, PAROLLES,
  HELENA, *and others*]

KING Go, call before me all the lords in court.
Sit, my preserver, by thy patient's side,
And with this healthful hand whose banished sense
Thou hast repealed, a second time receive
The confirmation of my promised gift,
Which but attends thy naming.
[*Enter four* LORDS]
Fair maid, send forth thine eye. This youthful parcel
Of noble bachelors stand at my bestowing,
O'er whom both sovereign power and father's voice
I have to use. Thy frank election make.
Thou hast power to choose, and they none to forsake.

HELENA To each of you one fair and virtuous
  mistress
Fall, when Love please. Marry, to each but one!

LAFEU [*Aside*] I'd give bay Curtal and his furniture
My mouth no more were broken than these boys',
And writ as little beard.

KING   Peruse them well.
Not one of those but had a noble father.

HELENA Gentlemen,
Heaven hath through me restored the King to health.

ALL We understand it, and thank heaven for you.

HELENA I am a simple maid, and therein wealthiest
That I protest I simply am a maid. –
Please it your majesty, I have done already.
The blushes in my cheeks thus whisper me:
'We blush that thou shouldst choose; but, be refused,
Let the white death sit on thy cheek for ever,
We'll ne'er come there again.'

KING   Make choice and see.
Who shuns thy love shuns all his love in me.

HELENA Now, Dian, from thy altar do I fly,
And to imperial Love, that god most high,
Do my sighs stream.
[*She addresses her to a* LORD]
                      Sir, will you hear my suit?

FIRST LORD And grant it.

HELENA   Thanks, sir. All the rest is mute.

LAFEU [*Aside*] I had rather be in this choice than
  throw ames-ace for my life.

HELENA [*To another* LORD] The honour, sir, that
  flames in your fair eyes,
Before I speak, too threat'ningly replies.
Love make your fortunes twenty times above
Her that so wishes, and her humble love.

SECOND LORD No better, if you please.

HELENA   My wish receive,
Which great Love grant. And so I take my leave.

> **'I'd give bay Curtal
> … writ as little beard.'**
>
> 'Curtal' is Lafeu's horse, which has been
> curtailed – that is, had its tail docked – and
> his 'furniture' is all its trappings. Lafeu would
> give away his horse if only he were young
> enough for his teeth not to be broken, or not
> to have been broken or trained (like a colt), or
> his voice had not yet broken – thus making
> him a suitable partner for young Helena.

LAFEU [*Aside*] Do all they deny her? An they were
sons of mine I'd have them whipped, or I would
send them to th' Turk, to make eunuchs of.

HELENA [*To another* LORD] Be not afraid that I
  your hand should take;
I'll never do you wrong for your own sake.
Blessing upon your vows, and in your bed
Find fairer fortune, if you ever wed.

LAFEU [*Aside*] These boys are boys of ice, they'll
none have her. Sure they are bastards to the English,
the French ne'er got 'em.

HELENA [*To another* LORD] You are too young,
  too happy, and too good
To make yourself a son out of my blood.

FOURTH LORD Fair one, I think not so.

LAFEU [*Aside*] There's one grape yet. I am sure thy
father drunk wine, but if thou be'st not an ass, I am
a youth of fourteen. I have known thee already.

HELENA [*To* BERTRAM] I dare not say I take you,
  but I give
Me and my service ever whilst I live
Into your guiding power. This is the man.

*Here, take her hand,
Proud scornful boy, unworthy this good gift*

KING Why, then, young Bertram, take her. She's
thy wife.

BERTRAM My wife, my liege! I shall beseech your
highness,
In such a business give me leave to use
The help of mine own eyes.

KING   Know'st thou not, Bertram,
What she has done for me?

BERTRAM   Yes, my good lord,
But never hope to know why I should marry her.

> **'Proud scornful boy, … to the beam'**
>
> **'Misprision' means 'contempt' or 'error'.
> Bertram's 'error' is not to see that when the
> King places himself on Helena's side of the
> weighing scales, they will outweigh Bertram
> (the king uses the royal 'we'). If Bertram
> persists in his error, he adds, he'll be thrown
> out of the court so fast he'll get the
> 'staggers' – a disease of the legs.**

KING Thou know'st she has raised me from my
sickly bed.

BERTRAM But follows it, my lord, to bring me down
Must answer for your raising? I know her well:
She had her breeding at my father's charge.
A poor physician's daughter, my wife! Disdain
Rather corrupt me ever!

KING 'Tis only title thou disdain'st in her, the which
I can build up. Strange is it that our bloods,
Of colour, weight, and heat, poured all together,
Would quite confound distinction, yet stands off
In differences so mighty. If she be
All that is virtuous, save what thou dislik'st –
A poor physician's daughter – thou dislik'st
Of virtue for the name; but do not so.
From lowest place when virtuous things proceed,
The place is dignified by the doer's deed.
Where great additions swell's, and virtue none,
It is a dropsied honour. Good alone
Is good without a name. Vileness is so.
The property by what it is should go,
Not by the title. She is young, wise, fair;
In these to nature she's immediate heir,
And these breed honour. That is honour's scorn
Which challenges itself as honour's born
And is not like the sire. Honours thrive
When rather from our acts we them derive
Than our foregoers. The mere word's a slave
Debauched on every tomb, on every grave

A lying trophy, and as oft is dumb
Where dust and damned oblivion is the tomb
Of honoured bones indeed. What should be said?
If thou canst like this creature as a maid,
I can create the rest. Virtue and she
Is her own dower; honour and wealth from me.

BERTRAM I cannot love her, nor will strive to do't.

KING Thou wrong'st thyself, if thou shouldst strive
to choose.

HELENA That you are well restored, my lord,
I'm glad.
Let the rest go.

KING My honour's at the stake, which to defeat
I must produce my power. Here, take her hand,
Proud scornful boy, unworthy this good gift,
That dost in vile misprision shackle up
My love and her desert; that canst not dream
We, poising us in her defective scale,
Shall weigh thee to the beam; that wilt not know
It is in us to plant thine honour where
We please to have it grow. Check thy contempt;
Obey our will, which travails in thy good;
Believe not thy disdain, but presently
Do thine own fortunes that obedient right
Which both thy duty owes and our power claims,
Or I will throw thee from my care for ever
Into the staggers and the careless lapse
Of youth and ignorance, both my revenge and hate
Loosing upon thee, in the name of justice,
Without all terms of pity. Speak. Thine answer.

BERTRAM Pardon, my gracious lord, for I submit
My fancy to your eyes. When I consider
What great creation and what dole of honour
Flies where you bid it, I find that she, which late
Was in my nobler thoughts most base, is now
The praisèd of the King; who, so ennobled,
Is as 'twere born so.

KING   Take her by the hand
And tell her she is thine; to whom I promise
A counterpoise, if not to thy estate
A balance more replete.

BERTRAM   I take her hand.

KING Good fortune and the favour of the King
Smile upon this contract, whose ceremony
Shall seem expedient on the now-born brief,
And be performed tonight. The solemn feast
Shall more attend upon the coming space,
Expecting absent friends. As thou lov'st her
Thy love's to me religious; else, does err.

Timon of Athens *c.1605-8*

ACT **4** | SCENE **3**

‘ **Lie where the light foam of the sea may beat
Thy gravestone daily.** ’

Timon of Athens

This play commemorates a time when the spendthrift James I was exhausting the royal treasury, and when Shakespeare's great contemporaries, Ben Jonson and Thomas Middleton, were exploring the dramatic possibilities of Europe's current obsession with money. The plot is simple: Timon is rich, becomes poor, and is abandoned by the well-heeled friends who flattered him in his prosperity.

The play's moral is sometimes taken to be simple too: money corrupts, the rich are hypocrites and Timon has good reason for the bitterness that grips him after his fall. But we should beware of trite moralizing. A poet who seeks Timon's patronage in Act 1 specializes in improving allegories, such as his famous account of Fortune's hill, with Timon at the top, then tumbling to the bottom, where he sprawls unaided. A painter praises the poem for showing Timon 'that mean eyes have seen / The foot above the head' – for warning him, that is, that social superiority cannot be taken for granted. But Timon pays no attention; he is too busy flattering the poet to analyse his work. And after his fall he gives the poet a beating, disgusted by the fictions on which he thrives: fake friendships and spurious pretensions to occupy the high moral ground.

The poet is wrong about Timon's fall, and so is Timon. When the tycoon loses his money he is not abandoned. Only his prosperous friends desert him, but their servants pity him, and his former employees are staggeringly loyal. One by one, as the rich refuse to help him, Timon's servants take centre stage to denounce ingratitude; and later they swear eternal fellowship with each other in Timon's name, despite the fact that he has renounced all human company. Their sympathy springs from his good treatment of them earlier – but also, perhaps, from the fact that he is now their peer, and that they understand his predicament. Timon's situation is not unique, whatever he thinks. His misanthropy, as the philosopher Apemantus tells him, is not earned; he would never have turned bitter if he had always been poor; and Timon confirms this when he claims he has better reason for cynicism than Apemantus, since unlike the philosopher he was not born to his current degradation.

For Timon, the loyalty of servants is unimportant because they were never his 'friends' – his allies or social equals. So when, in our extract, he rails on Apemantus, who never flattered him, his fury seems misguided; when he gives starving bandits some gold he has found and tells them to pillage Athens, his violent repudiation of the world seems as excessive to them as to us; and when he avers that his faithful steward Flavius is unique in his loyalty, Timon is a hypocrite, since he could have been surrounded by loyal comrades if he had recognized his staff as potential friends. Timon's best moment comes at the beginning of our extract, when he plans to locate his grave where 'the light foam of the sea may beat / [HIS] gravestone daily'. For once he seems to sense that, like all self-important people, he needs to lighten up a little – to pay attention to the 'daily' or everyday, instead of seeing himself as exceptional. It's a lesson some of his commentators, too, need to learn.

OPPOSITE The thieves interrupt Timon in his pit in the Royal Shakespeare Company's 1965 production.

[*Enter* TIMON *and* APEMANTUS]

TIMON Rogue, rogue, rogue!
I am sick of this false world, and will love nought
But even the mere necessities upon 't.
Then, Timon, presently prepare thy grave.
Lie where the light foam of the sea may beat
Thy gravestone daily. Make thine epitaph,
That death in me at others' lives may laugh.
[*He looks on the gold*]
O thou sweet king-killer, and dear divorce
'Twixt natural son and sire; thou bright defiler
Of Hymen's purest bed; thou valiant Mars;
Thou ever young, fresh, loved, and delicate wooer,
Whose blush doth thaw the consecrated snow
That lies on Dian's lap; thou visible god,
That solder'st close impossibilities
And mak'st them kiss; that speak'st with every tongue
To every purpose; O thou touch of hearts:
Think thy slave man rebels, and by thy virtue
Set them into confounding odds, that beasts
May have the world in empire.

APEMANTUS   Would 'twere so!
But not till I am dead. I'll say thou'st gold.
Thou wilt be thronged to shortly.

TIMON   Thronged to?

APEMANTUS   Ay.

TIMON Thy back, I prithee.

APEMANTUS   Live, and love thy misery.

TIMON Long live so, and so die. I am quit.

[*Enter* BANDITTI]

APEMANTUS More things like men. Eat, Timon,
    and abhor them. [*Exit*]

FIRST BANDIT Where should he have this gold? It
is some poor fragment, some slender ort of his
remainder. The mere want of gold and the falling-
from of his friends drove him into this melancholy.

SECOND BANDIT It is noised he hath a mass of
    treasure.

THIRD BANDIT Let us make the assay upon him. If
he care not for't, he will supply us easily. If he
covetously reserve it, how shall 's get it?

SECOND BANDIT True, for he bears it not about
    him; 'tis hid.

FIRST BANDIT Is not this he?

BANDITTI Where?

SECOND BANDIT 'Tis his description.

THIRD BANDIT He, I know him.

BANDITTI [*Coming forward*] Save thee, Timon.

TIMON Now, thieves?

BANDITTI Soldiers, not thieves.

TIMON   Both, too, and women's sons.

BANDITTI We are not thieves, but men that much
    do want.

TIMON Your greatest want is, you want much of meat.
Why should you want? Behold, the earth hath roots.

> **'thou bright defiler … lies on Dian's lap'**
>
> Hymen is the classical god of marriage; Mars,
> the god of war who 'defiled the bed of Hymen'
> by committing adultery with Venus, wife of
> Vulcan; the 'consecrated snow' is the snow
> of chastity, of which Diana was the goddess.
> Like each of these gods, gold solders together
> incompatible things ('impossibilities'):
> marriage with adultery, military honour with
> underhand dealings, chastity with sex.

Within this mile break forth a hundred springs,
The oaks bear mast, the briers scarlet hips,
The bounteous housewife nature on each bush
Lays her full mess before you. Want! Why want?

FIRST BANDIT We cannot live on grass, on berries,
    water,
As beasts and birds and fishes.

TIMON Nor on the beasts themselves, the birds and
    fishes;
You must eat men. Yet thanks I must you con
That you are thieves professed, that you work not
In holier shapes; for there is boundless theft
In limited professions. Rascal thieves,
Here's gold. Go, suck the subtle blood o' th' grape,
Till the high fever seethe your blood to froth,
And so scape hanging. Trust not the physician;
His antidotes are poison, and he slays
More than you rob. Take wealth and lives together.
Do villainy; do, since you protest to do't,
Like workmen. I'll example you with thievery.
The sun's a thief, and with his great attraction
Robs the vast sea. The moon's an arrant thief,
And her pale fire she snatches from the sun.
The sea's a thief, whose liquid surge resolves
The moon into salt tears. The earth's a thief,
That feeds and breeds by a composture stol'n
From general excrement. Each thing's a thief.
The laws, your curb and whip, in their rough power
Have unchecked theft. Love not yourselves. Away,
Rob one another. There's more gold. Cut throats;
All that you meet are thieves. To Athens go,
Break open shops; nothing can you steal
But thieves do lose it. Steal no less for this I give you,
And gold confound you howsoe'er. Amen.

THIRD BANDIT He's almost charmed me from my
    profession by persuading me to it.

FIRST BANDIT 'Tis in the malice of mankind that he
    thus advises us, not to have us thrive in our mystery.

SECOND BANDIT I'll believe him as an enemy,
    and give over my trade.

FIRST BANDIT Let us first see peace in Athens.
There is no time so miserable but a man may be true.

[*Exeunt* **BANDITTI**. *Enter* **FLAVIUS**]

FLAVIUS O you gods!
Is yon despised and ruinous man my lord,
Full of decay and failing? O monument
And wonder of good deeds evilly bestowed!
What an alteration of honour
Has desp'rate want made!
What viler thing upon the earth than friends,
Who can bring noblest minds to basest ends!
How rarely does it meet with this time's guise,
When man was wished to love his enemies!
Grant I may ever love, and rather woo
Those that would mischief me than those that do!
He's caught me in his eye. I will present
My honest grief unto him, and as my lord
Still serve him with my life. My dearest master!

TIMON Away! What art thou?

FLAVIUS   Have you forgot me, sir?

TIMON Why dost ask that? I have forgot all men;
Then if thou grant'st thou'rt man, I have forgot thee.

FLAVIUS An honest poor servant of yours.

TIMON Then I know thee not.
I never had honest man about me, I.
All I kept were knaves, to serve in meat to villains.

> *'do, since you protest to do't,*
> *… Each thing's a thief.'*
>
> **Timon urges the Bandits to do their job
> of robbing people like skilful artisans
> ('workmen'). He then gives examples of
> thieving. The moon is an 'arrant' (wandering,
> brazen) thief, stealing light from the sun.
> According to Renaissance science, the sea
> gets its tides by absorbing water from the
> moon. And the earth steals its sustaining
> compost from everyone's excrement.**

FLAVIUS The gods are witness,
Ne'er did poor steward wear a truer grief
For his undone lord than mine eyes for you.

TIMON What, dost thou weep? Come nearer.
    Then I love thee
Because thou art a woman, and disclaim'st
Flinty mankind whose eyes do never give
But thorough lust and laughter. Pity's sleeping.
Strange times, that weep with laughing, not with
    weeping!

FLAVIUS I beg of you to know me, good my lord,
T' accept my grief, [*Offers money*] and whilst this
    poor wealth lasts
To entertain me as your steward still.

TIMON Had I a steward
So true, so just, and now so comfortable?
It almost turns my dangerous nature mild.
Let me behold thy face. Surely, this man
Was born of woman.
Forgive my general and exceptless rashness,
You perpetual-sober gods! I do proclaim
One honest man – mistake me not, but one;
No more, I pray – and he's a steward.
How fain would I have hated all mankind,
And thou redeem'st thyself! But all save thee
I fell with curses.
Methinks thou art more honest now than wise,
For by oppressing and betraying me
Thou mightst have sooner got another service;
For many so arrive at second masters
Upon their first lord's neck. But tell me true –
For I must ever doubt, though ne'er so sure –
Is not thy kindness subtle, covetous,
A usuring kindness, and, as rich men deal gifts,
Expecting in return twenty for one?

FLAVIUS No, my most worthy master, in whose breast
Doubt and suspect, alas, are placed too late.
You should have feared false times when you did feast;
Suspect still comes where an estate is least.
That which I show, heaven knows, is merely love,
Duty and zeal to your unmatchèd mind,
Care of your food and living; and believe it,
My most honoured lord,
For any benefit that points to me,
Either in hope or present, I'd exchange
For this one wish: that you had power and wealth
To requite me by making rich yourself.

TIMON Look thee, 'tis so. Thou singly honest man,
Here, take. [*Gives gold*] The gods, out of my misery,
Have sent thee treasure. Go, live rich and happy,
But thus conditioned: thou shalt build from men,
Hate all, curse all, show charity to none,
But let the famished flesh slide from the bone
Ere thou relieve the beggar. Give to dogs
What thou deniest to men. Let prisons swallow 'em,
Debts wither 'em to nothing. Be men like blasted woods,
And may diseases lick up their false bloods!
And so farewell and thrive.

FLAVIUS   O, let me stay
And comfort you, my master.

TIMON   If thou hat'st curses,
Stay not. Fly whilst thou art blest and free.
Ne'er see thou man, and let me ne'er see thee.
[*Exeunt,* **TIMON** *to his cave,* **FLAVIUS** *another way*]

King Lear *c.1604-5*

ACT **3** | SCENE **2**

> Blow, winds, and crack your cheeks!

King Lear dismantles his kingdom and finds he has dismantled himself. As he prepares to retire, he stages a competition between his three daughters, arranged in such a way as to ensure that his favourite – Cordelia, the youngest – wins. She is to speak last, which gives her an advantage, and he opens the competition with the question: 'Which of you shall *we say* doth love us most?' – reserving the right to say what he likes, regardless of who speaks best. The winner of the competition will get the biggest portion of the kingdom when he withdraws from power.

But his plan goes wrong. Cordelia's sisters are prepared to utter overblown nonsense to get ahead; Goneril professes to love him 'more than word can wield the matter', which renders the competition meaningless, while Regan pronounces herself 'enemy to all other joys' but her father's love, which is yet more irrational. Cordelia, meanwhile, takes the whole thing as an intelligence test. 'I love your Majesty,' she declares, 'According to my bond; nor more nor less'; and in saying so she shows her understanding of how society works: there are other legitimate claims on her affection besides her father's. Lear does not understand; he must have all or nothing, and if she will not love him all, she will be nothing to him. In a dreadful speech he breaks his paternal bond with her, and with it all the complex bonds that connect him with those around him – linking king to subject, father to daughter, one human being to another. His loyal subject Kent points this out, but gets banished for his bluntness. The scene ends with the retired king preparing to live alternately with each of his elder daughters, possessed of 'the name, and all th'addition to a king' – an empty phrase – in a land where words and names have lost their functions, destroyed by the facile protestations of Regan, Goneril and Lear.

He soon learns how far his power depended on others. When his daughters' servants cease to address him as monarch; when his retinue is stripped from him, and his messenger – Kent, who has returned to his service in disguise – is put in the stocks for insubordination towards Regan; and when his daughters call him 'old man' and say he 'must needs taste his folly', he knows that his authority has gone. Storming from his daughters' presence, he finds himself, in our extract, in the middle of a thunderstorm. Arrogant as ever, he takes this as a commentary on his own situation, first inviting the elements to avenge him by destroying mankind, then accusing them of complicity with his daughters' ingratitude. Afterwards he makes the less self-centred suggestion that thunderclaps are 'dreadful summoners' calling *all* unpunished criminals to justice. Later still, his rage exhausted, his daughters unpunished, he learns to see something smaller: how 'necessities' such as shelter can become 'precious' under new circumstances. This is the first great shift in Lear's perspective – earlier he dismissed 'necessity' as having no relevance to a ruler – and he confirms the shift by asking after his fool's well-being. The scene marks a crucial stage in the play's relentless stripping-down of social life to the few essential components from which it's built; far fewer than most theatregoers tend to assume.

OPPOSITE *King Lear and the Fool in the Storm* – an 1836 painting by Louis Boulanger.

Britain – bare, open country

[*Enter* KING LEAR *and* FOOL]

LEAR

Blow, winds, and crack your cheeks! Rage, blow,
You cataracts and hurricanoes, spout
Till you have drenched our steeples, drowned the
   cocks!
You sulphurous and thought-executing fires,
Vaunt-couriers to oak-cleaving thunderbolts,
Singe my white head! And thou, all-shaking thunder,
Smite flat the thick rotundity o' th' world;
Crack Nature's moulds, all germens spill at once,
That make ingrateful man!

FOOL

O nuncle, court holy-water in a dry house is better
than this rain-water out o' door. Good nuncle, in,
and ask thy daughters' blessing! Here's a night pities
neither wise man nor fool.

> *'You cataracts and hurricanoes, spout*
> *Till you have drenched our steeples,*
> *drowned the cocks!*
> *You sulphurous and thought-*
> *executing fires,*
> *Vaunt-couriers to oak-cleaving*
> *thunderbolts'*
>
> **'Cataracts' are the floodgates of heaven,
> 'hurricanoes' waterspouts connecting sea
> and sky. Lear's 'cocks' are weathercocks at
> the tops of steeples, and the 'thought-
> executing fires' are lightning that strikes as
> swiftly as thought – or does what thought
> tells it to do. Thunderbolts are the weapons
> of the classical gods, and lightning precedes
> them as their herald or 'Vaunt-courier'.**

Things that love night
Love not such nights as these.

LEAR

Rumble thy bellyful! Spit, fire! Spout, rain!
Nor rain, wind, thunder, fire, are my daughters.
I tax not you, you elements, with unkindness;

I never gave you kingdom, called you children;
You owe me no subscription. Then let fall
Your horrible pleasure. Here I stand, your slave,
A poor, infirm, weak and despised old man;
But yet I call you servile ministers,
That have with two pernicious daughters joined
Your high-engendered battles 'gainst a head
So old and white as this. O, ho! 'Tis foul!

FOOL

He that has a house to put's head in has a good
   head-piece.
   The cod-piece that will house
     Before the head has any,
   The head and he shall louse,
     So beggars marry many.
   The man that makes his toe
     What he his heart should make
   Shall of a corn cry woe,
     And turn his sleep to wake.
For there was never yet fair woman but she made
   mouths in a glass.

[*Enter* KENT, *disguised*]

> *'The cod-piece that will house*
> *Before the head has any,*
> *The head and he shall louse,*
> *So beggars marry many.'*
>
> **The fool's words are often hard to gloss.
> Here, the codpiece is the 'house' of the
> penis, and those who have this kind of
> house without having a roof over their
> head are vagrants or beggars. Beggars
> are proverbially lice-infested, so any two
> beggars marry more than one living being,
> since there are many lice on the bridal
> couple's heads. In the second half of the
> song, the man who prefers his toe to his
> heart – as Lear valued Regan and Goneril
> above Cordelia – will find himself tormented
> by the inferior object of his affections, just
> as a man is tormented by his corns.**

Here I stand, your slave, A poor, infirm, weak and despised old man

LEAR

No, I will be the pattern of all patience;
I will say nothing.

KENT

Who's there?

FOOL

Marry, here's grace and a cod-piece; that's a wise
   man and a fool.

KENT

Alas, sir, are you here? Things that love night
Love not such nights as these. The wrathful skies
Gallow the very wanderers of the dark
And make them keep their caves. Since I was man
Such sheets of fire, such bursts of horrid thunder,
Such groans of roaring wind and rain, I never
Remember to have heard. Man's nature cannot carry
Th' affliction nor the fear.

LEAR

                            Let the great gods,
That keep this dreadful pother o'er our heads,
Find out their enemies now. Tremble, thou wretch
That hast within thee undivulgèd crimes
Unwhipped of justice. Hide thee, thou bloody hand;
Thou perjured, and thou simular man of virtue
That art incestuous; caitiff, to pieces shake,
That under covert and convenient seeming
Hast practised on man's life. Close pent-up guilts,
Rive your concealing continents, and cry
These dreadful summoners grace. I am a man
More sinned against than sinning.

KENT

                            Alack, bare-headed!
Gracious my lord, hard by here is a hovel;
Some friendship will it lend you 'gainst the tempest.
Repose you there, while I to this hard house –
More harder than the stones whereof 'tis raised,
Which even but now, demanding after you,

Denied me to come in – return, and force
Their scanted courtesy.

LEAR

                            My wits begin to turn.
Come on, my boy. How dost, my boy? Art cold?
I am cold myself. Where is this straw, my fellow?
The art of our necessities is strange,
That can make vile things precious. Come, your hovel.
Poor fool and knave, I have one part in my heart
That's sorry yet for thee.

FOOL [*Sings*]

   He that has and a little tiny wit,
      With hey, ho, the wind and the rain,
   Must make content with his fortunes fit,
      Though the rain it raineth every day.

LEAR

True, my good boy. Come, bring us to this hovel.

[*Exeunt* **KING LEAR** *and* **KENT**]

FOOL

This is a brave night to cool a courtezan.
I'll speak a prophecy ere I go:
   When priests are more in word than matter;
   When brewers mar their malt with water;
   When nobles are their tailors' tutors;
   No heretics burned, but wenches' suitors;
   When every case in law is right;
   No squire in debt, nor no poor knight;
   When slanders do not live in tongues,
   Nor cutpurses come not to throngs;
   When usurers tell their gold i' the field,
   And bawds and whores do churches build –
   Then shall the realm of Albion
   Come to great confusion.
   Then comes the time, who lives to see't,
   That going shall be used with feet.
This prophecy Merlin shall make, for I live before his
   time. [*Exit*]

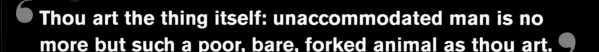

King Lear

c.1604-5

ACT 3 | **SCENE 4**

> **Thou art the thing itself: unaccommodated man is no more but such a poor, bare, forked animal as thou art.**

In the world of *King Lear*, the network of agreements, conventions, or bonds that hold a community together is both frail and arbitrary. Nobody knows this better than Edmund, bastard son of the Earl of Gloucester, who owes his illegitimacy to bad timing – the fact that he was born 'some twelve or fourteen moonshines' after his brother. He has been disinherited for a misdemeanour of his father's – though Gloucester has little sense of this; 'there was good sport at his making,' the earl observes cheerfully.

Gloucester is also superstitious, attributing to the influence of malevolent stars Lear's disowning of Cordelia and Kent's banishment. Edmund aims to show the world how easy it is to change the rules by human agency, without recourse to the workings of time or fate. He frames his brother for plotting against his father's life and gets him sentenced to death; then ingratiates himself with Lear's daughters and rises rapidly to political prominence. For much of the play, his flouting of the rules of his society pays ample dividends.

By smashing the familial and legal framework that held him and those around him in their place – as Lear did when he disowned Cordelia – Edmund unleashes a chain of devastating consequences. His brother Edgar takes on the disguise of the madman Poor Tom, whose broken language articulates the breakdown of all bonds, and the moral and emotional coldness that brought it about. In our extract, Tom describes himself as a former courtier, whose utterly conventional flouting of convention – breaking promises, sexual libertinism – led by degrees to Tom's present bestial condition, wandering witless among the foxes, wolves and lions he resembled when he lived at court. In this condition he meets Lear, whose mistreatment at the hands of his elder daughters makes him see all social structures as flawed, a perception that leads to a loss of mental stability, a 'tempest in my mind'. Lear's recognition of the flaws in his former assumptions is confirmed by his meeting with Tom. Any civilization that permits 'houseless poverty' to exist as Tom does is manifestly unjust, and the only proper thing to do when confronted with this injustice is to share the wretchedness of those who suffer by it. By removing his royal clothes, Lear disconnects himself from the system that imposes arbitrary distinctions between one man and another. In their nakedness and lunacy he and Tom are alike, and can speak together as equals, inhabitants of some bleak latter-day Eden.

Soon afterwards, the return of Cordelia to Britain seems to promise a restoration of all bonds that have been broken. Shakespeare could easily have given his play a happy ending, and for centuries it was performed with one, written for it by Nahum Tate in 1681. But he chose instead to have Cordelia die, as a result of more bad timing: an order for her execution, given by Edmund, that fails at the last minute to be retracted. Lear cannot bear her death – he dies of grief because of it. And both deaths leave the play's audiences with a new consciousness of the frailty of the world they re-enter as they leave the theatre – a fragility that has its most eloquent expression in Lear's encounter with Poor Tom.

OPPOSITE Kent (Andrew Cruikshank) with Lear (John Gielgud), the Fool (Alan Badel) and Edgar (Harry Andrews) in the Royal Shakespeare Company's 1950 production.

[*Enter* KING LEAR, KENT, *and* FOOL]

KENT Here is the place, my lord; good my lord, enter.
The tyranny of the open night's too rough
For nature to endure.

LEAR   Let me alone.

KENT Good my lord, enter here.

LEAR   Wilt break my heart?

KENT I had rather break mine own. Good my lord,
  enter.

LEAR Thou think'st 'tis much that this contentious
  storm
Invades us to the skin. So 'tis to thee;
But where the greater malady is fixed,
The lesser is scarce felt. Thou'dst shun a bear;
But if thy flight lay toward the raging sea,
Thou'dst meet the bear i' the mouth. When
  the mind's free,
The body's delicate; the tempest in my mind
Doth from my senses take all feeling else
Save what beats there. Filial ingratitude!
Is it not as this mouth should tear this hand
For lifting food to't? But I will punish home.

> **'laid knives … shadow for a traitor.'**
>
> These are all ways the 'foul fiend' seeks
> to tempt Tom to commit suicide and thus
> damn himself: by stabbing, hanging, or
> poison. A 'four-inched bridge' is too narrow
> to be ridden over safely, so crossing one
> on a horse might be suicidal. To 'course his
> own shadow for a traitor' is to hunt it as
> Edgar has been hunted – for treachery.

No, I will weep no more. In such a night
To shut me out! Pour on; I will endure.
In such a night as this! O Regan, Goneril!
Your old kind father, whose frank heart gave all –
O, that way madness lies; let me shun that;
No more of that.

KENT   Good my lord, enter here.

LEAR Prithee, go in thyself; seek thine own ease.
This tempest will not give me leave to ponder
On things would hurt me more. But I'll go in.
[*To the* FOOL] In, boy; go first. You houseless
  poverty –
Nay, get thee in. I'll pray, and then I'll sleep. [*Exit*
  FOOL]
Poor naked wretches, whereso'er you are,
That bide the pelting of this pitiless storm,
How shall your houseless heads and unfed sides,

Your looped and windowed raggedness, defend you
From seasons such as these? O, I have ta'en
Too little care of this! Take physic, pomp:
Expose thyself to feel what wretches feel,
That thou mayst shake the superflux to them,
And show the heavens more just.

EDGAR [*Within*] Fathom and half, fathom and
  half! Poor Tom!

[*Enter* FOOL *from hovel*]

FOOL Come not in here, nuncle, here's a spirit.
Help me, help me!

KENT   Give me thy hand. Who's there?

FOOL A spirit, a spirit! He says his name's poor Tom.

KENT What art thou that dost grumble there i' the
  straw?
Come forth.

[*Enter* EDGAR *disguised as a madman*]

EDGAR   Away! The foul fiend follows me!
Through the sharp hawthorn blows the cold wind.
Humh! Go to thy cold bed, and warm thee.

LEAR Didst thou give all to thy daughters? And art
  thou come to this?

EDGAR Who gives anything to poor Tom? Whom
the foul fiend hath led through fire and through
flame, through ford and whirlpool, o'er bog and
quagmire; that hath laid knives under his pillow
and halters in his pew; set ratsbane by his porridge;
made him proud of heart, to ride on a bay trotting-
horse over four-inched bridges, to course his own
shadow for a traitor. Bless thy five wits! Tom's a-
cold. O, do de, do de, do de. Bless thee from
whirlwinds, star-blasting, and taking! Do poor Tom
some charity, whom the foul fiend vexes. There
could I have him now – and there – and there again
– and there. [*Storm still*]

LEAR What, has his daughters brought him to this
  pass?
Couldst thou save nothing? Didst thou give them all?

FOOL Nay, he reserved a blanket, else we had been
  all shamed.

LEAR Now, all the plagues that in the pendulous air
Hang fated o'er men's faults light on thy daughters!

KENT He hath no daughters, sir.

LEAR Death, traitor! Nothing could have subdued
  nature
To such a lowness but his unkind daughters.

Is it the fashion that discarded fathers
Should have thus little mercy on their flesh?
Judicious punishment! 'Twas this flesh begot
Those pelican daughters.

EDGAR Pillicock sat on Pillicock-hill.
Halloo, halloo, loo, loo!

FOOL This cold night will turn us all to fools and
madmen.

EDGAR Take heed o' the foul fiend; obey thy
parents; keep thy word justly; swear not; commit
not with man's sworn spouse; set not thy sweet
heart on proud array. Tom's a-cold.

LEAR What hast thou been?

EDGAR A serving-man, proud in heart and mind;
that curled my hair; wore gloves in my cap; served
the lust of my mistress' heart, and did the act of
darkness with her; swore as many oaths as I spake
words, and broke them in the sweet face of heaven;
one that slept in the contriving of lust, and waked
to do it. Wine loved I deeply, dice dearly, and in
woman out-paramoured the Turk. False of heart,
light of ear, bloody of hand; hog in sloth, fox in
stealth, wolf in greediness, dog in madness, lion in
prey. Let not the creaking of shoes nor the rustling
of silks betray thy poor heart to woman. Keep thy
foot out of brothels, thy hand out of plackets, thy
pen from lenders' books, and defy the foul fiend.
Still through the hawthorn blows the cold wind:
    says suum, mun, nonny. Dolphin my boy, my boy,
    sessa! Let him trot by. [*Storm still*]

LEAR Why, thou wert better in thy grave than to
answer with thy uncovered body this extremity of the
skies. Is man no more than this? Consider him well.
Thou owest the worm no silk, the beast no hide, the
sheep no wool, the cat no perfume. Ha! Here's three
on's are sophisticated! Thou art the thing itself:
unaccommodated man is no more but such a poor,
bare, forked animal as thou art. Off, off, you lendings!
[*Tearing off his clothes*] Come, unbutton here.

FOOL Prithee, nuncle, be contented; 'tis a naughty
night to swim in. Now a little fire in a wild field
were like an old lecher's heart; a small spark, all the
rest on's body cold. Look, here comes a walking fire.

[*Enter* **GLOUCESTER** *with a torch*]

EDGAR This is the foul fiend Flibbertigibbet. He
begins at curfew, and walks till the first cock; he
gives the web and the pin, squinies the eye, and
makes the hare-lip; mildews the white wheat, and
hurts the poor creature of earth.

Swithold footed thrice the 'old;
He met the night-mare and her nine-fold;
    Bid her alight,
    And her troth plight,
And aroint thee, witch, aroint thee!

KENT How fares your grace?

LEAR What's he?

KENT Who's there? What is't you seek?

GLOUCESTER What are you there? Your names?

EDGAR Poor Tom; that eats the swimming frog,
the toad, the tadpole, the wall-newt and the water;
that in the fury of his heart, when the foul fiend
rages, eats cow-dung for sallets, swallows the old

> **'wore gloves in my cap
> … and defy the foul fiend.'**
>
> As a serving-man, Tom wore the gloves of his
> many mistresses in his cap to honour them –
> and had more women than the Turkish sultan
> had in his harem. He was hungry for gossip
> ('light of ear'), fashionable ('creaking shoes'
> were a modish affectation) and sex-mad
> ('foot' puns 'foutre', vulgar French for 'make
> love' and 'plackets' were slits in petticoats).

rat and the ditch-dog, drinks the green mantle of
the standing pool; who is whipped from tithing
to tithing, and stock-punished, and imprisoned;
who hath had three suits to his back, six shirts to
his body –
    Horse to ride, and weapon to wear;
    But mice and rats, and such small deer,
    Have been Tom's food for seven long year.
Beware my follower. Peace, Smulkin; peace, thou fiend!

GLOUCESTER What, hath your grace no better
company?

EDGAR The prince of darkness is a gentleman:
Modo he's called, and Mahu.

GLOUCESTER Our flesh and blood is grown so
vile, my lord,
That it doth hate what gets it.

EDGAR Poor Tom's a-cold.

GLOUCESTER Go in with me. My duty cannot suffer
To obey in all your daughters' hard commands.
Though their injunction be to bar my doors,
And let this tyrannous night take hold upon you,
Yet have I ventured to come seek you out,
And bring you where both fire and food is ready.

Macbeth *c.1606*

| ACT **1** | SCENE **7** |
| ACT **2** | SCENE **1** |

**❛Is this a dagger which I see before me,
The handle toward my hand?❜**

Written, scholars think, in the wake of the Gunpowder Plot – an attempt to assassinate King James I by blowing up Parliament – this tragedy plays on a number of James's fears: of witchcraft, of traitors who fail to recognize the divine right of kings, of the reasoning that leads to the overthrow of governments.

Two events spark off the killing spree that carries Macbeth to the throne of Scotland: a meeting with three witches for whom evil is good and good evil, and whose location in the order of things is so ambiguous that it's not even clear if they are male or female; and the praise he receives for killing a rebel. The witches make him think that he could be king instead of Duncan, regardless of moral objections; and his success as a soldier makes him think he can win still greater success by further killings. But the remarkable thing about Macbeth is not that he persuades himself these things are true, but that he *never* believes he has any right to murder Duncan and take his place. He embarks on his bloody career in full awareness that there is no justification for it, spurred on by the intensity with which he can imagine the whole process of getting power – and of being destroyed by it.

His awareness of the implications of his actions is nowhere clearer than in our first extract. At the beginning he urges himself to act quickly, as if speed can 'trammel up' the consequences of regicide like someone chasing after an unravelling ball of wool. He wishes he could leap across the intervening time between this moment, when he is contemplating the future, and the thing he desires: to be safely on the throne with Duncan dead. But he knows that killing Duncan will give 'bloody instructions' to other men, teaching them that assassination is an acceptable way to advance yourself and rendering Macbeth's future reign unstable. The speech ends with an apocalyptic vision of the murder giving birth to later events: the sudden appearance of 'pity, like a naked new-born babe', which will marshal the old king's allies against him, or of heaven's avenging cherubim, often pictured as infants in Renaissance paintings. Duncan's death will establish, not a new royal line founded by Macbeth, but an army of innocent imaginary children out to punish his guilt.

Sure enough, Macbeth's tyranny is most shockingly visited on children. After killing Duncan he kills Banquo – ancestor of James I – because the witches predicted he would found a royal dynasty. Next he intends to murder Banquo's young son Fleance, who escapes only just in time. Instead Macbeth kills the children of Macduff, who has fled to join Duncan's son Malcolm in England. In all this, Macbeth is taking literally the advice of his fearsome wife, Lady Macbeth, in our extract: that if he is truly ambitious, and man enough to show it, he should be willing to do something as dreadful as dash his own baby's brains out. Her words inaugurate her husband's new career, which is founded on the need to assassinate both real and imagined children. There has never been a more terrible representation than this of the perverse unreason of tyranny.

OPPOSITE Ian McKellen in the title role of Macbeth in the Royal Shakespeare Company's 1978 production.

[*Enter* MACBETH]

MACBETH If it were done when 'tis done, then
  'twere well
It were done quickly. If th' assassination
Could trammel up the consequence, and catch,
With his surcease, success; that but this blow
Might be the be-all and the end-all here –
But here, upon this bank and shoal of time –
We'd jump the life to come. But in these cases
We still have judgment here, that we but teach
Bloody instructions, which being taught return
To plague th' inventor. This even-handed justice
Commends th' ingredients of our poisoned chalice
To our own lips. He's here in double trust:
First, as I am his kinsman and his subject –
Strong both against the deed; then, as his host,
Who should against his murderer shut the door,
Not bear the knife myself. Besides, this Duncan
Hath borne his faculties so meek, hath been
So clear in his great office, that his virtues
Will plead like angels, trumpet-tongued, against
The deep damnation of his taking-off;
And pity, like a naked new-born babe,
Striding the blast, or heaven's cherubim, horsed
Upon the sightless couriers of the air,
Shall blow the horrid deed in every eye,
That tears shall drown the wind. I have no spur
To prick the sides of my intent, but only
Vaulting ambition, which o'erleaps itself
And falls on th' other.
[*Enter* LADY MACBETH]
                    How now! What news?

LADY MACBETH He has almost supped. Why have
  you left the chamber?

MACBETH Hath he asked for me?

LADY MACBETH   Know you not he has?

MACBETH We will proceed no further in this business.
He hath honoured me of late; and I have bought
Golden opinions from all sorts of people,
Which would be worn now in their newest gloss,
Not cast aside so soon.

LADY MACBETH   Was the hope drunk
Wherein you dressed yourself? Hath it slept since,
And wakes it now to look so green and pale
At what it did so freely? From this time
Such I account thy love. Art thou afeard
To be the same in thine own act and valour
As thou art in desire? Wouldst thou have that
Which thou esteem'st the ornament of life,
And live a coward in thine own esteem,
Letting 'I dare not' wait upon 'I would',
Like the poor cat i' th' adage?

> ***'If th' assassination …
> jump the life to come.'***
>
> **The images here are from fishing. If only,
> Macbeth thinks, we could assassinate
> Duncan and catch all the effects of the
> assassination as if in a 'trammel', or net –
> thus obtaining success at the moment of his
> ending ('surcease'). The 'bank and shoal of
> time' is the sandbar where Macbeth is doing
> his fishing – for a crown rather than a fish.**

MACBETH   Prithee, peace.
I dare do all that may become a man;
Who dares do more is none.

LADY MACBETH   What beast was't then
That made you break this enterprise to me?
When you durst do it, then you were a man;
And, to be more than what you were, you would
Be so much more the man. Nor time nor place
Did then adhere, and yet you would make both.
They have made themselves, and that their fitness now
Does unmake you. I have given suck, and know
How tender 'tis to love the babe that milks me.
I would, while it was smiling in my face,
Have plucked my nipple from his boneless gums
And dashed the brains out, had I so sworn
As you have done to this.

MACBETH   If we should fail?

LADY MACBETH   We fail!
But screw your courage to the sticking-place
And we'll not fail. When Duncan is asleep –
Whereto the rather shall his day's hard journey
Soundly invite him – his two chamberlains
Will I with wine and wassail so convince
That memory, the warder of the brain,
Shall be a fume, and the receipt of reason
A limbeck only. When in swinish sleep
Their drenchèd natures lie as in a death,
What cannot you and I perform upon
The unguarded Duncan? What not put upon
His spongy officers, who shall bear the guilt
Of our great quell?

MACBETH   Bring forth men-children only,
For thy undaunted mettle should compose
Nothing but males. Will it not be received,
When we have marked with blood those sleepy two
Of his own chamber, and used their very daggers,
That they have done't?

LADY MACBETH   Who dares receive it other,
As we shall make our griefs and clamour roar
Upon his death?

MACBETH   I am settled, and bend up
Each corporal agent to this terrible feat.
Away, and mock the time with fairest show.
False face must hide what the false heart doth
    know. [*Exeunt*]

ACT 2 | SCENE 1

Court of Macbeth's castle

[*Enter* BANQUO, *and* FLEANCE *bearing a torch
    before him*]

BANQUO How goes the night, boy?

FLEANCE The moon is down; I have not heard the
    clock.

BANQUO And she goes down at twelve.

FLEANCE   I take't, 'tis later, sir.

BANQUO Hold, take my sword. There's husbandry
    in heaven;
Their candles are all out. Take thee that too.
A heavy summons lies like lead upon me,
And yet I would not sleep. Merciful powers,
Restrain in me the cursèd thoughts that nature
Gives way to in repose!
[*Enter* MACBETH, *and a Servant with a torch*]
                    Give me my sword. Who's there?

MACBETH A friend.

BANQUO What, sir, not yet at rest? The King's a-bed.
He hath been in unusual pleasure, and
Sent forth great largess to your offices.
This diamond he greets your wife withal
By the name of most kind hostess, and shut up
In measureless content.

> **'Witchcraft celebrates … like a ghost.'**
>
> **'Hecate' is the Greek goddess of the moon,
> patroness of witchcraft and recipient of
> witches' sacrifices ('offerings'). At this time of
> night, Macbeth imagines, murder is 'alarumed'
> or roused by the wolf's 'watch' or watchword,
> and stalks towards its objective ('design') with
> the strides of Tarquin, the Roman prince who
> ravished Lucretia.**

MACBETH   Being unprepared,
Our will became the servant to defect,
Which else should free have wrought.

BANQUO   All's well.
I dreamt last night of the three weird sisters.
To you they have showed some truth.

MACBETH   I think not of them;
Yet, when we can entreat an hour to serve,

We would spend it in some words upon that
    business,
If you would grant the time.

BANQUO   At your kind'st leisure.

MACBETH If you shall cleave to my consent, when 'tis,
It shall make honour for you.

BANQUO   So I lose none
In seeking to augment it, but still keep
My bosom franchised and allegiance clear,
I shall be counselled.

MACBETH   Good repose the while!

BANQUO Thanks, sir. The like to you.

[*Exeunt* BANQUO *and* FLEANCE]

MACBETH Go bid thy mistress, when my
    drink is ready,
She strike upon the bell. Get thee to bed.
[*Exit Servant*]
 Is this a dagger which I see before me,
The handle toward my hand? Come, let me
    clutch thee.
I have thee not, and yet I see thee still.
Art thou not, fatal vision, sensible
To feeling as to sight? Or art thou but
A dagger of the mind, a false creation
Proceeding from the heat-oppressèd brain?
I see thee yet, in form as palpable
As this which now I draw.
Thou marshall'st me the way that I was going;
And such an instrument I was to use.
Mine eyes are made the fools o' th' other senses,
Or else worth all the rest. I see thee still,
And on thy blade and dudgeon gouts of blood,
Which was not so before. There's no such thing;
It is the bloody business which informs
Thus to mine eyes. Now o'er the one half-world
Nature seems dead, and wicked dreams abuse
The curtained sleep. Witchcraft celebrates
Pale Hecate's offerings, and withered murder,
Alarumed by his sentinel the wolf,
Whose howl's his watch, thus with his stealthy pace,
With Tarquin's ravishing strides, towards his design
Moves like a ghost. Thou sure and firm-set earth,
Hear not my steps which way they walk, for fear
Thy very stones prate of my whereabout
And take the present horror from the time,
Which now suits with it. Whiles I threat, he lives.
Words to the heat of deeds too cold breath gives.
[*A bell rings*]
I go, and it is done. The bell invites me.
Hear it not, Duncan, for it is a knell
That summons thee to heaven or to hell.
[*Exit*]

Macbeth *c.1606*

ACT **3** | SCENE **4**

❝ **Thou canst not say I did it. Never shake
Thy gory locks at me.** ❞

In our previous extract, Macbeth saw a 'dagger of the mind' and made it real by drawing his own dagger, which he later used to murder Duncan. In this tragedy the imagination makes things happen, and Macbeth's is the most active in Scotland, rendering solid first the prophecies of the witches, then the airy dagger and finally his expectations that he will be destroyed by violence, no matter how he struggles to avert this. If Shakespeare's medium is the imagination, Macbeth's knife represents its terrible potency.

But the weapon also raises questions of responsibility. One of the debating points of the play is: who's to blame for its atrocities? Macbeth, the witches, fate, Lady Macbeth? The dagger makes these questions irrelevant. We don't know if it's a vision or an hallucination – a symptom of the pressure Macbeth exerts on his mind by contemplating regicide. It points the way he's already going, he says; so it does not affect his actions. Unlike Hamlet, Macbeth has no motive or cue for killing; yet he kills. And in doing so he makes nonsense of our limited understanding of the relationship between causes and effects.

If Macbeth's killings cannot be explained, their consequences too must be beyond explanation. Our next scene takes place after Banquo's assassination, which was ordered by Macbeth so as to forestall part of the witches' prophecy in Act 1: that the crown he wins will pass to Banquo's descendants. This second assassination violates the laws of friendship, just as Duncan's broke the laws of obligation between subject and monarch, host and guest (he was staying at Macbeth's castle when he died). But after Banquo's death, Macbeth goes on to act the part of royal host as if it still had some meaning. He invites his lords to supper, and claims to miss his friend when he doesn't turn up. The gulf between this dignified performance and his secret law-breaking leads to the disintegration of yet further laws: that dead men stay buried, for example. Banquo's ghost arrives during the meal and sits on the stool reserved for Macbeth; and a murderer comes too, with the news that Banquo's son Fleance has escaped his clutches. As he contemplates these two unwelcome presences – those of the ghost and Fleance – Macbeth begins to understand that he is losing his control over the effects of his regicide – its children, as it were – and that nothing he can do will recover it.

Yet he strives to maintain the *appearance* of control – just as Lady Macbeth still strives to control her husband by appealing to his masculinity. His strangest effort to stay in charge comes when he tells the ghost, 'Thou canst not say I did it'. This is literally true, since Macbeth only *ordered* Banquo's murder – he did not commit it; yet it seems absurd to try to pull the wool over the eyes of a vengeful spirit. So we are wryly amused when Macbeth begins to reminisce about the happy days when corpses *stayed* dead and refrained from stealing other people's stools at dinnertime. Those days ended when Macbeth allowed himself to think that living people might reasonably be made into corpses, and that law-breaking might get him total command of the law.

OPPOSITE *The Ghost of Banquo* – 19th-century painting by Théodore Chassériau.

[*Enter* MACBETH, LADY MACBETH, ROSS,
LENNOX, LORDS, *and Attendants*]

MACBETH You know your own degrees; sit down.
   At first
And last the hearty welcome.

> ### 'My royal lord … to meat is ceremony'
>
> Lady Macbeth waxes obscure as she berates
> her husband. Macbeth, she says, does not
> welcome his guests ('give the cheer'), which
> is essential, since those guests might as
> well have paid for the feast if they are not
> repeatedly assured of their welcome. Mere
> eating ('To feed') can be done at home; but
> when dining out ('From thence') one desires
> ceremony with one's meals.

LORDS   Thanks to your majesty.

MACBETH Ourself will mingle with society
And play the humble host.
Our hostess keeps her state, but in best time
We will require her welcome.

LADY MACBETH Pronounce it for me, sir, to all
   our friends,
For my heart speaks they are welcome.

[FIRST MURDERER *appears at the door*]

MACBETH See, they encounter thee with their
   hearts' thanks.
Both sides are even. Here I'll sit i' th' midst.
Be large in mirth; anon we'll drink a measure
The table round. [*Aside to* MURDERER]
There's blood upon thy face.

FIRST MURDERER [*Aside*] 'Tis Banquo's then.

MACBETH [*Aside*] 'Tis better thee without than
   he within.
Is he dispatched?

FIRST MURDERER [*Aside*] My lord, his throat is cut;
That I did for him.

MACBETH [*Aside*] Thou art the best o' th' cut-throats.
Yet he's good that did the like for Fleance.
If thou didst it, thou art the nonpareil.

FIRST MURDERER [*Aside*] Most royal sir –
   Fleance is scaped.

MACBETH [*Aside*] Then comes my fit again. I had
   else been perfect,
Whole as the marble, founded as the rock,
As broad and general as the casing air,
But now I am cabined, cribbed, confined, bound in
To saucy doubts and fears. But Banquo's safe?

FIRST MURDERER [*Aside*] Ay, my good lord. Safe
   in a ditch he bides,
With twenty trenchèd gashes on his head,

The least a death to nature.

MACBETH [*Aside*]   Thanks for that.
There the grown serpent lies; the worm that's fled
Hath nature that in time will venom breed,
No teeth for th' present. Get thee gone. Tomorrow
We'll hear, ourselves, again. [*Exit* FIRST
MURDERER]

LADY MACBETH   My royal lord,
You do not give the cheer. The feast is sold
That is not often vouched, while 'tis a-making,
'Tis given with welcome. To feed were best at home.
From thence the sauce to meat is ceremony;
Meeting were bare without it.

[*Enter the* GHOST OF BANQUO *and sits in*
   MACBETH's *place*]

MACBETH   Sweet remembrancer!
Now good digestion wait on appetite,
And health on both!

LENNOX   May't please your highness sit?

MACBETH Here had we now our country's honour
   roofed
Were the graced person of our Banquo present,
Who may I rather challenge for unkindness
Than pity for mischance.

ROSS   His absence, sir,
Lays blame upon his promise. Please't your
   highness
To grace us with your royal company?

MACBETH The table's full.

LENNOX   Here is a place reserved, sir.

MACBETH Where?

LENNOX   Here, my good lord.
What is't that moves your Highness?

MACBETH Which of you have done this?

LORDS   What, my good lord?

MACBETH Thou canst not say I did it. Never shake
Thy gory locks at me.

ROSS Gentlemen, rise. His Highness is not well.

LADY MACBETH Sit, worthy friends. My lord is
   often thus,
And hath been from his youth. Pray you, keep seat.
The fit is momentary; upon a thought
He will again be well. If much you note him
You shall offend him and extend his passion.
Feed, and regard him not. [*Aside to* MACBETH] Are
   you a man?

MACBETH [*Aside*] Ay, and a bold one that dare
   look on that
Which might appal the devil.

LADY MACBETH [*Aside*]   O proper stuff!

This is the very painting of your fear:
This is the air-drawn dagger which you said
Led you to Duncan. O, these flaws and starts,
Impostors to true fear, would well become
A woman's story at a winter's fire,
Authorized by her grandam. Shame itself!
Why do you make such faces? When all's done,
You look but on a stool.

MACBETH [*Aside*] Prithee see there. Behold! Look!
    Lo! How say you?

Why, what care I? [*To* GHOST] If thou canst nod,
    speak too.

If charnel-houses and our graves must send
Those that we bury back, our monuments
Shall be the maws of kites. [*Exit* GHOST]

LADY MACBETH [*Aside*] What, quite unmanned
    in folly?

MACBETH [*Aside*] If I stand here, I saw him.

LADY MACBETH [*Aside*]   Fie, for shame!

MACBETH [*Aside*] Blood hath been shed ere now, i'
    th' olden time,

Ere human statute purged the gentle weal;
Ay, and since too, murders have been performed
Too terrible for the ear. The times have been
That, when the brains were out, the man would die,
And there an end; but now they rise again,
With twenty mortal murders on their crowns,
And push us from our stools. This is more strange
Than such a murder is.

LADY MACBETH [*Aside*] My worthy lord,
Your noble friends do lack you.

MACBETH [*Aside*]   I do forget.
[*Aloud*] Do not muse at me, my most worthy friends.
I have a strange infirmity, which is nothing
To those that know me. Come, love and health to all;
Then I'll sit down. Give me some wine, fill full.
[*Re-enter* GHOST]
I drink to th' general joy o' the whole table,
And to our dear friend Banquo, whom we miss.
Would he were here! To all, and him, we thirst,
And all to all.

'Augurs and understood … secret'st man of blood.'

'Augurs' are auguries – prophecies acquired through the study of signs. 'Understood relations' are relationships between cause and effect that were once hidden, but are now revealed. Magpies, choughs and rooks were traditionally sacrificed by augurers. A 'man of blood' is a man with blood on his hands – a murderer.

LORDS   Our duties, and the pledge.

MACBETH [*To* GHOST]
Avaunt, and quit my sight! Let the earth hide thee!
Thy bones are marrowless, thy blood is cold;
Thou hast no speculation in those eyes
Which thou dost glare with!

LADY MACBETH [*To Lords*]
                    Think of this, good peers,
But as a thing of custom. 'Tis no other;
Only it spoils the pleasure of the time.

MACBETH [*To* GHOST] What man dare, I dare.
Approach thou like the rugged Russian bear,
The armed rhinoceros, or th' Hyrcan tiger;
Take any shape but that, and my firm nerves
Shall never tremble. Or be alive again,
And dare me to the desert with thy sword;
If trembling I inhabit then, protest me
The baby of a girl. Hence, horrible shadow!
Unreal mock'ry, hence! [*Exit* GHOST] Why so,
    being gone,
I am a man again. Pray you, sit still.

LADY MACBETH You have displaced the mirth,
    broke the good meeting
With most admired disorder.

MACBETH   Can such things be,
And overcome us like a summer's cloud,
Without our special wonder? You make me strange
Even to the disposition that I owe,
When now I think you can behold such sights
And keep the natural ruby of your cheeks
When mine is blanched with fear.

ROSS   What sights, my lord?

LADY MACBETH I pray you speak not. He grows
    worse and worse;
Question enrages him. At once, good night.
Stand not upon the order of your going,
But go at once.

LENNOX   Good night; and better health
Attend his Majesty!

LADY MACBETH   A kind good night to all!

[*Exeunt all but* MACBETH *and* LADY MACBETH]

MACBETH It will have blood, they say. Blood will
    have blood.
Stones have been known to move, and trees to speak;
Augurs and understood relations have
By maggot-pies and choughs and rooks brought forth
The secret'st man of blood. What is the night?

LADY MACBETH Almost at odds with morning,
    which is which.

Antony and Cleopatra

c.1606-7

ACT **2** | SCENE **2**

❝Age cannot wither her, nor custom stale
Her infinite variety.❞

This tragedy is Shakespeare's great celebration of older lovers. In *Julius Caesar* he gave his audience a young, astute Antony, who constructed a posthumous image of the assassinated leader so powerful it sustained him and Octavius in their defeat of Caesar's assassins. But now all Antony's achievements are behind him, and his efforts to build up his own image are riddled with inconsistencies.

He brags about his military triumphs, but his lieutenant tells us: 'Caesar and Antony have ever won / More in their officer than person' – that is, they depend on their subordinates to win their battles for them. And despite Antony's pretensions to heroism, he follows the fleeing Cleopatra from the battlefield at Actium 'like a doting mallard', and later botches his suicide attempt, thus shaming himself in the eyes of his fellow Romans. He may once have 'glowed like plated Mars', but in middle age cracks have appeared in his persona.

He is not, however, alone in his inconsistency; the condition is universal in the ancient world as it stumbles towards civil war. Octavius Caesar, Antony's colleague in the uneasy triumvirate that rules the Roman Empire, considers himself a model of Roman virtues, especially those of reason, order, manliness and constancy. But he too is deeply inconstant, like his namesake Julius: breaking his promise to the young rebel Pompey, betraying Lepidus (the third member of the triumvirate), and encouraging dozens of traitors to desert from Antony's army, then placing them in the vanguard of his own to be hacked down by their former comrades as punishment for their treachery. Caesar despises Cleopatra for her slipperiness, but he is equally slippery, and in Act 3 he tries to turn her, too, against Antony, assuming that she is as faithless as he is. As the Emperor Augustus, Octavius later presided over the Golden Age of Roman culture; but, if it took its tone from him, Shakespeare implies that this culture may not have been wholly admirable.

Cleopatra's inconstancy is what makes her great. As Antony's friend Enobarbus says in our extract, variety is her element, time her plaything, and conventions irrelevant to her: 'Age cannot wither her, nor custom stale / Her infinite variety.' The scene begins with the Romans planning a marriage of convenience, where emotion will be subservient to political expediency. Antony is to marry a woman of 'general graces', Caesar's sister Octavia, in the interest of consolidating the shaky alliance between them; and Antony bluntly describes the match as 'business'. Enobarbus knows full well such a marriage cannot compete against Cleopatra's dazzling charms – and that its collapse will trigger the inevitable war between Caesar and Antony. He shows how inevitable this is in one of the most dazzling speeches Shakespeare wrote, where Cleopatra floats down the river Cydnus in a barge whose very rigging seems aroused at her presence, whose sailors are women and boys, and whose oars and sails contaminate the elements with passion. Cleopatra is never described: she has the pervasive presence of the 'strange invisible perfume' that emanates from her, and anyone can imagine her as they please. Cleopatra's Egypt may be part of the Roman empire, and she herself may be past her prime, but she represents all that the empire cannot circumscribe and which the Romans therefore long to crush: above all, the ever-changing shapes of desire.

OPPOSITE An 1883 painting by Sir Lawrence Alma-Tadema depicting Enobarbus's description of Cleopatra on her barge.

A house in Rome

[*Enter* MARK ANTONY, OCTAVIUS CAESAR, LEPIDUS, MAECENAS, AGRIPPA, *and* ENOBARBUS]

AGRIPPA Give me leave, Caesar.

CAESAR Speak, Agrippa.

AGRIPPA Thou hast a sister by the mother's side,
Admired Octavia. Great Mark Antony
Is now a widower.

CAESAR   Say not so, Agrippa.
If Cleopatra heard you, your reproof
Were well deserved of rashness.

ANTONY I am not married, Caesar. Let me hear
Agrippa further speak.

AGRIPPA To hold you in perpetual amity,
To make you brothers, and to knit your hearts
With an unslipping knot, take Antony
Octavia to his wife; whose beauty claims
No worse a husband than the best of men;
Whose virtue and whose general graces speak
That which none else can utter. By this marriage
All little jealousies which now seem great,
And all great fears which now import their dangers,
Would then be nothing. Truths would be tales
Where now half-tales be truths. Her love to both
Would each to other and all loves to both
Draw after her. Pardon what I have spoke,
For 'tis a studied, not a present thought,
By duty ruminated.

ANTONY   Will Caesar speak?

CAESAR Not till he hears how Antony is touched
With what is spoke already.

ANTONY What power is in Agrippa,
If I would say, 'Agrippa, be it so',
To make this good?

CAESAR   The power of Caesar, and
His power unto Octavia.

ANTONY   May I never
To this good purpose, that so fairly shows,
Dream of impediment! Let me have thy hand.
Further this act of grace, and from this hour
The heart of brothers govern in our loves
And sway our great designs.

CAESAR   There is my hand.
A sister I bequeath you whom no brother
Did ever love so dearly. Let her live
To join our kingdoms and our hearts; and never
Fly off our loves again.

LEPIDUS   Happily, amen.

ANTONY I did not think to draw my sword 'gainst Pompey;
For he hath laid strange courtesies and great
Of late upon me. I must thank him only,
Lest my remembrance suffer ill report;
At heel of that, defy him.

LEPIDUS   Time calls upon's.
Of us must Pompey presently be sought,
Or else he seeks out us.

ANTONY   Where lies he?

CAESAR About the Mount Misena.

ANTONY   What is his strength
By land?

> **'Whose virtue … none else can utter.'**
>
> **Whose virtue and graces speak for themselves. A few lines later, 'Truths would be tales / Where now half-tales be truths' is a wonderfully convoluted utterance, meaning something like: unwelcome truths would be taken as fabrications ('tales'), whereas at present vicious rumours are taken as truths. This hardly makes it sound as if the marriage will improve the situation.**

CAESAR   Great and increasing, but by sea
He is an absolute master.

ANTONY   So is the fame.
Would we had spoke together. Haste we for it.
Yet ere we put ourselves in arms, dispatch we
The business we have talked of.

CAESAR   With most gladness,
And do invite you to my sister's view,
Whither straight I'll lead you.

> **'May I never … Dream of impediment!'**
>
> **These lines refer to the Anglican marriage service, where the priest asks if anyone knows of any cause or just impediment to prevent the joining of the couple in holy matrimony. Antony's reference to dreaming might make us doubt his words, since Cleopatra is more attuned to dreams than Octavia. 'So fairly shows' means 'looks so attractive' – which also makes the marriage seem superficial and temporary.**

ANTONY   Let us, Lepidus,
Not lack your company.

LEPIDUS   Noble Antony,
Not sickness should detain me.

[*Exeunt* OCTAVIUS CAESAR, MARK ANTONY, *and* LEPIDUS]

MAECENAS [*To* ENOBARBUS] Welcome from Egypt, sir.

ENOBARBUS Half the heart of Caesar, worthy Maecenas! My honourable friend, Agrippa!

AGRIPPA Good Enobarbus!

MAECENAS We have cause to be glad that matters are so well digested. You stayed well by't in Egypt.

ENOBARBUS Ay, sir; we did sleep day out of countenance, and made the night light with drinking.

MAECENAS Eight wild boars roasted whole at a breakfast, and but twelve persons there – is this true?

ENOBARBUS This was but as a fly by an eagle. We had much more monstrous matter of feast, which worthily deserved noting.

MAECENAS She's a most triumphant lady, if report be square to her.

ENOBARBUS When she first met Mark Antony, she pursed up his heart upon the river of Cydnus.

AGRIPPA There she appeared indeed, or my reporter devised well for her.

ENOBARBUS I will tell you.
The barge she sat in, like a burnished throne,
Burned on the water. The poop was beaten gold;
Purple the sails, and so perfumèd that
The winds were love-sick with them. The oars were
    silver,
Which to the tune of flutes kept stroke, and made
The water which they beat to follow faster,
As amorous of their strokes. For her own person,
It beggared all description. She did lie
In her pavilion – cloth-of-gold, of tissue –
O'er-picturing that Venus where we see
The fancy outwork nature. On each side her
Stood pretty dimpled boys, like smiling Cupids,
With divers-coloured fans, whose wind did seem
To glow the delicate cheeks which they did cool,
And what they undid did.

AGRIPPA   O rare for Antony!

ENOBARBUS Her gentlewomen, like the Nereides,
So many mermaids, tended her i' th' eyes,
And made their bends adornings. At the helm
A seeming mermaid steers. The silken tackle
Swell with the touches of those flower-soft hands
That yarely frame the office. From the barge

A strange invisible perfume hits the sense
Of the adjacent wharfs. The city cast
Her people out upon her; and Antony,
Enthroned i' th' market-place, did sit alone,
Whistling to th' air; which, but for vacancy,
Had gone to gaze on Cleopatra too,
And made a gap in nature.

AGRIPPA   Rare Egyptian!

ENOBARBUS Upon her landing, Antony sent
    to her,
Invited her to supper. She replied
It should be better he became her guest,
Which she entreated. Our courteous Antony,
Whom ne'er the word of 'No' woman heard speak,
Being barbered ten times o'er, goes to the feast,
And for his ordinary pays his heart
For what his eyes eat only.

AGRIPPA   Royal wench!
She made great Caesar lay his sword to bed.
He ploughed her, and she cropped.

ENOBARBUS   I saw her once
Hop forty paces through the public street;
And having lost her breath, she spoke and panted,
That she did make defect perfection,
And, breathless, pow'r breathe forth.

*The barge she sat in,
like a burnished throne,
Burned on the water.*

MAECENAS   Now Antony
Must leave her utterly.

ENOBARBUS   Never. He will not.
Age cannot wither her, nor custom stale
Her infinite variety. Other women cloy
The appetites they feed, but she makes hungry
Where most she satisfies; for vilest things
Become themselves in her, that the holy priests
Bless her when she is riggish.

MAECENAS If beauty, wisdom, modesty, can settle
The heart of Antony, Octavia is
A blessèd lottery to him.

AGRIPPA   Let us go.
Good Enobarbus, make yourself my guest
Whilst you abide here.

ENOBARBUS   Humbly, sir, I thank you. [*Exeunt*]

Antony and Cleopatra

c.1606-7

> Give me my robe, put on my crown; I have Immortal longings in me.

When Cleopatra dies, she does it 'after the high Roman fashion' – by committing suicide like her lover Antony – and declares that in her resolution she has 'nothing / Of woman in me'. She has been practising for this moment throughout the play. The queen of Egypt has never had any patience for the crude gender distinctions the Romans favour, where men are tough enough to drink horse-piss (as Caesar says of Antony), while women, like Octavia, stay rigidly faithful to their menfolk.

Cleopatra likes to dress Antony in her clothes while she wears his 'sword Philippan' – the sword with which he defeated Brutus in *Julius Caesar*. When she decides to join him in battle she plans to 'Appear there for a man', and when she flees she takes his 'manhood' with her (as one of his soldiers rages). Her gender is one of the many areas in which she refuses to be pinned down.

More remarkably, perhaps, she dies many times before her suicide. When Antony announces he is leaving Egypt in Act 1, Enobarbus says this will kill Cleopatra, and adds: 'I have seen her die twenty times upon far poorer moment.' She passes away, he observes, with as much enthusiasm as if death 'commits some loving act on her'. Later, the queen waxes jealous when Antony's first wife Fulvia dies: '*Can* Fulvia die?' she asks incredulously, and then quickly finds sympathy for her: 'Now I see … In Fulvia's death how mine received shall be.' She is, in fact, so keen to know how her death will be received that she stages a dress rehearsal for it in Act 4, when Antony accuses her of betraying him: she promptly flees to her monument, then sends word to him that she has killed herself – which is what drives him to his own botched act of suicide. But death is Cleopatra's territory. After Antony's demise she constructs an image for him more sublime than any he made for Julius Caesar, as a giant whose 'legs bestrid the ocean'. And her own suicide – which occurs in our second extract – is a triumph over Rome, a theatrical alternative to the military victory that Antony could never achieve against Caesar.

She contrives this death scene as competition for the 'triumphs' or victory processions in which Caesar would make her take part if she went with him to Rome. It is designed to outshine the celebrated Roman theatre, where 'Some squeaking Cleopatra' would 'boy' her greatness if she didn't pre-empt this boy's performance with a far greater one. Her suicide – by the erotic bite of a poisonous snake – 'conquers' the 'absurd intents' of her captors; mocks the 'luck' of Caesar, which has been Antony's bane throughout the play; and enables her to 'call great Caesar ass / Unpolicied', since she beats him at his own political game. As it happens, it also suits Caesar's policies very well, since her death augments 'his glory which / Brought [her] to be lamented', thus providing the ideal start to his reign as emperor. But Caesar is moved by the dead Cleopatra into an uncharacteristic moment of poetry: 'she looks', he says, 'As she would catch another Antony / In her strong toil of grace.' So if his imperial reign was famous for verse, we know exactly who to thank.

OPPOSITE Peggy Ashcroft as Cleopatra, with Charmian (Jean Wilson) and Iras (Mary Watson) in the Royal Shakespeare Company's 1953 production.

Egypt – Cleopatra's monument

[*Enter* CLEOPATRA *and* IRAS]

CLEOPATRA Now, Iras, what think'st thou?
Thou, an Egyptian puppet shalt be shown
In Rome, as well as I. Mechanic slaves
With greasy aprons, rules, and hammers, shall
Uplift us to the view. In their thick breaths,
Rank of gross diet, shall be enclouded,
And forced to drink their vapour.

IRAS   The gods forbid!

CLEOPATRA Nay, 'tis most certain, Iras. Saucy lictors
Will catch at us like strumpets; and scald rhymers
Ballad us out o' tune. The quick comedians
Extemporally will stage us, and present
Our Alexandrian revels. Antony
Shall be brought drunken forth, and I shall see
Some squeaking Cleopatra boy my greatness
I' th' posture of a whore.

IRAS   O, the good gods!

CLEOPATRA Nay, that's certain.

IRAS I'll never see 't, for I am sure my nails
Are stronger than mine eyes.

CLEOPATRA   Why, that's the way
To fool their preparation and to conquer
Their most absurd intents.

[*Enter* CHARMIAN]

                         Now, Charmian!
Show me, my women, like a queen. Go fetch
My best attires. I am again for Cydnus,
To meet Mark Antony. Sirrah Iras, go.
Now, noble Charmian, we'll dispatch indeed,
And when thou hast done this chore I'll give thee leave
To play till doomsday. – Bring our crown and all.
[*Exit* IRAS. *A noise within*]
Wherefore's this noise?

[*Enter a* GUARD]

GUARD   Here is a rural fellow
That will not be denied your highness' presence.
He brings you figs.

CLEOPATRA Let him come in. [*Exit* GUARD]
   What poor an instrument
May do a noble deed! He brings me liberty.
My resolution's placed, and I have nothing
Of woman in me. Now from head to foot
I am marble-constant. Now the fleeting moon
No planet is of mine.

[*Re-enter* GUARD, *and* CLOWN *with a basket*]

GUARD   This is the man.

CLEOPATRA Avoid, and leave him. [*Exit* GUARD]
                    Hast thou the pretty worm
Of Nilus there, that kills and pains not?

CLOWN Truly, I have him; but I would not be the
party that should desire you to touch him, for his
biting is immortal. Those that do die of it do seldom
or never recover.

CLEOPATRA Remember'st thou any that have died on't?

CLOWN Very many, men, and women too. I heard of
one of them no longer than yesterday, a very honest
woman, but something given to lie, as a woman
should not do but in the way of honesty; how she died
of the biting of it, what pain she felt – truly, she makes
a very good report o' th' worm; but he that will believe
all that they say shall never be saved by half that they
do. But this is most falliable: the worm's an odd worm.

CLEOPATRA Get thee hence, farewell.

CLOWN I wish you all joy of the worm.

CLEOPATRA Farewell.

CLOWN You must think this, look you, that the worm
  will do his kind.

CLEOPATRA Ay, ay; farewell.

CLOWN Look you, the worm is not to be trusted but
in the keeping of wise people; for indeed there is no
goodness in the worm.

CLEOPATRA Take thou no care; it shall be heeded.

CLOWN Very good. Give it nothing, I pray you, for it
  is not worth the feeding.

CLEOPATRA Will it eat me?

CLOWN You must not think I am so simple but I
know the devil himself will not eat a woman. I know
that a woman is a dish for the gods, if the devil dress
her not. But truly, these same whoreson devils do the
gods great harm in their women; for in every ten that
they make, the devils mar five.

CLEOPATRA Well, get thee gone, farewell.

CLOWN Yes, forsooth. I wish you joy o' th' worm.
[*Exit, leaving the basket*]

[*Re-enter* IRAS *with a robe, crown, and other jewels*]

CLEOPATRA Give me my robe, put on my crown; I have
Immortal longings in me. Now no more
The juice of Egypt's grape shall moist this lip.
Yare, yare, good Iras, quick – methinks I hear
Antony call. I see him rouse himself
To praise my noble act. I hear him mock
The luck of Caesar, which the gods give men
To excuse their after wrath. Husband, I come.
Now to that name my courage prove my title!
I am fire and air; my other elements
I give to baser life. So, have you done?
Come then, and take the last warmth of my lips.
Farewell, kind Charmian. Iras, long farewell.
[*Kisses them.* IRAS *falls and dies*]
Have I the aspic in my lips? Dost fall?

If thou and nature can so gently part,
The stroke of death is as a lover's pinch,
Which hurts and is desired. Dost thou lie still?
If thus thou vanishest, thou tell'st the world
It is not worth leave-taking.

CHARMIAN Dissolve, thick cloud, and rain, that
I may say
The gods themselves do weep.

CLEOPATRA   This proves me base.
If she first meet the curlèd Antony
He'll make demand of her, and spend that kiss
Which is my heaven to have.
[*She takes an aspic from the basket and
puts it to her breast*]
Come, thou mortal wretch,
With thy sharp teeth this knot intrinsicate
Of life at once untie. Poor venomous fool,
Be angry, and dispatch. O, couldst thou speak,
That I might hear thee call great Caesar ass
Unpolicied!

CHARMIAN O eastern star!

CLEOPATRA   Peace, peace.
Dost thou not see my baby at my breast,
That sucks the nurse asleep?

CHARMIAN   O, break! O, break!

CLEOPATRA As sweet as balm, as soft as air, as
gentle –
O Antony! – Nay, I will take thee too.
[*Applying another aspic to her arm*]
What should I stay – [*Dies*]

CHARMIAN   In this vile world? So, fare thee well.
Now boast thee, death, in thy possession lies
A lass unparalleled. Downy windows, close;
And golden Phoebus never be beheld
Of eyes again so royal. Your crown's awry.
I'll mend it, and then play –
[*Enter GUARD, rushing in*]

FIRST GUARD Where's the Queen?

CHARMIAN   Speak softly, wake her not.

FIRST GUARD Caesar hath sent –

> ### 'I am fire and air … to baser life.'
> The four elements that composed the human body were earth, air, fire and water. Earth and water were particularly associated with women, and Cleopatra is often linked with both in the play (the mud of the Nile; the Nile itself). By disclaiming these two elements, she is declaring herself to have jettisoned her womanhood – as she declared earlier when she said, 'My resolution's placed, and I have nothing / Of woman in me'.

I am fire and air; my other elements I give to baser life.

CHARMIAN Too slow a messenger. [*Applies an aspic*]
O come apace, dispatch! I partly feel thee.

FIRST GUARD Approach, ho! All's not well.
Caesar's beguiled.

SECOND GUARD There's Dolabella sent from
Caesar. Call him.

[*Exit a GUARD*]

FIRST GUARD What work is here! Charmian, is
this well done?

CHARMIAN It is well done, and fitting for a princess
Descended of so many royal kings. Ah, soldier! [*Dies*]

[*Enter DOLABELLA*]

DOLABELLA How goes it here?

SECOND GUARD   All dead.

DOLABELLA   Caesar, thy thoughts
Touch their effects in this. Thyself art coming
To see performed the dreaded act which thou
So sought'st to hinder.

ALL   A way there, a way for Caesar!
[*Enter OCTAVIUS CAESAR and all his train, marching*]

DOLABELLA O sir, you are too sure an augurer.
That you did fear is done.

CAESAR   Bravest at the last,
She levelled at our purposes, and, being royal,
Took her own way. The manner of their deaths?
I do not see them bleed.

DOLABELLA   Who was last with them?

FIRST GUARD A simple countryman that brought
her figs.
This was his basket.

CAESAR   Poisoned, then.

FIRST GUARD   O Caesar,
This Charmian lived but now; she stood and spake.
I found her trimming up the diadem
On her dead mistress; tremblingly she stood,
And on the sudden dropped.

CAESAR   O noble weakness!
If they had swallowed poison, 'twould appear
By external swelling; but she looks like sleep,
As she would catch another Antony
In her strong toil of grace.

Pericles

c.1607-8

ACT 5 | SCENE 1

'Give me a gash, put me to present pain,
Lest this great sea of joys rushing upon me
O'erbear the shores of my mortality'

***Pericles* is the first of Shakespeare's romances – the series of late plays that draw on the ancient art of popular storytelling. Characteristic of these plays is their coverage of vast tracts of space and time, together with drastic shifts of fortune, as the characters lurch from misery to joy to misery again before reaching the safe haven of a happy ending.**

Miracles occur, as when a physician brings Pericles's wife back from the dead, or Marina restores her father to his senses. And the process of storytelling is foregrounded in each play: most obviously, here, in the presence of the 15th-century poet Gower, who introduces each section with a narrative in medieval English. In raising Gower's ghost, Shakespeare stresses the validity of other ways of mapping human lives besides the privileged genre of chronicle history, which is sponsored by governments and policed by censors. *Pericles* shows both governments and censorship in a poor light, and sets stories up in opposition to them, as a means of separating the wholesome from the poisonous, the worthwhile from the corrupt.

Telling things as they are, in stories or plain statements, is a problem that besets Pericles and his daughter Marina. The play opens with Pericles's arrival at Antioch, determined to solve a riddle that will win him the country's princess. But the solution shocks him into silence, exposing as it does an incestuous relationship between the girl and her father. Fearful of saying what he knows, Pericles flees from Antioch pursued by an assassin. His inability to speak openly about royal incest, and the king's murderous determination to stop him speaking, is what starts him on his travels, in the course of which he loses his wife and daughter and ends up floating speechless on the waves, unable to articulate his tribulations. Marina, meanwhile, undergoes similar traumas, but retains her ability to express them in art. Throughout her trials – attempted assassination, kidnapping, being sold to a pimp – she remains a matchless singer, a fine needlewoman and an eloquent speaker, who can dissuade a brothel's customers from libertinism and tell tales that change their hearers' lives. In our scene, she restores her father's sanity by telling him her story and making him recognize it as his own. There could hardly be a more elegant summation of the storyteller's craft.

At the beginning of the extract, after long separation neither Pericles nor Marina has any notion of each other's identity. She has been brought aboard his vessel as an attested verbal healer, but as she speaks she grows embarrassed by Pericles's passionate responses to her narrative, convinced that he is mocking her for the strange events she unfolds. Pericles isn't laughing, however; as at Antioch, he knows the truths that are hidden under seeming strangeness. Indeed, he gets so involved in her tale that his gender becomes somehow mixed with hers: he describes himself as 'great with woe' – pregnant with it – and says that in curing him 'Thou… beget'st him that did thee beget', as if she were a father. Her storytelling, then, effects a redemptive version of the incest that opened the play. There are terrible things in the world, Shakespeare suggests, but there are also wonders; and the 'great sea of joys' that accompanies the latter may almost, at times, make suffering seem worthwhile.

OPPOSITE Marina (Suzan Sylvester), Pericles (Nigel Terry) and Thaisa (Sally Edwards) finally reunited, in the Royal Shakespeare Company's 1989 production.

[*Enter* PERICLES, MARINA, LYSIMACHUS, HELICANUS, *and others*]

MARINA Hail, sir! My lord, lend ear.

PERICLES Hum, ha!
[*He roughly repulses her*]

MARINA I am a maid,
My lord, that ne'er before invited eyes,
But have been gazed on like a comet. She speaks,
My lord, that maybe hath endured a grief
Might equal yours, if both were justly weighed.
Though wayward fortune did malign my state,
My derivation was from ancestors
Who stood equivalent with mighty kings,
But time hath rooted out my parentage,
And to the world and awkward casualties
Bound me in servitude. [*Aside*] I will desist.
But there is something glows upon my cheek,
And whispers in mine ear, 'Stay till he speak.'

PERICLES My fortunes – parentage – good
   parentage –
To equal mine? Was it not thus? What say you?

MARINA I said if you did know my parentage,
My lord, you would not do me violence.

PERICLES I do think so. Pray you, turn your eyes
   upon me.
You are like something that – what countrywoman?
Here of these shores?

MARINA   No, nor of any shores,
Yet I was mortally brought forth, and am
No other than I seem.

PERICLES I am great with woe, and shall deliver
   weeping.
My dearest wife was like this maid, and such
My daughter might have been: my queen's square
   brows;

'Yet thou dost look …
Extremity out of act.'

Pericles means that Marina looks like the personified virtue of Patience, which can endure anything – even the deaths of kings – and smile at the worst possible situations ('Extremity') so calmly that they are no longer extreme. The last phrase may also imply that she can dissuade people from committing the most extreme of human acts, suicide, simply by smiling. In the next line, 'kind' has both its modern meaning and the obsolete meaning of 'related by blood'; Pericles already suspects Marina to be his daughter.

Her stature to an inch; as wand-like straight;
As silver-voiced; her eyes as jewel-like,
And cased as richly; in pace another Juno;
Who starves the ears she feeds, and makes them
   hungry
The more she gives them speech. Where do you
   live?

MARINA Where I am but a stranger. From the deck
You may discern the place.

PERICLES   Where were you bred?
And how achieved you these endowments, which
You make more rich to owe?

MARINA If I should tell my history, it would seem
Like lies disdained in the reporting.

PERICLES   Prithee speak.
Falseness cannot come from thee; for thou look'st
Modest as Justice, and thou seem'st a palace
For the crowned Truth to dwell in. I will
   believe thee,
And make my senses credit thy relation
To points that seem impossible. Thou show'st
Like one I loved indeed. What were thy friends?
Didst thou not say, when I did push thee back –
Which was when I perceived thee – that thou cam'st
From good descending?

MARINA   So indeed I did.

PERICLES Report thy parentage. I think thou said'st
Thou hadst been tossed from wrong to injury,
And that thou thought'st thy griefs might equal
   mine,
If both were opened.

MARINA   Some such thing I said,
And said no more but what my circumstance
Did warrant me was likely.

PERICLES   Tell thy story.
If thine considered prove the thousandth part
Of my endurance, thou art a man, and I
Have suffered like a girl. Yet thou dost look
Like Patience gazing on kings' graves, and smiling
Extremity out of act. What were thy friends?
How lost thou them? Thy name, my most kind virgin?
Recount, I do beseech thee. Come, sit by me.

MARINA My name, sir, is Marina.

PERICLES   O, I am mocked,
And thou by some incensèd god sent hither
To make the world to laugh at me.

MARINA   Patience, good sir,
Or here I'll cease.

PERICLES   Nay, I'll be patient.
Thou little know'st how thou dost startle me
To call thyself Marina.

MARINA The name
Was given me by one that had some power:
My father, and a king.

PERICLES   How! A king's daughter?
And called Marina?

MARINA You said you would believe me;
But, not to be a troubler of your peace,
I will end here.

PERICLES   But are you flesh and blood?
Have you a working pulse and are no fairy?
Motion as well? Speak on. Where were you born,
And wherefore called Marina?

You think me an impostor. No, good faith,
I am the daughter to King Pericles,
If good King Pericles be.

PERICLES Ho, Helicanus!

HELICANUS   Calls my lord?

PERICLES Thou art a grave and noble counsellor,
Most wise in gen'ral. Tell me if thou canst
What this maid is, or what is like to be,
That thus hath made me weep?

HELICANUS   I know not; but
Here is the regent, sir, of Mytilene
Speaks nobly of her.

LYSIMACHUS   She would never tell
Her parentage. Being demanded that,
She would sit still and weep.

Now blessing on thee! Rise; thou art my child.

MARINA   Called Marina
For I was born at sea.

PERICLES   At sea? What mother?

MARINA My mother was the daughter of a king,
Who died the minute I was born,
As my good nurse Lychorida hath oft
Delivered weeping.

PERICLES   O, stop there a little!
[*Aside*] This is the rarest dream that e'er dull sleep
Did mock sad fools withal. This cannot be;
My daughter's buried. [*To* MARINA] Well, where
   were you bred?
I'll hear you more, to th' bottom of your story,
And never interrupt you.

MARINA You scorn. Believe me, 'twere best I did
   give o'er.

PERICLES I will believe you by the syllable
Of what you shall deliver. Yet give me leave:
How came you in these parts? Where were you bred?

MARINA The King my father did in Tarsus
   leave me,
Till cruel Cleon, with his wicked wife,
Did seek to murder me; and having wooed
A villain t' attempt it, who having drawn to do't,
A crew of pirates came and rescued me;
Brought me to Mytilene. But, good sir,
Whither will you have me? Why do you weep? It
   may be

PERICLES O Helicanus, strike me, honoured sir,
Give me a gash, put me to present pain,
Lest this great sea of joys rushing upon me
O'erbear the shores of my mortality
And drown me with their sweetness. [*To* MARINA]
   O, come hither,
Thou that beget'st him that did thee beget,
Thou that wast born at sea, buried at Tarsus,
And found at sea again! O Helicanus,
Down on thy knees, thank the holy gods as loud
As thunder threatens us. This is Marina.
What was thy mother's name? Tell me but that,
For truth can never be confirmed enough,
Though doubts did ever sleep.

MARINA   First, sir, I pray,
What is your title?

PERICLES I am Pericles of Tyre. But tell me now
My drowned queen's name, as in the rest you said
Thou hast been godlike perfect,
The heir of kingdoms and another life
To Pericles thy father.

MARINA Is it no more to be your daughter than
To say my mother's name was Thaisa?
Thaisa was my mother, who did end
The minute I began.

PERICLES Now blessing on thee! Rise; thou art
   my child.

Coriolanus
c.1608

ACT **5** | SCENE **3**

❝ Thou hast never in thy life
Showed thy dear mother any courtesy. ❞

If Shakespeare's late plays are committed to seeking out what remains constant through all the vicissitudes of history, *Coriolanus* focuses on a hero who is destroyed by excessive constancy. An aristocratic Roman, Coriolanus has been brought up to idolize warfare, self-reliance and aggressive masculinity. His admirers liken him to a stone, an unshifting oak, or a relentless machine: 'When he walks, he moves like an engine, and the ground shrinks before his treading.'

These qualities are ideally suited to war, where he refuses to acknowledge physical frailty, and sets about the business of bloodshed with exultation, greeting soldiers like lovers: 'O! Let me clip ye / In arms as sound as when I wooed'. But in time of peace his unshakable convictions become a liability. He articulates the aristocrats' disdain for commoners with a directness that shocks even the aristocracy, and enrages the elected representatives of the ordinary people of Rome. His refusal to adapt to the demands of urban living wins him powerful enemies, and leads at last to his banishment, despite all the glory he amassed when fighting to defend his people.

As he trudges into exile, Coriolanus pronounces his own sentence on Rome – 'I banish you!' – as if *he* were the city, not the cluster of buildings he leaves behind. This conviction that he is Rome sustains him as he goes to offer his services to Rome's arch-enemies, the Volsces. He won his surname, 'Coriolanus', when he seized the Volscian city of Corioli virtually single-handed; but now it becomes a sign of his commitment to the Volscian cause. Marching at the head of their army he aims to win a new title by conquering his old country; he becomes 'a kind of nothing, titleless', till he has 'forged himself a name i' th' fire / Of burning Rome'. He stands, in fact, for a perverseness in his culture's conception of personal and national identity, which makes it appropriate for men to name themselves after places they have smashed.

Nevertheless, Coriolanus is no machine, nor is he self-reliant; and our extract captures the moment when he sees this for the first time. Sitting in state beside the Volscian general Aufidius (with whom he has formed a pact like a second marriage), having rejected all pleas for clemency from the Romans, he is suddenly faced by a family group – his mother, wife and son, with their friend Valeria – and at once begins a lengthy capitulation. It was his mother, Volumnia, who fed his principles to him along with her breast-milk, and it's she whose rhetorical skills are later credited by the Romans with turning him back from Rome. But the real conqueror of Coriolanus is his constancy: his continuing capacity to feel shame when she tells him off; his continuing delight in his wife's kiss and his child's liveliness. No matter how he tries, Coriolanus cannot act a role that's different from the one Volumnia taught him; before she even opens her mouth he admits that 'Like a dull actor now / I have forgot my part', abandoning his show of indifference to old bonds. His decision to stop the Volscian army before it reaches Rome is suicidal; but it's one he was trained to commit at his mother's knee; and it finally makes him likeable enough to be tragic.

OPPOSITE Coriolanus is confronted by his family in this 18th-century painting by Giovanni Battista Pittoni.

🎭 | ACT **5** | SCENE **3**
The Volscian camp, near Rome

[*Enter* CORIOLANUS, AUFIDIUS, VIRGILIA, VOLUMNIA, *young* MARCIUS, *and others*]

CORIOLANUS These eyes are not the same I wore
  in Rome.

VIRGILIA The sorrow that delivers us thus changed
Makes you think so.

CORIOLANUS   Like a dull actor now
I have forgot my part, and I am out
Even to a full disgrace. Best of my flesh,
Forgive my tyranny, but do not say,
'For that, forgive our Romans.' [*She kisses him*]
    O, a kiss
Long as my exile, sweet as my revenge!
Now, by the jealous queen of heaven, that kiss
I carried from thee, dear, and my true lip
Hath virgined it e'er since. You gods! I prate,
And the most noble mother of the world
Leave unsaluted. Sink, my knee, i' th' earth; [*Kneels*]
Of thy deep duty more impression show
Than that of common sons.

VOLUMNIA   O, stand up blest!
Whilst with no softer cushion than the flint
I kneel before thee, and unproperly
Show duty, as mistaken all this while
Between the child and parent. [*Kneels*]

CORIOLANUS   What's this?
Your knees to me, to your corrected son?
Then let the pebbles on the hungry beach
Fillip the stars; then let the mutinous winds
Strike the proud cedars 'gainst the fiery sun,
Murd'ring impossibility, to make
What cannot be slight work.

VOLUMNIA   Thou art my warrior;
I holp to frame thee. Do you know this lady?

CORIOLANUS The noble sister of Publicola,
The moon of Rome, chaste as the icicle
That's candied by the frost from purest snow,
And hangs on Dian's temple – dear Valeria!

VOLUMNIA This is a poor epitome of yours,
Which by th' interpretation of full time
May show like all yourself.

CORIOLANUS   The god of soldiers,
With the consent of supreme Jove, inform
Thy thoughts with nobleness, that thou mayst prove
To shame unvulnerable, and stick i' th' wars

Like a great sea-mark, standing every flaw,
And saving those that eye thee!

VOLUMNIA   Your knee, sirrah.

CORIOLANUS That's my brave boy.

VOLUMNIA Even he, your wife, this lady, and myself,
Are suitors to you.

CORIOLANUS   I beseech you, peace.
Or, if you'd ask, remember this before:
The thing I have forsworn to grant may never
Be held by you denials. Do not bid me
Dismiss my soldiers, or capitulate
Again with Rome's mechanics. Tell me not
Wherein I seem unnatural. Desire not
T' allay my rages and revenges with
Your colder reasons.

VOLUMNIA   O, no more, no more!
You have said you will not grant us anything –
For we have nothing else to ask but that
Which you deny already. Yet we will ask,
That, if you fail in our request, the blame
May hang upon your hardness. Therefore hear us.

> ### 'Your knees to me … be slight work.'
> **Coriolanus feels 'corrected' (rebuked) by Volumnia's ironic show of self-abasement in kneeling to him. Her gesture constitutes for him an action as unnatural as if stones from the beach should strike at ('fillip') the stars. Such a thing would 'murder impossibility' – make nothing impossible – with the result that 'what cannot be' would become easy ('slight work').**

CORIOLANUS Aufidius and you Volsces, mark,
  for we'll
Hear nought from Rome in private. Your request?

VOLUMNIA Should we be silent and not speak, our
  raiment
And state of bodies would bewray what life
We have led since thy exile. Think with thyself
How more unfortunate than all living women
Are we come hither, since that thy sight, which
  should
Make our eyes flow with joy, hearts dance with
  comforts,
Constrains them weep and shake with fear and
  sorrow,
Making the mother, wife, and child to see

The son, the husband, and the father tearing
His country's bowels out. And to poor we
Thine enmity's most capital. Thou barr'st us
Our prayers to the gods, which is a comfort
That all but we enjoy. For how can we,
Alas, how can we for our country pray,
Whereto we are bound, together with thy victory,
Whereto we are bound? Alack, or we must lose
The country, our dear nurse, or else thy person,
Our comfort in the country. We must find
An evident calamity, though we had
Our wish which side should win. For either thou
Must as a foreign recreant be led
With manacles thorough our streets, or else
Triumphantly tread on thy country's ruin,
And bear the palm for having bravely shed
Thy wife and children's blood. For myself, son,
I purpose not to wait on fortune till
These wars determine. If I cannot persuade thee
Rather to show a noble grace to both parts
Than seek the end of one, thou shalt no sooner
March to assault thy country than to tread –
Trust to't, thou shalt not – on thy mother's womb
That brought thee to this world.

VIRGILIA   Ay, and mine,
That brought you forth this boy to keep your name
Living to time.

BOY   A shall not tread on me!
I'll run away till I am bigger, but then I'll fight.

CORIOLANUS Not of a woman's tenderness to be
Requires nor child nor woman's face to see.
I have sat too long. [*Rising*]

VOLUMNIA   Nay, go not from us thus.
If it were so that our request did tend
To save the Romans, thereby to destroy
The Volsces whom you serve, you might
   condemn us
As poisonous of your honour. No, our suit
Is that you reconcile them: while the Volsces
May say 'This mercy we have showed', the Romans
'This we received', and each in either side
Give the all-hail to thee and cry 'Be blest
For making up this peace!' Thou know'st, great son,
The end of war's uncertain; but this certain:
That if thou conquer Rome, the benefit
Which thou shalt thereby reap is such a name
Whose repetition will be dogged with curses,
Whose chronicle thus writ: 'The man was noble,
But with his last attempt he wiped it out,
Destroyed his country, and his name remains

To th' ensuing age abhorred.' Speak to me, son.
Thou hast affected the fine strains of honour,
To imitate the graces of the gods,
To tear with thunder the wide cheeks o' th' air,
And yet to charge thy sulphur with a bolt
That should but rive an oak. Why dost not speak?
Think'st thou it honourable for a noble man
Still to remember wrongs? Daughter, speak you,
He cares not for your weeping. Speak thou, boy.
Perhaps thy childishness will move him more

O mother, mother! What have you done?

Than can our reasons. There's no man in the world
More bound to 's mother, yet here he lets me prate
Like one i' th' stocks. Thou hast never in thy life
Showed thy dear mother any courtesy,
When she, poor hen, fond of no second brood,
Has clucked thee to the wars and safely home,
Loaden with honour. Say my request's unjust,
And spurn me back; but if it be not so,
Thou art not honest, and the gods will plague thee
That thou restrain'st from me the duty which
To a mother's part belongs. He turns away.
Down, ladies; let us shame him with our knees.
[*They kneel*]
To his surname Coriolanus 'longs more pride
Than pity to our prayers. Down! An end.
This is the last. So we will home to Rome,
And die among our neighbours. Nay, behold 's:
This boy, that cannot tell what he would have
But kneels and holds up hands for fellowship,
Does reason our petition with more strength
Than thou hast to deny 't. Come, let us go.
This fellow had a Volscian to his mother;
His wife is in Corioli, and this child
Like him by chance. Yet give us our dispatch.
I am hushed until our city be a-fire,
And then I'll speak a little.
[*He holds her by the hand, silent*]

CORIOLANUS   O mother, mother!
What have you done? Behold, the heavens do ope,
The gods look down, and this unnatural scene
They laugh at. O my mother, mother! O!
You have won a happy victory to Rome;
But for your son – believe it, O, believe it! –
Most dangerously you have with him prevailed,
If not most mortal to him. But let it come.

The Winter's Tale

c.1609-11

ACT **5** SCENE **3**

" What fine chisel
Could ever yet cut breath? "

Our scene comes at the end of the longest period of time spanned by any of Shakespeare's plays. Sixteen years elapse between the third and fourth acts of *The Winter's Tale*, as if the ageing Shakespeare were seeking to subject playgoers of all ages to the experience of getting older. In between the acts the figure of Time appears, speaking like a playwright: 'I that please some, try all ... it is in my power ... To plant and o'erwhelm custom.' Experimental, ever controversial, Shakespeare like Time has challenged customs and conventions theatrical and social, delighting and enraging his audiences in equal measure.

This strange old story – the second of his 'romances' after *Pericles* – seems in part a celebration of the art of storytelling he had practised for so long, and its ability to mimic and shape the lives of its sympathetic auditors.

The two halves of the play pay homage to two genres. In the tragic first half Leontes, King of Sicily, becomes insanely jealous of his wife Hermione and their guest, Polixenes of Bohemia, and orders his courtier Camillo to assassinate the Bohemian. When Camillo and Polixenes instead flee to safety, Leontes takes out his rage on his wife and baby daughter, abandoning the bastard girl (as he thinks her) on a distant shore and putting Hermione on trial for treason. When he declares her guilty in the teeth of the evidence – including a verdict of 'innocent' from the Delphic Oracle itself – his son Mamillius dies of grief, and Hermione dies too at the news of the boy's death. But, after Time's intervention in Act 4, the play turns comic. Shepherds dance and play at a sheep-shearing festival, presided over by Leontes's daughter – now grown into an articulate young woman, Perdita – and attended by her lover Prince Florizel, son of Polixenes. Despite Polixenes's objections to their union, the irrepressible young couple flee to Sicily, where Perdita is reunited with her father, Polixenes and Leontes are reconciled, and Leontes's long period of penance for the death of Hermione finally comes to an end.

In our scene – the last – the veteran playwright springs the greatest theatrical surprise of his career. Hermione's friend Paulina – who stood by her at the trial and presided over Leontes's penance – invites everyone to visit her house, where she will unveil a new statue of the dead queen. The statue is a miracle of the sculptor's art; and when it moves and speaks, it testifies to the artistry of Renaissance scientist-magicians, who could animate stone images with their wizardry. But more than sculpture or magic, the statue celebrates the art of the theatre. For it really is alive: what looked like marble is in fact warm with blood. And more than this, it really is the person it seemed only to represent – Hermione, who did not die after all, but has been kept alive by Paulina until the moment when she could meet her long-lost daughter. Theatre's imitation of life, this living statue seems to say, participates in the substance of life like no other artistic medium; which is why it's an art 'lawful as eating', as Leontes puts it, and perhaps even as necessary as eating for the health of its participants.

OPPOSITE Leontes is startled as Paulina tells Hermione that it's time to 'be stone no more' in this 18th-century engraving by Robert Thew.

ACT 5 | SCENE 3
Sicilia – Paulina's house

[*Enter* LEONTES, POLIXENES, FLORIZEL, PERDITA, CAMILLO, PAULINA, *Lords, and Attendants*]

LEONTES O grave and good Paulina, the great comfort
That I have had of thee!

PAULINA   What, sovereign sir,
I did not well, I meant well. All my services
You have paid home, but that you have vouchsafed
With your crowned brother and these young contracted
Heirs of your kingdoms my poor house to visit,
It is a surplus of your grace which never
My life may last to answer.

LEONTES   O Paulina,
We honour you with trouble. But we came
To see the statue of our queen. Your gallery
Have we passed through, not without much content
In many singularities; but we saw not
That which my daughter came to look upon,
The statue of her mother.

PAULINA   As she lived peerless,
So her dead likeness, I do well believe,
Excels whatever yet you looked upon
Or hand of man hath done; therefore I keep it
Lonely, apart. But here it is. Prepare
To see the life as lively mocked as ever
Still sleep mocked death. Behold, and say 'tis well.
[PAULINA *draws a curtain, and reveals the figure of* HERMIONE *standing like a statue*]
I like your silence; it the more shows off
Your wonder. But yet speak; first, you, my liege.
Comes it not something near?

LEONTES   Her natural posture!
Chide me, dear stone, that I may say indeed
Thou art Hermione; or rather, thou art she
In thy not chiding, for she was as tender
As infancy and grace. But yet, Paulina,
Hermione was not so much wrinkled, nothing
So agèd as this seems.

POLIXENES   O, not by much.

PAULINA So much the more our carver's excellence,
Which lets go by some sixteen years, and makes her
As she lived now.

LEONTES   As now she might have done,
So much to my good comfort as it is
Now piercing to my soul. O, thus she stood,
Even with such life of majesty – warm life,
As now it coldly stands – when first I wooed her!
I am ashamed. Does not the stone rebuke me
For being more stone than it? O royal piece,

There's magic in thy majesty, which has
My evils conjured to remembrance, and
From thy admiring daughter took the spirits,
Standing like stone with thee.

PERDITA   And give me leave,
And do not say 'tis superstition, that
I kneel and then implore her blessing. Lady,
Dear Queen, that ended when I but began,
Give me that hand of yours to kiss.

> ### 'We honour you with trouble.'
> **Of all Shakespeare's works, this play has some of the most elaborate courtly compliments in it – which is what helped to make Leontes jealous (his wife Hermione was obeying his instructions to persuade Polixenes to stay in Sicily a little longer, and succeeded all too well). This means 'what you take to be an honour is putting you to a great deal of trouble'.**

PAULINA   O, patience!
The statue is but newly fixed; the colour's
Not dry.

CAMILLO [*To* LEONTES] My lord, your sorrow was too sore laid on,
Which sixteen winters cannot blow away,
So many summers dry. Scarce any joy
Did ever so long live; no sorrow
But killed itself much sooner.

POLIXENES [*To* LEONTES] Dear my brother,
Let him that was the cause of this have power
To take off so much grief from you as he
Will piece up in himself.

PAULINA [*To* LEONTES] Indeed, my lord,
If I had thought the sight of my poor image
Would thus have wrought you – for the stone is mine –
I'd not have showed it.
[*She makes to draw the curtain*]

LEONTES   Do not draw the curtain.

PAULINA No longer shall you gaze on't, lest your fancy
May think anon it moves.

LEONTES   Let be, let be.
Would I were dead but that methinks already.
What was he that did make it? See, my lord,
Would you not deem it breathed, and that those veins
Did verily bear blood?

POLIXENES   Masterly done.
The very life seems warm upon her lip.

LEONTES The fixture of her eye has motion in't,
As we are mocked with art.

PAULINA I'll draw the curtain.
My lord's almost so far transported that
He'll think anon it lives.

LEONTES O sweet Paulina,
Make me to think so twenty years together!
No settled senses of the world can match
The pleasure of that madness. Let 't alone.

PAULINA I am sorry, sir, I have thus far stirred you; but
I could afflict you farther.

LEONTES Do, Paulina,
For this affliction has a taste as sweet
As any cordial comfort. Still methinks
There is an air comes from her. What fine chisel
Could ever yet cut breath? Let no man mock me,
For I will kiss her.

PAULINA Good my lord, forbear.
The ruddiness upon her lip is wet;
You'll mar it if you kiss it, stain your own
With oily painting. Shall I draw the curtain?

LEONTES No, not these twenty years.

PERDITA So long could I
Stand by, a looker-on.

PAULINA Either forbear,
Quit presently the chapel, or resolve you
For more amazement. If you can behold it,
I'll make the statue move indeed, descend,
And take you by the hand; but then you'll think –
Which I protest against – I am assisted
By wicked powers.

LEONTES What you can make her do,
I am content to look on; what to speak,
I am content to hear; for 'tis as easy
To make her speak as move.

PAULINA It is required
You do awake your faith. Then, all stand still.
Or those that think it is unlawful business
I am about, let them depart.

> ## 'Would I were dead but that
> methinks already.'
>
> **May I die if I don't already think that
> (i.e. that the statue moves). Later he adds,
> 'The fixture of her eye has motion in't' – the
> set of her eye makes it look as if it's moving.
> Leontes's emotional reaction to the statue's
> motion confirms Paulina's statement that it
> has 'wrought' him – made him distraught,
> or fashioned him like another statue.**

LEONTES Proceed.
No foot shall stir.

PAULINA Music, awake her; strike! [*Music*]
'Tis time; descend; be stone no more; approach;
Strike all that look upon with marvel. Come,
I'll fill your grave up. Stir. Nay, come away.
Bequeath to death your numbness, for from him
Dear life redeems you. You perceive she stirs.
[**HERMIONE** *slowly descends*]
Start not. Her actions shall be holy as
You hear my spell is lawful. Do not shun her
Until you see her die again, for then
You kill her double. Nay, present your hand.
When she was young you wooed her; now in age
Is she become the suitor?

LEONTES O, she's warm!
If this be magic, let it be an art
Lawful as eating.

POLIXENES She embraces him.

CAMILLO She hangs about his neck.
If she pertain to life, let her speak too.

POLIXENES Ay, and make it manifest where
she has lived,
Or how stol'n from the dead.

PAULINA That she is living,
Were it but told you, should be hooted at
Like an old tale. But it appears she lives,
Though yet she speak not. Mark a little while.
[*To* **PERDITA**] Please you to interpose, fair madam.
Kneel,
And pray your mother's blessing. Turn, good lady,
Our Perdita is found.

HERMIONE You gods, look down
And from your sacred vials pour your graces
Upon my daughter's head! Tell me, mine own.
Where hast thou been preserved? Where lived?
How found
Thy father's court? For thou shalt hear that I,
Knowing by Paulina that the oracle
Gave hope thou wast in being, have preserved
Myself to see the issue.

PAULINA There's time enough for that,
Lest they desire upon this push to trouble
Your joys with like relation. Go together,
You precious winners all; your exultation
Partake to every one. I, an old turtle,
Will wing me to some withered bough, and there
My mate, that's never to be found again,
Lament till I am lost.

Cymbeline

c.1609-10

❝ 'Tis her breathing that
Perfumes the
chamber thus. ❞

Like other romances, *Cymbeline* is packed with incident: love, exile, treachery, disguise, assassination, warfare and eventual reconciliation; but through it all one woman stays stable – Princess Imogen of Britain, who quickly becomes the touchstone for all value in the play. Imogen has no time for the superficial values that govern other people. Class, for instance, means nothing to her, and she marries the base-born Posthumus in defiance of her father, Cymbeline, in order to 'proclaim how she esteemed … his virtue'.

When Posthumus is banished, Imogen is disgusted by the snobbish Prince Cloten, who seeks to supplant him in her affections. Her love for her husband, on the other hand, convinces her she can communicate with him in exile – they will pray at certain hours and 'encounter … with orisons, i.e. [prayers] in heaven. When she hears he has returned to Britain she plans to 'glide' a week's journey in a day in her hurry to meet him. Later, having disguised herself as the boy Fidele in order to escape from Cymbeline's court, she meets two young mountaineers who fall in love with her at once; when Fidele seems to die they compose him one of the loveliest elegies in English. Later still, the newly revived Fidele is taken into service by a Roman officer, who falls in love with him as passionately as the mountaineers did. Imogen's qualities, then, transcend distinctions of gender and nation, drawing strangers together into a kind of scattered family. In the last scene she finds herself surrounded by all the people who love her: husband, father, mountaineers (who turn out to be her long-lost brothers), the old courtier who raised them, the Roman officer – she regards them all as relatives, looking from one to another with an egalitarian gaze that astonishes Cymbeline: 'she, like harmless lightning, throws her eye / On him, her brothers, me, her master, hitting / Each object with a joy.' No woman in Shakespeare's work engineers such a happy ending against such overwhelming odds.

Our extract marks the moment when Imogen's status as the touchstone of value is jeopardized by the Italian Iachimo, who bets Posthumus he can seduce her in her husband's absence. When he fails, Iachimo slips into her bedchamber hidden in a trunk, emerging at night to make a list of the room's furnishings and of intimate marks on Imogen's sleeping body; details that will convince Posthumus he has slept with her. As a result of this deception, Posthumus orders his servant to kill her – triggering a chain of traumatic events that does not end till the final act. The power of our scene stems from the creeping horror with which Iachimo observes himself reducing Imogen to an 'inventory': a financial valuation of her body, with its lips like rubies, breath like perfume, and honour like 'treasure' which he dare not touch. Lovers usually wish that night would linger; Iachimo yearns for its rapid passing: 'Swift, swift, you dragons of the night', he cries, desperate to escape from a room that has become hell to him through self-disgust. But Iachimo finds no escape from his damnation, since his inventory has violated his sense of value itself – as he shows when he goes ahead with his plan to convince Posthumus of Imogen's infidelity, despite his loathing for the treason he commits. From this moment on, nothing can ever seem precious to Iachimo again – until Posthumus forgives him at the play's astounding close.

OPPOSITE Tim Piggot-Smith as Iachimo and Geraldine James as Imogen in the 1988 National Theatre production.

ACT **2** | SCENE **1**

Britain – outside Cymbeline's palace

[*Enter* CLOTEN, FIRST LORD, *and* SECOND LORD]

FIRST LORD Did you hear of a stranger that's come to court tonight?

CLOTEN A stranger, and I not know on't?

SECOND LORD [*Aside*] He's a strange fellow himself, and knows it not.

FIRST LORD There's an Italian come, and, 'tis thought, one of Leonatus's friends.

CLOTEN Leonatus? A banished rascal; and he's another, whatsoever he be. Who told you of this stranger?

FIRST LORD One of your lordship's pages.

CLOTEN Is it fit I went to look upon him? Is there no derogation in't?

SECOND LORD You cannot derogate, my lord.

CLOTEN Not easily, I think.

SECOND LORD [*Aside*] You are a fool granted; therefore your issues, being foolish, do not derogate.

CLOTEN Come, I'll go see this Italian. What I have lost today at bowls I'll win tonight of him. Come, go.

SECOND LORD I'll attend your lordship.

[*Exeunt* CLOTEN *and* FIRST LORD]

That such a crafty devil as is his mother
Should yield the world this ass! A woman that
Bears all down with her brain; and this her son
Cannot take two from twenty, for his heart,
And leave eighteen. Alas, poor princess,
Thou divine Imogen, what thou endur'st,
Betwixt a father by thy step-dame governed,
A mother hourly coining plots, a wooer

> ### 'Our Tarquin thus … The chastity he wounded.'
>
> **Sextus Tarquinius raped a chaste Roman wife, Lucretia, as she lay in her bed (Shakespeare told the story in his poem *The Rape of Lucrece*). He is 'our Tarquin' because he, like Iachimo, came from Italy. The 'rushes' are reeds, often strewn on the floor of seventeenth-century houses. Cytherea in the following line is a name for Venus, goddess of love and beauty, since it's the island where she first set foot after being born from the sea-foam.**

More hateful than the foul expulsion is
Of thy dear husband, than that horrid act
Of the divorce he'd make! The heavens hold firm
The walls of thy dear honour, keep unshaked
That temple, thy fair mind, that thou mayst stand
T'enjoy thy banished lord and this great land!
[*Exit*]

> ### 'the arras; figures … contents o' th' story.'
>
> **The arras is a wall-hanging, a tapestry; this one has 'figures' on it that act out a 'story'. The story's contents are given in Act 2, Scene 4: the tapestry shows the meeting between Cleopatra and Antony described by Enobarbus in our first extract from *Antony and Cleopatra*.**

ACT **2** | SCENE **2**

Imogen's chamber

[IMOGEN *in bed, reading; a* LADY *attending; a trunk by the bed*]

IMOGEN Who's there? my woman Helen?

LADY   Please you, madam.

IMOGEN What hour is it?

LADY   Almost midnight, madam.

IMOGEN I have read three hours then. Mine eyes are weak.
Fold down the leaf where I have left. To bed.
Take not away the taper; leave it burning,
And if thou canst awake by four o' th' clock,
I prithee call me. Sleep hath seized me wholly.
[*Exit* LADY]
To your protection I commend me, gods.
From fairies and the tempters of the night
Guard me, beseech ye. [*Sleeps*]

[IACHIMO *comes from the trunk*]

IACHIMO The crickets sing, and man's o'er-laboured sense
Repairs itself by rest. Our Tarquin thus
Did softly press the rushes, ere he wakened
The chastity he wounded. Cytherea,
How bravely thou becom'st thy bed! Fresh lily,
And whiter than the sheets! That I might touch!
But kiss, one kiss! Rubies unparagoned,
How dearly they do't! 'Tis her breathing that
Perfumes the chamber thus. The flame o' th' taper
Bows toward her, and would under-peep her lids,

O sleep, thou ape of death, lie dull upon her

To see th' enclosèd lights, now canopied
Under these windows, white and azure-laced
With blue of heaven's own tinct. But my design –
To note the chamber. I will write all down.
Such and such pictures; there the window; such
The adornment of her bed; the arras; figures,
Why, such and such; and the contents o' th' story.
Ah, but some natural notes about her body
Above ten thousand meaner movables
Would testify t' enrich mine inventory.
O sleep, thou ape of death, lie dull upon her,
And be her sense but as a monument,
Thus in a chapel lying. Come off, come off.
[*He takes the bracelet from her arm*]
As slippery as the Gordian knot was hard!
'Tis mine, and this will witness outwardly,
As strongly as the conscience does within,
To th' madding of her lord. On her left breast
A mole cinque-spotted, like the crimson drops
I' th' bottom of a cowslip. Here's a voucher
Stronger than ever law could make. This secret
Will force him think I have picked the lock and ta'en
The treasure of her honour. No more. To what end?
Why should I write this down, that's riveted,
Screwed to my memory? She hath been reading late,
The tale of Tereus. Here the leaf's turned down
Where Philomel gave up. I have enough.
To the trunk again, and shut the spring of it.
Swift, swift, you dragons of the night, that dawning
May bare the raven's eye! I lodge in fear;
Though this' a heavenly angel, hell is here.
[*Clock strikes*]
One, two, three. Time, time!
[*Exit into the trunk. The scene closes*]

ACT **2** | SCENE **3**
Outside Imogen's chamber

[*Enter* CLOTEN *and two* LORDS]

FIRST LORD Your lordship is the most patient man
  in loss, the most coldest that ever turned up ace.

CLOTEN It would make any man cold to lose.

FIRST LORD But not every man patient after the
noble temper of your lordship. You are most hot
and furious when you win.

CLOTEN Winning will put any man into courage. If

I could get this foolish Imogen I should have gold
enough. It's almost morning, is't not?

FIRST LORD Day, my lord.

CLOTEN I would this music would come. I am
advised to give her music o' mornings; they say it
will penetrate. [*Enter* MUSICIANS] Come on, tune.
If you can penetrate her with your fingering,
so; we'll try with tongue too. If none will do, let

> ### 'As slippery as the Gordian knot was hard!'
>
> **The mythical Gordian knot, too hard to be loosed, was tied by King Gordius, who announced that anyone who untied it would become ruler of Asia. Alexander the Great slashed through it with one blow of his sword, and duly went on to conquer what he took to be the world.**

her remain, but I'll never give o'er. First, a very
excellent good-conceited thing; after, a wonderful
sweet air with admirable rich words to it – and
then let her consider.

MUSICIAN [*Sings*]
  Hark, hark! The lark at heaven's gate sings,
    And Phoebus 'gins arise,
  His steeds to water at those springs
    On chaliced flowers that lies;
  And winking Mary-buds begin
    To ope their golden eyes.
  With everything that pretty is,
    My lady sweet, arise;
      Arise, arise!

CLOTEN So, get you gone. If this penetrate, I will
consider your music the better; if it do not, it is a
vice in her ears which horsehairs and calves' guts,
nor the voice of unpaved eunuch to boot, can never
amend.

The Tempest

c.1610-11

ACT 1 | SCENE 2

 You taught me language, and my profit on't
Is I know how to curse.

***The Tempest* is in a sense one long last scene. After an opening spectacle designed to catch our attention – the tempest of the title – the Duke of Milan, Prospero, settles down to tell his daughter Miranda the tale of his deposition by his brother, and of how he and she were cast adrift in a rudderless boat, which brought them to the shores of the island where they have lived ever since.**

On this island spirits dwell, among them Ariel, with whose help Prospero honed his magical skills until he possessed the power to engineer what he hopes will be the happy ending of the story he told her. The tempest was a work of magic art, which capsized a ship containing Antonio (Prospero's treacherous brother), Alonso King of Naples, and Alonso's brother Sebastian and son Ferdinand. With Prospero and Miranda, these people constitute the cast of Prospero's valedictory show; and the show consists of him moving them around his island like chess pieces until he has them where he wants them and can dispense justice, as he sees it, before sending everybody home.

But this intended happy ending proves difficult to accomplish. Complications arise: Sebastian plots with Antonio to murder the king; a drunken butler and a jester plot to murder Prospero; the wicked characters stubbornly refuse to learn anything from the elaborate moral lessons taught them by Ariel at Prospero's behest. More seriously, Prospero himself has doubts about the efficacy of his project. His past has taught him to fear the intervention of chance and human corruption in the best-laid plans, and he is acutely conscious that the intended star of his show – his daughter Miranda, who he has kept in isolation to protect her from the perils to which he fell prey – is immensely vulnerable to abuse by men. His fears for her, as well as his futile wish to keep her under his protection, render him irascible. In the second part of our extract, even Miranda's falling in love with the man he intends for her – Prince Ferdinand – reminds Prospero how little she knows; she lacks the experience to judge whether Ferdinand is handsome. And it reminds him, too, how little he can influence her future. He decides, somewhat half-heartedly, to test the young couple's new love for each other 'lest too light winning / Make the prize light', and enslaves Ferdinand for no very good reason; but the trials he imposes on him don't last long, and are finally irrelevant. The boy will either be faithful to Miranda or he won't, and there's nothing her father can do about it.

Prospero's penchant for enslaving people is the most disturbing aspect of his desperate need for control. Ariel is his slave, and Prospero seems deeply reluctant to set this attractive spirit free. And his other slave is Caliban, the island's original human inhabitant – though Prospero likes to deny his humanity. In our extract, Caliban points out that Prospero too is a usurper, taking the island from Caliban by stealth, and giving him in exchange a few words and some water flavoured with berries. Prospero, then, participates in the corruption from which he yearns to protect Miranda: it's already present on the island before ever his happy ending gets under way.

OPPOSITE Prospero is restrained by Miranda while Ferdinand looks on in this 19th-century painting by William Hamilton.

Prospero's island

[*Enter* PROSPERO *and* MIRANDA]

PROSPERO Thou poisonous slave, got by the
  devil himself
Upon thy wicked dam, come forth!

[*Enter* CALIBAN]

CALIBAN As wicked dew as e'er my mother brushed
With raven's feather from unwholesome fen
Drop on you both! A southwest blow on ye
And blister you all o'er!

PROSPERO For this be sure tonight thou shalt
  have cramps,
Side-stitches that shall pen thy breath up. Urchins
Shall, for that vast of night that they may work,
All exercise on thee; thou shalt be pinched
As thick as honeycomb, each pinch more stinging
Than bees that made 'em.

CALIBAN   I must eat my dinner.
This island's mine, by Sycorax my mother,
Which thou tak'st from me. When thou cam'st first,
Thou strok'st me and made much of me, wouldst
  give me
Water with berries in't, and teach me how
To name the bigger light, and how the less,
That burn by day and night; and then I loved thee,
And showed thee all the qualities o' th' isle,
The fresh springs, brine-pits, barren place and fertile.
Cursed be I that did so! All the charms
Of Sycorax, toads, beetles, bats, light on you!
For I am all the subjects that you have,
Which first was mine own king, and here you sty me
In this hard rock, whiles you do keep from me
The rest o' th' the island.

PROSPERO   Thou most lying slave,
Whom stripes may move, not kindness! I have
  used thee,
Filth as thou art, with human care, and lodged thee
In mine own cell, till thou didst seek to violate
The honour of my child.

CALIBAN O ho, O ho! Would't had been done!
Thou didst prevent me; I had peopled else
This isle with Calibans.

MIRANDA   Abhorrèd slave,
Which any print of goodness wilt not take,
Being capable of all ill! I pitied thee,
Took pains to make thee speak, taught thee each hour
One thing or other. When thou didst not, savage,
Know thine own meaning, but wouldst gabble like
A thing most brutish, I endowed thy purposes
With words that made them known. But thy vile race,
Though thou didst learn, had that in't which good
  natures

Could not abide to be with; therefore wast thou
Deservedly confined into this rock,
Who hadst deserved more than a prison.

CALIBAN You taught me language, and my
  profit on't
Is I know how to curse. The red plague rid you
For learning me your language!

PROSPERO Hag-seed, hence!
Fetch us in fuel. And be quick, thou'rt best,
To answer other business. Shrug'st thou, malice?
If thou neglect'st or dost unwillingly
What I command, I'll rack thee with old cramps,
Fill all thy bones with aches, make thee roar,
That beasts shall tremble at thy din.

CALIBAN   No, pray thee.
[*Aside*] I must obey. His art is of such power
It would control my dam's god Setebos,
And make a vassal of him.

PROSPERO   So, slave; hence! [*Exit* CALIBAN]

[*Enter* ARIEL, *invisible, playing and singing,*
  followed by FERDINAND]

ARIEL [*Sings*]
  Come unto these yellow sands,
    And then take hands;
  Curtsied when you have and kissed
    The wild waves whist.
  Foot it featly here and there,
  And, sweet sprites, the burden bear.
    Hark, hark!
[SPIRITS *within*] Bow-wow!
  The watch-dogs bark.
[SPIRITS *within*]Bow-wow!
    Hark, hark! I hear
  The strain of strutting Chanticleer
    Cry, 'cock-a-diddle-dow'.

FERDINAND Where should this music be?
  I' th' air or th' earth?
It sounds no more; and sure it waits upon
Some god o' th' island. Sitting on a bank,
Weeping again the King my father's wreck,
This music crept by me upon the waters,
Allaying both their fury and my passion
With its sweet air. Thence I have followed it,
Or it hath drawn me rather. But 'tis gone.
No, it begins again.

ARIEL [*Sings*]
  Full fathom five thy father lies.
    Of his bones are coral made;
  Those are pearls that were his eyes;
    Nothing of him that doth fade
  But doth suffer a sea-change

The Tempest

'A single thing … does I weep.'

Ferdinand means that he and the King of Naples are 'a single thing' – the same thing; but he also means he is alone and helpless. When he says 'He hears me', Ferdinand means that he himself – as King of Naples, now that he thinks his father drowned – can hear himself speaking. Prospero later pretends to be sceptical of these claims.

Into something rich and strange.
Sea-nymphs hourly ring his knell:
[SPIRITS *within*] Ding dong.
      Hark, now I hear them.
[SPIRITS *within*] Ding-dong bell.

FERDINAND The ditty does remember my
   drowned father.
This is no mortal business, nor no sound
That the earth owes. I hear it now above me.

PROSPERO [*To* MIRANDA] The fringèd curtains
   of thine eye advance,
And say what thou seest yond.

MIRANDA   What is't? A spirit?
Lord, how it looks about! Believe me, sir,
It carries a brave form. But 'tis a spirit.

PROSPERO No, wench. It eats and sleeps, and
   hath such senses
As we have, such. This gallant which thou seest
Was in the wreck, and but he's something stained
With grief, that's beauty's canker, thou mightst call him
A goodly person. He hath lost his fellows,
And strays about to find 'em.

MIRANDA   I might call him
A thing divine, for nothing natural
I ever saw so noble.

PROSPERO [*Aside*]   It goes on, I see,
As my soul prompts it. [*To* ARIEL] Spirit, fine
   spirit, I'll free thee
Within two days for this.

FERDINAND   Most sure, the goddess
On whom these airs attend! Vouchsafe my prayer
May know if you remain upon this island,
And that you will some good instruction give
How I may bear me here. My prime request,
Which I do last pronounce, is – O you wonder! –
If you be maid or no?

MIRANDA   No wonder, sir,
But certainly a maid.

FERDINAND My language! Heavens!
I am the best of them that speak this speech,
Were I but where 'tis spoken.

PROSPERO   How, the best?
What wert thou if the King of Naples heard thee?

FERDINAND A single thing, as I am now, that
   wonders
To hear thee speak of Naples. He does hear me,
And that he does I weep. Myself am Naples,
Who with mine eyes, never since at ebb, beheld
The King my father wrecked.

MIRANDA   Alack, for mercy!

FERDINAND Yes, faith, and all his lords, the Duke
   of Milan
And his brave son being twain.

PROSPERO [*Aside*]   The Duke of Milan
And his more braver daughter could control thee,
If now 'twere fit to do't. At the first sight
They have changed eyes. Delicate Ariel,
I'll set thee free for this. [*To* FERDINAND] A word,
   good sir.
I fear you have done yourself some wrong. A word.

MIRANDA [*Aside*] Why speaks my father so
   ungently? This
Is the third man that e'er I saw, the first
That e'er I sigh'd for. Pity move my father
To be inclined my way.

FERDINAND   O, if a virgin,
And your affection not gone forth, I'll make you
The Queen of Naples.

PROSPERO   Soft, sir! One word more.
[*Aside*] They are both in either's powers; but this
   swift business
I must uneasy make, lest too light winning
Make the prize light. [*To* FERDINAND] One word
   more. I charge thee
That thou attend me. Thou dost here usurp
The name thou ow'st not; and hast put thyself
Upon this island as a spy, to win it
From me, the lord on't.

FERDINAND   No, as I am a man.

MIRANDA There's nothing ill can dwell in such a
   temple.
If the ill spirit have so fair a house,
Good things will strive to dwell with't.

'My prime request … maid or no?'

'Wonder' means 'miracle', punning on Miranda's name. 'Maid' means 'virgin', but Ferdinand is also asking if Miranda was 'made' by God or if she is immortal. Later he makes clear his intentions in asking about her virginity: 'O, if a virgin, / And your affection not gone forth,' – i.e. your love not already given to somebody else – 'I'll make you / The Queen of Naples'.

The Tempest

c.1610-11

ACT **3** SCENE **2**

"The isle is full of noises,
Sounds, and sweet airs, that
give delight and hurt not."

The Tempest

The island in *The Tempest* is full of ideals: dreams of better ways of living than those that prevail in the world beyond its shores. Prospero dreams of a fairy-tale marriage for Miranda. The old courtier Gonzalo seeks to comfort the King of Naples, who thinks Ferdinand to be drowned, with a tale about the utopian state they might found on the island, where all things would be held in common and Nature would provide 'all foison, all abundance' for the 'innocent people'.

When Stephano the butler and Trinculo the jester first meet Caliban they intend to exploit him, as Prospero did; but after giving him a drink or two – which fuel his fantasies of a better life, so that he sings about freedom – their plans become more equitable. In our scene, Stephano, who has crowned himself king of the island with Caliban's consent (again, unlike Prospero), offers him and Trinculo the rank of viceroy. In fact, Stephano does what he can to treat his 'subjects' fairly: when he thinks the jester is abusing Caliban he tells him off ('he shall not suffer indignity') – though he quickly forgives him, and offers him a singularly un-monarchic apology. There is something touching, then, about the song Stephano sings with Trinculo, with its chorus of 'Thought is free'. These humble characters do indeed have freedom in their thoughts, as Gonzalo did.

All these people see the island as a place of infinite potential: and the audience is invited to share this vision in our scene, when Caliban describes it in some of Shakespeare's finest lyrical verses: 'The isle is full of noises, / Sounds, and sweet airs, that give delight and hurt not'. Caliban's use of verse makes nonsense of Prospero's attempts to dehumanize him: verse is in Shakespeare's plays the medium of royalty, so Caliban's language confirms his claim to be the island's legitimate heir. But none of the ideals in the play seems to have a chance of becoming reality. Gonzalo's utopia is mocked by his fellow courtiers; Stephano and Trinculo are hounded by Prospero's spirits; and the fragility of Prospero's own hopes is expressed by the masque he puts on for Ferdinand and Miranda. In the middle of the performance he remembers Caliban's plot against his life and stops the show before it can reach a happy ending; and this abrupt termination makes him think of the instability of life itself, despite art's efforts to make it enduringly lovely: 'the great globe itself, / Yea, all which it inherit, shall dissolve, / And, like this insubstantial pageant faded, / Leave not a rack behind.' At this point, the play looks set to end in mournful resignation.

But this is to reckon without the optimism of the young. For Miranda, the promise of a better life lies beyond the island's shores, and when she meets the rest of the cast in Act 5 she has nothing but praise for them: 'O brave new world, that has such people in it!' Prospero's announcement of his retirement in the epilogue, like Shakespeare's withdrawal to Stratford not long afterwards, may indicate his exhaustion after a lifetime of staggering artistry; but he leaves us with a vision of hope, Miranda, whose joy in newness will inhabit our hearts long after the end of the action.

OPPOSITE Stephano (Terence Rigby) with Caliban (Tony Haygarth) and Ariel (Steven Mackintosh) in the National Theatre's 1988 production.

[*Enter* CALIBAN, STEPHANO, *and* TRINCULO]

STEPHANO Tell not me. When the butt is out we will drink water, not a drop before. Therefore bear up and board 'em. Servant monster, drink to me.

TRINCULO Servant monster? The folly of this island! They say there's but five upon this isle. We are three of them; if th' other two be brained like us, the state totters.

STEPHANO Drink, servant-monster, when I bid thee. Thy eyes are almost set in thy head.

TRINCULO Where should they be set else? He were a brave monster indeed if they were set in his tail.

STEPHANO My man-monster hath drowned his tongue in sack. For my part, the sea cannot drown me. I swam, ere I could recover the shore, five and thirty leagues, off and on. By this light, thou shalt be my lieutenant, monster, or my standard.

TRINCULO Your lieutenant if you list; he's no standard.

STEPHANO We'll not run, Monsieur Monster.

TRINCULO Nor go neither; but you'll lie like dogs, and yet say nothing neither.

STEPHANO Moon-calf, speak once in thy life, if thou beest a good moon-calf.

CALIBAN How does thy honour? Let me lick thy shoe. I'll not serve him; he is not valiant.

> ### *'Therefore bear up and board 'em'*
>
> Stephano often uses nautical terminology. This is a sailor's command to attack ('bear up') and board an enemy vessel. 'Board' also means take on board (i.e. drink). Later, the butler claims to have swum 100 miles ('five and twenty leagues') while tacking from side to side ('off and on').

STEPHANO Marry, will I. Kneel and repeat it. I will stand, and so shall Trinculo.

[*Enter* ARIEL, *invisible*]

CALIBAN As I told thee before, I am subject to a tyrant, a sorcerer, that by his cunning hath cheated me of the island.

ARIEL Thou liest.

CALIBAN [*To* TRINCULO] Thou liest, thou jesting monkey, thou.
I would my valiant master would destroy thee!
I do not lie.

STEPHANO Trinculo, if you trouble him any more in's tale, by this hand, I will supplant some of your teeth.

TRINCULO Why, I said nothing.

STEPHANO Mum, then, and no more.
[*To* CALIBAN] Proceed.

This will prove a brave kingdom to me, where I shall have my music for nothing.

TRINCULO Thou liest, most ignorant monster! I am in case to jostle a constable. Why, thou deboshed fish, thou, was there ever man a coward that hath drunk so much sack as I today? Wilt thou tell a monstrous lie, being but half a fish and half a monster?

CALIBAN Lo, how he mocks me! Wilt thou let him, my lord?

TRINCULO 'Lord' quoth he? That a monster should be such a natural!

CALIBAN Lo, lo, again! Bite him to death, I prithee.

STEPHANO Trinculo, keep a good tongue in your head. If you prove a mutineer – the next tree. The poor monster's my subject, and he shall not suffer indignity.

CALIBAN I thank my noble lord. Wilt thou be pleased To hearken once again to the suit I made to thee?

CALIBAN I say, by sorcery he got this isle;
From me he got it. If thy greatness will
Revenge it on him – for I know thou dar'st,
But this thing dare not –

STEPHANO That's most certain.

CALIBAN Thou shalt be lord of it, and I'll serve thee.

STEPHANO How now shall this be compassed?
Canst thou bring me to the party? [*Strikes him*]

CALIBAN Yea, yea, my lord. I'll yield him thee asleep
Where thou mayst knock a nail into his head.

ARIEL Thou liest, thou canst not.

CALIBAN What a pied ninny's this! [*To* TRINCULO]
Thou scurvy patch!
[*To* STEPHANO] I do beseech thy greatness, give him blows,
And take his bottle from him. When that's gone
He shall drink nought but brine, for I'll not show him
Where the quick freshes are.

STEPHANO Trinculo, run into no further danger. Interrupt the monster one word further, and, by this hand, I'll turn my mercy out o' doors and make a stock-fish of thee.

TRINCULO Why, what did I? I did nothing. I'll go farther off.

STEPHANO Didst thou not say he lied?

ARIEL Thou liest.

STEPHANO Do I so? Take thou that. [*Strikes* **TRINCULO**] As you like this, give me the lie another time.

TRINCULO I did not give the lie. Out o' your wits and hearing too? A pox o' your bottle! This can sack and drinking do. A murrain on your monster, and the devil take your fingers!

CALIBAN Ha, ha, ha!

STEPHANO Now, forward with your tale.
  [*To* **TRINCULO**] Prithee stand farther off.

CALIBAN Beat him enough. After a little time I'll beat him too.

STEPHANO [*To* **TRINCULO**] Stand farther.
  [*To* **CALIBAN**] Come, proceed.

> ### 'This is the tune of our catch … Nobody.'
>
> 'Nobody' was a character in a popular satirical comedy, *Nobody and Somebody*, who had no torso, and was depicted on the title page with breeches up to his neck. 'Nobody' was also the pseudonym adopted by the wily traveller Ulysses so as to conceal his true identity from the man-eating Cyclops Polyphemus; so it's a name associated with trickery.

CALIBAN Why, as I told thee, 'tis a custom with him
I' th' afternoon to sleep. There thou mayst brain him,
Having first seized his books, or with a log
Batter his skull, or paunch him with a stake,
Or cut his weasand with thy knife. Remember
First to possess his books, for without them
He's but a sot as I am, nor hath not
One spirit to command – they all do hate him
As rootedly as I. Burn but his books.
He has brave utensils, for so he calls them,
Which when he has a house he'll deck withal.
And that most deeply to consider is
The beauty of his daughter. He himself
Calls her a nonpareil. I never saw a woman
But only Sycorax my dam and she,
But she as far surpasseth Sycorax
As great'st does least.

STEPHANO   Is it so brave a lass?

CALIBAN Ay, lord. She will become thy bed, I warrant,
And bring thee forth brave brood.

STEPHANO Monster, I will kill this man. His daughter and I will be king and queen – save our graces! – and Trinculo and thyself shall be viceroys. Dost thou like the plot, Trinculo?

TRINCULO Excellent.

STEPHANO Give me thy hand. I am sorry I beat thee; but while thou liv'st, keep a good tongue in thy head.

CALIBAN Within this half hour will he be asleep. Wilt thou destroy him then?

STEPHANO Ay, on mine honour.

ARIEL This will I tell my master.

CALIBAN Thou mak'st me merry; I am full of pleasure.
Let us be jocund. Will you troll the catch
You taught me but while-ere?

STEPHANO At thy request, monster, I will do reason, any reason. Come on, Trinculo, let us sing.

STEPHANO and TRINCULO [*Sing*]
  Flout 'em and scout 'em
  And scout 'em and flout 'em
    Thought is free.

CALIBAN That's not the tune.

[**ARIEL** *plays the tune on a tabor and pipe*]

STEPHANO What is this same?

TRINCULO This is the tune of our catch, played by the picture of Nobody.

STEPHANO [*Calls towards* **ARIEL**] If thou beest a man, show thyself in thy likeness. If thou beest a devil, take't as thou list.

TRINCULO O, forgive me my sins!

STEPHANO He that dies pays all debts. [*Calls*] I defy thee. Mercy upon us!

CALIBAN Art thou afeard?

STEPHANO No, monster, not I.

CALIBAN Be not afeard. The isle is full of noises,
Sounds, and sweet airs, that give delight and hurt not.
Sometimes a thousand twangling instruments
Will hum about mine ears, and sometime voices
That if I then had waked after long sleep
Will make me sleep again; and then in dreaming
The clouds methought would open and show riches
Ready to drop upon me, that when I waked
I cried to dream again.

STEPHANO This will prove a brave kingdom to me, where I shall have my music for nothing.

Henry VIII

c.1612-13

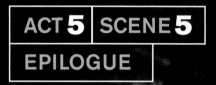

ACT **5** | SCENE **5**

EPILOGUE

❝In her days every man shall eat in safety
Under his own vine what he plants, and sing
The merry songs of peace to all his neighbours.❞

Our selection closes with a scene that may not be by Shakespeare. *Henry VIII* or *All Is True* is one of three plays Shakespeare co-authored with John Fletcher, as the younger man prepared to succeed him as principal playwright for the King's Men. *All Is True* is the better title, since this is an investigation of the nature of historical and personal truth.

The story takes place in the prelude to that great battle over truth, the Reformation; it concerns Henry's divorce from Katherine of Aragon – which led to England's split from Rome – and the downfall of Cardinal Wolsey; and its treatment of all three characters, and the religions they represent, eschews simplicity. As if in homage to the play's joint authorship, there are two sides to every personality and incident, and this double vision pervades our extract, the last scene of the play.

Everyone agrees that Katherine is 'true' in the sense of 'faithful'; but it's also 'true' that she may never 'truly' have been Henry's wife at all, since their marriage was possibly incestuous. Henry's fears concerning the marriage seem 'true' too, but he is not 'true' as a husband, since his doubts about incest are always getting mixed up with his desire for Anne Boleyn. And Wolsey has a yet more vexed relationship to truth. He promises that the trial he sets up to push through the divorce will be 'just and noble', and seems to believe it. When Katherine says he is 'not … a friend to truth' he seems genuinely aggrieved. But when his disgrace comes, Wolsey reacts with relief, as if the burden of sustaining incompatible truths has been lifted from him at last, and he can commit himself wholeheartedly to the simple business of dying – which makes him '*truly* happy'. And when he dies he gets two elegies (a negative one from Katherine, a positive one from her usher), both of which are equally accurate. By this stage, 'All Is True' seems a comment on the complexities of history, to which pity seems a more appropriate response than any absolute judgement.

So Cranmer's famous prophecy in our extract, which he admits resembles 'flattery' more than 'truth', is not as simple as it seems. Uttered at the christening of the future Elizabeth I, it paints a glowing picture of her reign and that of her successor, James I, as a time when 'Peace, plenty, love, truth, terror' will flourish like a vine. But everyone in the playhouse would have been able to judge how far this picture resembled reality, and their views would presumably have varied. Is this what Cranmer means when he says 'few now living can behold that goodness': that not only will he and others die by violence before she's crowned, but that some listeners may be sceptical as to his picture's accuracy? The simple joy of the occasion, which Henry affirms when he declares, 'Never before / This happy child did I get anything', is complicated by the fact that this is not true: Henry *did* beget children before Elizabeth, one of them Katherine's daughter Mary, in whose reign Cranmer died. The speech, then, describes an ideal to be yearned for, perhaps nostalgically remembered; but it's not designed to erase the painful truths of history, which Shakespeare had so often exposed on the London stage.

OPPOSITE Donald Sinden in the title role in the Royal Shakespeare Company's 1970 production.

[*Enter trumpets, sounding. Then two Aldermen, Lord Mayor,* GARTER *King of Arms,* CRANMER *the Archbishop of Canterbury, the Duke of* NORFOLK *with his marshal's staff, the Duke of* SUFFOLK, *two Noblemen bearing great standing-bowls for the christening gifts; then four Noblemen bearing a canopy, under which is the Duchess of Norfolk, godmother, bearing the child* ELIZABETH *richly habited in a mantle, whose train is borne by a Lady. Then follows the Marchioness Dorset, the other godmother, and ladies. The troop pass once about the stage, and* GARTER *speaks.*]

GARTER
Heaven, from thy endless goodness, send prosperous life, long, and ever happy, to the high and mighty Princess of England, Elizabeth!

[*Flourish. Enter* KING HENRY VIII *and Guard*]

> '*Saba was never*
> *More covetous of wisdom and*
> *fair virtue*
> *Than this pure soul shall be.*'

The Queen of Saba or Sheba came to visit the biblical King Solomon in Jerusalem to learn wisdom from him. She was therefore the model for wise women, just as Solomon was for wise men.

CRANMER [*Kneeling*]
And to your royal grace, and the good Queen!
My noble partners and myself thus pray
All comfort, joy, in this most gracious lady,
Heaven ever laid up to make parents happy,
May hourly fall upon ye.

KING   Thank you, good Lord Archbishop.
What is her name?

CRANMER   Elizabeth.

KING   Stand up, lord. [CRANMER *rises*]
[*To* ELIZABETH] With this kiss take my
    blessing. [*Kisses her*] God protect thee,
Into whose hand I give thy life.

CRANMER   Amen.

KING
My noble gossips, ye have been too prodigal.
I thank ye heartily. So shall this lady,
When she has so much English.

CRANMER   Let me speak, sir,
For heaven now bids me, and the words I utter
Let none think flattery, for they'll find 'em truth.
This royal infant – heaven still move about her! –
Though in her cradle, yet now promises
Upon this land a thousand thousand blessings
Which time shall bring to ripeness. She shall be –
But few now living can behold that goodness –
A pattern to all princes living with her,
And all that shall succeed. Saba was never
More covetous of wisdom and fair virtue
Than this pure soul shall be. All princely graces
That mould up such a mighty piece as this is,
With all the virtues that attend the good,
Shall still be doubled on her. Truth shall
    nurse her,
Holy and heavenly thoughts still counsel her.
She shall be loved and feared. Her own shall
    bless her;
Her foes shake like a field of beaten corn,
And hang their heads with sorrow. Good grows
    with her.
In her days every man shall eat in safety
Under his own vine what he plants, and sing
The merry songs of peace to all his neighbours.
God shall be truly known, and those about her
From her shall read the perfect ways of honour,

the words I utter
Let none think flattery, for they'll find 'em truth.

And by those claim their greatness, not by blood.
Nor shall this peace sleep with her, but, as when
The bird of wonder dies – the maiden phoenix –
Her ashes new create another heir
As great in admiration as herself,
So shall she leave her blessèdness to one,
When heaven shall call her from this cloud of
   darkness,
Who from the sacred ashes of her honour
Shall star-like rise as great in fame as she was,
And so stand fixed. Peace, plenty, love, truth, terror,
That were the servants to this chosen infant,
Shall then be his, and like a vine grow to him.
Wherever the bright sun of heaven shall shine,
His honour and the greatness of his name
Shall be, and make new nations. He shall flourish,
And like a mountain cedar reach his branches
To all the plains about him. Our children's children
Shall see this, and bless heaven.

KING   Thou speakest wonders.

CRANMER
She shall be, to the happiness of England,
An agèd princess. Many days shall see her,
And yet no day without a deed to crown it.
Would I had known no more. But she must die –
She must, the saints must have her – yet a virgin,
A most unspotted lily shall she pass
To th' ground, and all the world shall mourn her.

KING
O Lord Archbishop,
Thou hast made me now a man. Never before
This happy child did I get anything.
This oracle of comfort has so pleased me
That when I am in heaven I shall desire
To see what this child does, and praise my Maker.
I thank ye all. To you, my good Lord Mayor,
And your good brethren, I am much beholden.
I have received much honour by your presence,
And ye shall find me thankful. Lead the way, lords.
Ye must all see the Queen, and she must thank ye,
She will be sick else. This day, no man think
He's business at his house, for all shall stay.
This little one shall make it holiday. [*Exeunt*]

> **'as when**
> **The bird of wonder dies**
> **– the maiden phoenix –**
> **Her ashes new create another heir**
> **As great in admiration as herself'**
>
> The phoenix is a mythical Arabian bird of
> which there is only ever one. Every hundred
> years it reproduces by setting itself on fire,
> then rising anew from the ashes. Elizabeth
> was often likened to a phoenix, as were
> many royal or aristocratic women. Her
> phoenix-like successor is James I, but may
> also be his daughter Elizabeth, for whose
> wedding this play may have been written.

Our children's children
Shall see this,
and bless heaven.

EPILOGUE

'Tis ten to one this play can never please
All that are here. Some come to take their ease,
And sleep an act or two; but those, we fear,
We've frighted with our trumpets, so 'tis clear
They'll say 'tis naught. Others, to hear the city
Abused extremely, and to cry, 'That's witty!' –
Which we have not done neither; that, I fear,
All the expected good we're like to hear
For this play at this time is only in
The merciful construction of good women;
For such a one we showed 'em. If they smile,
And say 'twill do, I know within a while
All the best men are ours; for 'tis ill hap
If they hold when their ladies bid 'em clap. [*Exit*]

Index

For K, B and G, with love and thanks

Quercus Publishing Plc
21 Bloomsbury Square
London
WC1A 2NS

First published in 2008

Copyright © R W Maslen and Michael Schmidt 2008

The moral rights of R W Maslen and Michael
Schmidt to be identified as the authors of this
work have been asserted in accordance with the
Copyright, Design and Patents Act, 1988.

Editorial and project management: JMS Books LLP
Design: Austin Taylor
Picture research: Josine Meijer

A catalogue record of this book is available from
the British Library

Cloth case edition:
ISBN 13: 978 1 84724 615 8

Printed case edition:
ISBN 13: 978 1 84724 194 8

Printed and bound in China

10 9 8 7 6 5 4 3 2 1